DISTRIBUTED PROCESSING SYSTEMS

Distributed Processing Systems

END OF THE MAINFRAME ERA?

Judson Breslin
and
C. Bradley Tashenberg

 a division of American Management Associations

Library of Congress Cataloging in Publication Data

Breslin, Judson.
    Distributed processing systems.

    Includes index.
    1. Business—Data processing. 2. Management—Data
processing. 3. Electronic data processing—Distributed
processing. 4. Miniature computers. I. Tashenberg,
C. Bradley, joint author. II. Title.
HF5548.2.B735   658'.05'4   77-16398
ISBN 0-8144-5457-7

© 1978 AMACOM
A division of American Management Associations, New York.

Third Printing

To
R.L.T., whose policy of mutual trust and
confidence made this book possible,

and to
E.S.T. and W.W.B., whose encouragement
and enthusiasm inspired the confidence
to meet the challenge.

PREFACE

We are coming to the end of an era in which data processing was characterized by a computer processing ability that apparently outstripped business's ability to manage it. The computer's revolutionary development has been the source of great dissatisfaction because (1) data processing costs have escalated to an uncontrollable level; (2) the promised benefits from computers have not been realized; and (3) data processing is often ineffective, providing information that may not be accurate, timely, or in the desired format. In fact, in some instances, the growth in computer and data processing costs indicates that the computer is too large for the applications it processes.

Top management and the data processing professionals are equally responsible for this unhappy state of affairs. Top management has abdicated control over the data processing function. They have decided that it is too technical, too complicated, and too specialized to be managed. They preface each contact with data processing personnel by declaring, "You know I don't understand anything about computers." Yet top managers don't hesitate to make important decisions on research and development or manufacturing investments, which may be just as technical and foreign. When data processing first came on the scene, it was viewed as just another administrative tool—not worth the trouble to understand. Now, when a computer shutdown can bring airline reservations, banking operations, or an assembly line to a halt, it *is* worth the trouble to understand, but management has lost the will and the ability to do so.

The data processing professionals, on the other hand, have pursued their freedom in ways that have not been in their employers' best interests. Instead of serving the information and paperwork processing needs of the organizations they work for, many professionals have been more interested in developing their own technical expertise to the highest level possible. Simply stated, this meant obtaining the most sophisticated computer gear, whether it was needed or not. If the data processing function had been subjected to the usual management disciplines of accountability and return-on-investment justification, this could not have happened. But these controls were applied only infrequently, and, worse yet, procedures and systems were often modified to adapt to the computer, rather than vice versa.

Recent advancements in computer technology have put larger, faster, more sophisticated computer mainframes on the market, which have led to a cost spiral that is accelerating continually. Management in many organizations is beginning to show concern, and fortunately, a solution has now appeared—distributed data processing combined with the minicomputer. Advances in integrated circuitry now offer tremendous data processing power in small computers of a relatively low cost. Furthermore, minicomputers permit decentralization of data processing. This puts the control back in the hands of the user organizations, who are more familiar with their problems and requirements than some remote data processing department that attempts to serve a wide variety of users.

As we see it, the minicomputer era will commence with a managerial conflict between top management and the data processing function. Management's desire for decentralized user operations and for improved service at less cost will clash directly with the professional's imperial interest in ever larger central organizations with huge computers and overflowing technical staffs.

This book attempts to help some organizations avoid a crisis while they are in the process of adopting distributed data processing. It is directed to top management, data processing users, and data processing professionals, to both the layman and the technical expert. Although it contains essential technical information, this book is fundamentally concerned with the management of the data processing function. Since many managers lack even the basic knowledge of data processing, we have included considerable background information about data processing and a description of how computers work. The more sophisticated reader may wish to skip these sections, but the presence of this information should not lead one to conclude that the book is not for the professional. It definitely is, for just as the manager must come to understand data processing, so must the professional come to understand the management problems, the current crisis, and how he will have to adapt if he is to be successful in the future.

We believe that this book serves an important purpose in helping solve a complex problem. We are simply asking management to manage the data processing function and to provide the leadership that will help the technician regain his professionalism and objectivity.

In the world of how-to books, this should be considered a why-to book. It asks if we are ready to end the mainframe era and begin the minicomputer era. It is designed to challenge readers to put aside old beliefs and passions and consider the potentials of a really marvelous new system that can realize the previously unfulfilled promises of data processing.

We would like to express our appreciation to John C. W. Schaie for his help and counsel.

Judson Breslin
C. Bradley Tashenberg

CONTENTS

1

The End of an Era

Responsibility—with the necessary authority—is the very essence of management in today's complex private and governmental environments. But in the area of data processing over the past 20 years, a great many, and perhaps most, top managers abdicated their responsibility by defaulting to their technically oriented data processing managers in all matters pertaining to computers and computing systems. Authority all but went with it. And this default from the top has been costly. During this abdication, encouraged by the brilliant marketing strategy of a few computer manufacturers, a philosophy of computer evolution filled the managerial void and became institutionalized. It remains institutionalized today.

Evolution in our computer world means continual escalation in size, speed, storage capacity, and, ultimately, the costs of computers. The organization finds itself in a position of planned incremental cost increases, unable to stop, to step back, to evaluate its requirements in terms of actual needs. Computer evolution was encouraged by a marketing strategy geared to an awareness that complexity and mystique also increase with the size and cost of computing power. Too many competent managers have taken the position that data processing decisions are "not for them," the mystique having won and the evolutionary spiral begun.

This evolutionary growth, fostered initially by the manager's neglect, has resulted in internal cost increases, which has led to product cost increases and contributed to our inflationary economy. We must question whether management has acted in the best interest of the organization or the economy.

The government argues that the computer industry is a monopoly; it is more serious than that! In many organizations the computer manufacturer and the data processing professionals have promoted a kind of conspiracy that perpetuates large central computer facilities, permanent positions in data

1

processing, and spiraling costs. The computer manufacturer literally monopolizes, restricts, and dramatically affects internal decision making in many American organizations today by promoting evolutionary increases in data processing expenditures and propagating a fear of change. It may be true that this monopoly, this conspiracy, and the fear of change have engendered a major disservice to American business. And it is clear that management is to blame, not the computer manufacturer.

Computers as we know them today have been in existence for only 26 years, yet in that short period of time they have managed to penetrate the core of all major corporations. The computer manufacturer worked closely with the company, assuming the responsibility for maintaining and supporting the computer systems. The computer became a status symbol of corporate success.

In the early days of computers, performance was not the prime factor, and progress took place at the rate the computer manufacturer recommended and could control. The manufacturer's representative, frequently the most knowledgeable about the system and thus an essential part of the data processing organization, directed the end user during a period when technological advances were occurring at too fast a rate to follow.

In the history of commerce, no industry has had such an impact in so many areas of business as the computer industry. Its representatives often controlled the major decision making of the data processing departments of large corporations with the largest manufacturer, IBM, advising them to *THINK*. The influence of the computer industry on business is unparalleled. As a result, the computer industry today is seen not as an industry but as an institution to which the user may well dedicate his loyalty before his own company.

It is often difficult for management to understand the makeup of its own data processing personnel, but the industry understands these personalities and knows how to establish a demand for new products. To upper management this would normally be considered a conspiracy, but to data processing management it is just the way business is done. In most cases upper management is not aware of this relationship anyway.

That 26-year history has been a strange and unique one, to be sure. Commercially, it started simply enough with the old unit record equipment. Unit record means a single card with holes punched in it to represent alphabetic and numeric characters. Through electrical impulses, machines were able to read these characters, store the data in counters, and perform simple mathematical calculations. They became status symbols early in the game and human nature dictated the enthusiastic acquisition of unit record equipment by many companies during the 1940s and the 1950s.

The record shows that unit record equipment was leased and the era of data processing began. And, for the very first time, a unique department of data processing was born. It normally reported directly to the controller as a separate function. It also separated the accounting data from the accountant as it eliminated his quill pen and ink-stained ledger. The new department of data processing became responsible for:

Designing the specific accounting systems that would be run on the unit record equipment.

Preparing the data with keypunching and verifying for the unit record equipment.

Reporting the data from the unit.

It was a new world, really. The head of this department of data processing assumed a shared responsibility with the accountant for the accuracy and timeliness of reports. In other words, the data processing department now shared a responsibility that formerly had been clearly vested. With shared responsibility came shared authority.

And the computing device was mysterious from the beginning. Managers simply did not understand how it worked. The accountants and the controller did not understand it well, although it was, in fact, an elementary calculator. In all fairness, the unit record department was made up of several machines: sorters; collaters, which matched sets of cards with identical codes; and interpreters, which printed the letters or numbers that had been punched into those cards. Of course, the mystery of how those punched cards could speed through the sorter, falling into lots of slots, and how that adder and subtracter did its thing, remained.

The mystery was there and so were the machines. And systems responsibility took a remote step away from the accountant, the one who used the machines.

ABDICATION OF RESPONSIBILITY

It is not strange to us that management did not get involved in data processing. We can speculate that the overall impact of computing and data processing was just not that apparent in the early days. For example, the new department did not typically report to the senior management. The person who was made supervisor was not an executive, but an electrical engineer, a timekeeper, or a lower-level accountant. And the early applications, because of the elementary capabilities of the computing device, were confined to the more mundane business necessities, such as payroll and accounts payable.

The computing machines and the new departments were different from the rest of the business. They spoke their own language, dealt with special machines, and didn't really disrupt marketing and manufacturing functions. Furthermore, at that time, data processing costs did not represent a large chunk of the total company expenditures. In most cases, since the data processing department was new and did have unique machines, it required guidance and assistance. Where could it turn? The data processing manager could not turn to the controller if his machine reported that one plus one was three. Out of necessity, he turned to the one person who understood his problem—the machine manufacturer. This was a novel solution. Normally companies have engineers and machinists to handle sick machinery; but neither of these disciplines was prepared to fix the new computing machine or solve the data processor's problem.

Also, a new discipline was born: programming, or the wiring of electronic boards, to make the machines think. Inevitably, problems arose. Now, when one plus one became four, where could you go for help? Again, the only source of help for the beleaguered data processor was the equipment manufacturer. And the very real wall separating data processing from the user thickened (along with the plot). But the tie between the data processor and the manufacturer was strengthened. Management had its mind on other matters.

By 1955, the first commercially feasible computers hit the market. They were greeted with about the same reaction that had been accorded the unit record machines: "If the competitor has one, we'll get one." Only now, certain things had changed. Cost justifications did not seem necessary and the need for computers was not questioned. The remote data processing organization, with its centralized systems manager, was firmly established. The major manufacturers, at this time, were IBM and UNIVAC. Data processing technology jumped a quantum. The data processor again turned to the manufacturer as his only source of guidance, advice, and, in times of trouble, salvation.

Another generation of computers was announced in 1964–1965. This third generation brought with it a new level of sophistication and complexity. It also opened new avenues into business because of tremendously increased capabilities. The computer was now capable of tackling marketing, forecasting, and manufacturing. It could serve the organization as a whole, and hit at the very heart of the operation. It remained centralized; it preferred to be characterized as "different" and not subject to normal control and direction or to the normal performance measurements levied on marketing and production. And management acquiesced, because it had indeed become a complex discipline, run by specialized people, most of whom were very young. In 1963, McKinsey & Co., the premier management consultants, issued a study in which it was made very clear that management was quite uninvolved. The report was called "Getting the Most Out of Your Computer."

The concept of projects and project management surfaced. Most systems were unique and separate in the data processing world because of the machine's propensity to "do one thing at a time." Yet project management was far from a science. The records will show that data processors added to their mystique through long projects that included such things as system design, programming, and conversion.

Beyond doubt, the evolutionary spiral of inflation was with us in the mid-1960s, when third-generation computers were introduced. Since then there has been no major breakthrough. Rather, computers, with the same basic architecture, have grown in size and complexity. Companies continue to move up the data processing ladder to bigger and bigger models of the same machine. The larger models have more capacity, more memory, faster printers, and *higher costs.*

For both the second and third generations, data processing people sought frantically to add more applications to the computer. "We must use this device. Idleness is worse than Godlessness," was their motto. But this is as absurd as rushing to make more calculations on a calculator that is sitting idly on an accountant's desk. And when the computer was full, the obvious next step was to get a bigger and faster copy of the same model. Justification came from the data processor. And management listened and accepted without undertaking the same rigorous return-on-investment analysis it made on lesser expenditures. Manufacturers stayed close by and encouraged this "progress." And they were not to blame.

Arnold E. Keller wrote that the largest manufacturer, IBM, has a mental monopoly on the entire marketplace today—meaning that IBM dictates to the data processor, who has a blind loyalty to this manufacturer because of its long history of the togetherness we alluded to earlier. It is a sound market strategy from a tremendously successful company. But there is something very wrong with this mental monopoly, if it does exist. It creates an untenable situation in which many data processors are more loyal to IBM than they are to the company for which they work and by which they get paid.

No one computer manufacturer, not even IBM, always has the best product, any more than General Motors always has the best automobile. Yet many competitive products are shunned by the data processor, who feels it is safer to stick with IBM. These "safe" installations are sometimes the ones with massive cost increases and escalating data processing budgets, and as we will prove, they are often ineffective and inefficient; they are simply overloaded with hardware and are limping along with outdated software.

IBM does not have a monopoly on installations that perform poorly, nor are they responsible for all the cost escalations that occur. But according to some experts, "It is ironic that many data processing managers will squeeze the last penny out of cards and forms suppliers and never even question additions recommended by the IBM salesman. This think-IBM-only syndrome may be a tribute to skilled marketing, but it is a sad commentary on the state of professionalism among data processing people." *

It is also a sad reflection on management. When the mental monopoly was beginning and when it matured, management was saying, "Data processing decisions are not for me. Leave them to those young fellows." And managers are now paying the price.

PROOF OF THE PROBLEM

Today, these same managers must acknowledge the cost evolution and the real potential of a mental monopoly. In 1967, a major executive in the consumer market industry told us that he was afraid even to consider any manufacturer other than IBM, although the IBM proposal was higher in cost than competitive proposals by Burroughs, NCR, and Honeywell. This executive and other managers must recognize their contribution to cost escalation; the evolutionary spiral of data processing costs could not have occurred without their unconscious submission. Our proof is extensive. First we have the early McKinsey study, which concluded that management was not involved. Also, as a seminar entitled Data Center Performance Evaluation held in Chicago in August 1976, Peat, Marwick & Mitchell, the large CPA firm, revealed that less than one-third of the management in the companies they interviewed were satisfied with the services they were receiving from their data processing departments.

A third item is an internal IBM memorandum released during the current antitrust hearings, which showed that management did not consider computer decisions to be cost-justifiable. The memorandum pointed out that the early decisions on unit record equipment were based on *cost displacement,* that is, how much it would cost to replace some manual operations with a mechanical device. But then, according to the memo, when the value

* Arnold E. Keller, Editorial, *Infosystems,* March 1975, p. 31.

of computers began to be understood, newer, larger models were acquired, not on the basis of cost justification, but because they were better, and because the need for them had been established. In addition, the memorandum pointed out, prestige was definitely a factor. Other things resulted in upgrading to more costly equipment without any management guidance or any appreciable cost justification. They were, according to the IBM memorandum:

1. The mystique of the computer.
2. Management's unwillingness to learn or to become involved.
3. The slow awareness of the fact that these costs were escalating rapidly.
4. The data processing professionals' unwillingness to get management involved, which would threaten their stronghold and unique position.

So management, duped by the data processing professionals, abdicated its role and, in some dramatic documentation from the Federal District Court in New York, management simply ignored competitive bidding for computers in favor of sole-source procurements. In multimillion-dollar decisions, this is a costly practice.

The document on competitive bidding showed that such bids are taken less than 20 percent of the time, depending on the size of the computer. This document is summarized in Table 1. The findings are astounding. In the first place, for some computers, 88 percent of the decisions are made without any competition. Second, the vast majority of these selections goes to one manu-

Table 1. Computer decisions and competitive bidding.

Size of System	Year	Competitive Bid	Noncompetitive Bid	Competitive Success Rate (%)	Noncompetitive Bids (%)
Very large	1970	N/A	N/A	50	88
Large	1970	N/A	N/A	59	81
Medium	1970	133	1,013	38	88
	1971	N/A	N/A	64	73
Small to medium	1970	302	1,636	37	84
Intermediate	1970	760	915	31	55
	1971	597	2,411	40	80
Small	1970	1,326	4,989	42	79

SOURCE: *Computerworld*, May 1976.

facturer. And yet, with no attempt to downgrade anyone, the success rate in competition is not impressive—less than 50 percent in most categories.

The selected manufacturer frequently experienced a head-to-head win rate of about 36 percent, as shown in Table 1. This can only mean one thing: There are good computers marketed by several computer manufacturers, which should be evaluated. Failure to review competitive bids shows negligence and irresponsibility. Competition, the report proves, results in selection of several manufacturers, not just one.

It is dramatic proof that competent managers are letting technical people, who are not always in the best position to evaluate overall company needs, make critical—even million-dollar—decisions without support. In what other area of decision making would an intelligent manager agree to a selection without reviewing alternatives or competitors? What more convincing argument can there be? Direction? Supervision? Responsibility? Who is in charge here?

Companies are run by systems and systems are run by computers. There are manufacturing systems, payroll systems, accounts payable and receivable systems, and management information systems, all of which are now dominated by computers. By neglecting this responsibility, managers have launched a potential disaster. Few other areas could have been quite so costly or could have so devastating an effect on the total organization as the abdication of responsibility for systems and data processing. It is part of a new reality that managers can no longer take this position by ignoring their responsibility for data processing while maintaining their roles as directors of the organization.

THE ARGUMENTS

Effectiveness

Naturally, the data processing staff will say it isn't so. Although costs may, in fact, have skyrocketed, there has also been a phenomenal growth in the effectiveness of data processing. But this holds only in some instances. As we shall see in the next chapter, the rush to new generations and larger models and the insane quest for "capacity" was achieved at the expense of improved systems design. The effectiveness of the systems effort certainly suffered in the process. The Peat, Marwick & Mitchell study showed it, and so does experience. Too many managers have complained to us about the ineffectiveness of their computing centers, and too much is being said and written to consider today's data processing efficient and cost-effective.

In the first place, the vendors sold their larger models, promising ease of conversion from the old system to the new, larger one. This approach has, in fact, been successful in discouraging management from changing vendors. The ease of conversion, however, translates into putting existing systems on a newer machine. In one specific, documented installation, a major manufacturer proposed that conversion to its new computer could be implemented in one weekend. But why? Ineffective systems, which were cited as one of the reasons for seeking another computer, would be just as ineffective after conversion. It is a fallacy to assume that a system will be more effective if it runs on a computer rated at 400 nanoseconds instead of a computer rated at 900 nanoseconds. It is not the computer speed that creates the bottleneck or the factor of ineffectiveness.

The result of these conversions, in many cases, is that systems designed for older, smaller, and slower-generation computers are still running on the newer and larger computer. But more on that in the next chapter. Suffice it to say here that the old system is just as ineffective as it ever was, but the total cost of processing the same system has soared way above what it was on the old machines. If you take a look at the majority of data processing installations you will be amazed at how many have systems running in emulation, simulation, duplication, and liberation. This is your first clue to the problem.

In Phase with the Times?

How many data processing people can prove the cost-effectiveness of their functions? How many managers even ask for such a justification? There are means to measure cost-effectiveness. Both hardware and software monitors are available. According to a 1970 study conducted by A. T. Kearney, Inc., in many instances computers were operating at less than 48 percent efficiency, and in many large installations, the effective use was less than 65 percent. But these measuring devices are not often used by the security-wise data processing manager.

Despite the wide availability of these tools, it is surprising how rarely they are used. The Peat, Marwick study found that only 30% of the responding organizations were using quantified measures of computer performance. And only 25% had even attempted the trickier question of measuring the return from data-processing investments. The study showed, by the way, that there was a high correlation between those who were satisfied with their data-processing operation and those who used performance-evaluated techniques.*

* Special report, "Getting Control of the System," *Dun's Review,* July 1977, p. 77.

Many managers feel that this type of analysis is worthless anyway, because they are captive users of computers.

The Mystique Has Won Too Often

There is another fallacy to the argument that effectiveness has increased with the escalated cost. In most instances, the computer is not in phase with the business. In manufacturing, for example, the business process is continuous. The plant manufactures its product all day, at night on the second shift, and, it is hoped, on a third shift in good times. But the large-scale computer generally operates in a batch mode, with only one system running at a time. Each system is run sequentially. Batch-type processing necessitates a cutoff time in the plant to allow time to prepare the manufacturing information for its scheduled computer run.

While this data processing cutoff is in effect, the plant continues to operate. Shipments are made and received, products are produced, and the world continues. But this activity will not be reported until after the next cutoff, which is the next day. Somewhere, someone is keypunching the information into punched cards while someone else is scheduling the computer, which is now completely out of phase with the real world.

It is the same with all record-keeping functions, such as a general ledger. Holding any financial information to await month-end batch processing means that computer-generated balances are not current. Balance sheets are only valid for a moment. And you have to wait until the next time your job is scheduled to run so you can get an update. This is ineffective data processing. And it is literally costing a fortune. Furthermore, it perpetuates the need for a centralized data processing organization to schedule and process the batch system.

This is the era of large-scale computers. It is the era of large expenditures and marginal effectiveness. It is the era that saw management turn over the reins to the technician for which it is now paying the price. If it doesn't have to be this way, who will authorize a change?

THE END OF AN ERA

The problem is not a simple one. If it were, we would not be writing this book. Costs are soaring. The computer is out of phase with the real world of business. A centralized computer organization separates the systems execution from the systems user, confusing the responsibilities for timeliness and accuracy. Managers have abdicated their responsibility by allowing the technician to control data processing. And everyone, except the manufacturer and the data processing people, says "It's a mystery to me."

This era has to come to an end. For a cost-effective solution is available: First, we must return systems responsibility to the users, second, we must get the computer back in phase with the business at hand, and third, we must cut escalating costs. All of this is possible, but managers must understand and control the data processing function so that they can properly direct the data processing professionals and make the computer work for them. We shall call this the end of an era.

2

Returning Control to Management

Why did we ever go to centralized data processing and remove systems responsibility and integrity from the end user? Back in the beginning, the user understood his system. He used to design the system and act as controller, treasurer, manufacturing manager, or market analyst. Today, the user no longer designs his own systems and he surely does not control the destiny of his own data processing—or have the necessary control over his own systems. Why did we allow his responsibility to be dissipated? Was it because of limited capabilities of the early computers, which required special training and new skills? Or was it the costs, which led to one central computing function? This book will prove that those excuses are not valid.

The computer was originally designed to handle one task at a time, a very expensive operation. Accountants could not afford to support individual computers of their own. We shall see later that the early days of typewriters dictated the same need for centralization. But, as with the typewriter, it is desirable to keep the tools of the trade with the knowledgeable user, except from the point of view of those who wish to perpetuate a centralized empire.

The costly computer is a carry-over from the old era; it is obsolete. Centralized data processing as we know it today will also become a thing of the past as it becomes recognized that decentralization, or putting computing power in the hands of the users, will eliminate the unavoidable bottleneck in the centralized approach.

KEEPING IN PHASE

It is management's responsibility to keep the organization in phase with the real world. How else can a company in the private sector remain competitive? How can a social service organization or a government provide adequate services? When the computer is providing the information for making decisions, it must be current and supplied when needed. Otherwise, decisions cannot be made under the best conditions, and the opportunity for making poor decisions is greatly enhanced.

An example of in-phase processing is the airline reservation clerk's immediate need to determine the availability of space on the flights. This situation cannot rely on a batch process, which would have the clerk tell the customer to wait until tomorrow's computer report on space availability. The computer has to be in phase with the customer's immediate demand. This relatively new concept is essential in today's competitive, service-oriented society. At one time only such large companies as the airlines could afford it. This is no longer true.

The emerging concept is called *distributed processing*. It means redistributing the power of the computer back to the users, making the data immediately available to them. It means that the machine assumes its rightful position as a tool rather than as a dehumanizing centralized mystifier. The concept requires management to distribute both the data *and* the processing. Not being fond of acronyms, we nevertheless feel that one is appropriate here for clarity. We shall call this distributed data and processing ADDAPT for Automated Distributed Data And Processing Technique. The "and" is the key because it points up the responsibility for returning the data *and* the processing of it back to the user by the most efficient and cost-effective method available. This processing scheme is now feasible on both counts through a new computer technology which has emerged during the past ten years. This is important—the idea is not new, but the feasibility is because of the new computing power.

ENTER THE MINICOMPUTER

The new technology is the fourth-generation computer—the new minicomputers. These versatile, inexpensive computers were designed to fill the void of timeliness between the user and the large-scale computer. We believe it is the people-oriented machine that lets users talk directly to the computer. It cuts into the mystique that grew out of management's abdication of its organizational role as director and supervisor. It is a low-cost yet powerful computer, far superior to the large-scale batch computers in solving the very real day-to-day business processing requirements of any dynamic organization. And the user does not need to know exactly how the thing is engineered to give him his answer.

As computer technology advanced to larger and more powerful systems from 1950 to 1965, a group of young companies led by Digital Equipment Corporation of Maynard, Mass., uncovered a market for a small-scale computer with limited capability, but high reliability. Out of their efforts emerged the new generation of computers.

The compactness of the new computers resulted in the term minicomputer. From 1966 through 1968, this term was an appropriate description of the device in terms of compactness and capability. However, since 1968, there has been a tremendous growth and advance in the industry, and the term "mini" is no longer appropriate in describing the "maxi" capability of the more recent announcements. But it still describes its compact size and reasonable cost.

The development of the minicomputers has been so rapid and prolific that there is no comparison with the earlier units. Memory capabilities are comparable to the large-scale computers, called *mainframes*. Minicomputers can execute at speeds that stagger the imagination, operating in many instances at significantly faster rates than their big brothers, the mainframes. They can support all the peripheral devices the mainframe can, with about half the hardware.

What, then, is the advantage of the mainframe processors over these powerful new-generation computers? In an on-line, real-time environment—none. The difference is about a million dollars—saved. Even some extremely complicated and sophisticated overhead software in the larger systems has done very little to improve the throughput of the mainframe. Conversion to the minicomputer means gaining control over your data. This is achieved with on-line, decentralized processing, which enables the department manager to gain the benefits of the computer directly, rather than indirectly through the traditional channel of a data processing department. The minicomputer can handle the load. There are really only two features that make this computer a minicomputer—the cost and the space requirement.

The misnamed minicomputer computes just like the mainframe computers manufactured by Honeywell, IBM, Burroughs, National Cash Register (NCR), and UNIVAC. Its smaller size has been achieved through miniaturized electronic circuitry. It is cheaper to manufacture and is sold to customers at substantially lower prices. UNIVAC has been manufacturing large-scale 1100-model computers for years. Yet Data General, one of the leading minicomputer manufacturers, makes more computers in a single month than UNIVAC has made of the entire 1100 series.

The minicomputer is an on-line system, which means that users can "talk" to their computer through video display terminals more frequently than through the conventional cards with punched holes. Low cost combined with the on-line feature opens the door to control over the computer function. Today, the minicomputer offers an alternative method of processing data and controlling systems and costs for those companies saddled with a large, expensive central data processing department responsible for all systems and processing of data.

The developer of the minicomputer, Kenneth H. Olsen, an MIT engineer and now president of Digital Equipment Corporation, realized a weakness in the mainframe computer approach. Being batch oriented, the mainframe frequently did not respond satisfactorily to user demands for accurate data within a reasonable time frame. His answer was a user-oriented computer that could provide interactive conversation between the user and the computer without the need for a middle man.

The efficiency and low production cost of the minicomputer opens the door for new systems to satisfy user demands. A network of computers or a distribution of terminal devices may accomplish this need for responsiveness and accuracy, which is enormously expensive with the mainframe. Recall our acronym for distributed data and processing, ADDAPT. We will define distributed processing in Chapter 6 and will clarify the distinction between multiple computers in a network and multiple terminals tied to one host computer. We define how this approach can return management of the data processing function to management.

This approach may well signal the end of an era—an era of spiraling costs and large, centralized computers that could not keep pace with demand. We hope to open eyes and put to rest the myths that have existed for too long. Our purpose is undeniably to place data processing in perspective with the overall objectives of the organization. The goal is to return to management the responsibility for planning of data and data systems, for controlling costs, and for achieving the stated, but unrealized, expectations of data processing.

For, really, a computer is nothing more than a marvelous machine, a sophisticated calculator, which, in addition to fantastic processing speeds and accuracy, has two unique characteristics:

A computer can store and save large volumes of records, transactions, and historical data on magnetic tape, diskettes, cards, and/or magnetic disks similar to long-playing records.

A computer can be programmed to perform a logical sequence of events through our ability to direct it with *languages*—COBOL, FORTRAN, BASIC, and REPORT PROGRAM GENERATOR (RPG) are four of the most frequently used languages.

Getting down to its most elementary features, a computer is a superfast adder, subtracter, multiplier, and divider. It can also make comparisons of data. Its ability to store data and logically follow a sequence of defined instructions makes it possible for computers to rapidly, accurately, and economically calculate payroll, generate checks from accounts payable, and provide information needed to control inventory and schedule production.

To be sure, there are complex technical aspects to data processing. But, the control of data, scheduling of information priorities, and control of costs do not require an in-depth knowledge of these mechanics any more than accounting control requires an understanding of the engineering of calculators or turning on a light requires a knowledge of electronics.

How can the organization control its information using our marvelous computing machine? What information is needed? If the system's user can write his own "simple" reports, why are reams of reports needed? These are the questions that need attention, not the relationship between synchronous and asynchronous communications. Managers, manage!

To help reorient management, we have documented a method. This is not a presentation of theory, but is founded in actual experience gained over a period of several years. The results will be improved information systems, increased computing power, and cuts in the data processing budget of up to 45 percent. Of more importance, however, is the fact that management is the decision maker and the guiding force in the information revolution.

Once it is seen that a computer can be a practical machine, and not a Space Age enigma, direction can be elevated to the level of the president and the board of directors.

This is not our idea alone. Two mainframe manufacturers, Honeywell and NCR, have recently altered their marketing strategies with the new generation of computers and are becoming major proponents of ADDAPTing. Each of these leading companies has established policies that will bring more retailers, bankers, and manufacturers into the electronic age. According to the chief executive officer of one computer manufacturer, computers used to be thought of as "general-purpose machines designed for the programmer and the data processing technician." Honeywell and NCR now say they are making computing devices for the retailer, banking teller, and manufacturing planner. This is the direction of many banks and several Fortune 500 companies. It is the direction from which we came—looking at the organization's needs and the specific requirements of the various departments, not the data processing department. We are witnessing a change of philosophy to more responsive systems from many companies. These systems, including those of the Bank of America, Lowe's Retailers, and Citibank, are discussed in Chapter 5. The responsive minicomputer system eliminates the bottleneck problem experienced with the large-scale centralized computer

and places information entry and retrieval devices out in the user departments. These systems make distributed processing a reality while putting
management back in charge.

WHAT DO WE WANT OUT OF DATA PROCESSING?

What are we really trying to accomplish here? Decentralization? Are we trying to shift responsibilities? Are we trying to penalize, or even criticize, data
processing professionals? Certainly, it is not the latter. What we are present-
ing is an alternative for managers that can improve the effectiveness of data
processing for the organization. If data can be handled more efficiently with
manual systems, fine. If a very large-scale multimillion-dollar computer is
the only answer, so be it. But over the past ten years, we have observed that
management is *not* in charge of the vital systems functions, and certain
unnecessary inefficiencies have become institutionalized. Without management's direction, this may remain the case.

We believe that the time for evaluation and change has arrived. We
believe it is the end of an era of unproductive systems and inflationary costs.
We want you to know about it. Leadership can finally end the ineffective
processing we have all experienced. The first step is to step back and see
where we are by getting down to the zero base of demand and need.

Zero-Base Computing

The Small Organization. Returning control to management should begin
with an evaluation of the need for data processing. In the smaller organizations, where no data processing capability exists today, management should
undertake a detailed analysis of its present operations to determine the real
need for a computer, or even a service bureau, to process the workload at a
remote location. This evaluation should begin with an internal audit without
the intervention of a manufacturer whose self-interest almost certainly pre-
cludes an objective review.

The question here is: Do you need a computer at all, or will manual
processing be sufficient to handle the workload at a reasonable cost and in a
reasonable timetable? Guidelines are available for the so-called computer
feasibility studies. The small firm may want to review these guidelines, or it
may request assistance from its auditor or from a reputable consulting firm.
But management must control this study and not be overwhelmed by any
technical ramifications at this evaluation phase.

The idea is to evaluate the cost benefits of installing a computer—a return to the original concept of *cost displacement*. It is not the mystery it may seem. A computer costs money—does it save you any? Do you eliminate salaries? Do you even want to eliminate salaries? Does increased computing power reduce receivables, or speed payables, to take better advantage of discounts? Does a better inventory system potentially reduce inventory levels or not? These questions can and should be answered. During the second-generation era, and the third to a lesser extent, many companies found that all a computer accomplished was increasing costs and making information more inaccessible than with the old manual records.

The intangible benefits cannot be quantified, but they must be included in the equation. Improved customer service, for example, may not be quantifiable, but it is real. These so-called intangible benefits must be documented and analyzed. The cost and the method to attain them must also be quantified. The result of such an analysis may be that a computer could be feasible, at which time, to use a government phrase, a *request for proposal* should be prepared for the computer manufacturer. This request will generate a plethora of activity from manufacturers to respond. We will discuss this request for proposal later to provide managers with the essential ingredients of this very effective and commonly eye-opening documentation.

The Medium-Size Organization. Medium-size companies that already have computers have a somewhat different problem. These companies pay a monthly computer rental of $1,000 to $25,000. In this vast range, the minicomputer represents a very real alternative. For, as we shall see, the range of the minicomputer's capability is as vast as the mainframe's but with a much smaller price tag.

The challenge is to try to step back and evaluate existing computerized and manual systems. Cost displacement is still involved in that a lower-priced computer may well replace an expensive mainframe.

Which computerized systems are effective in providing timely and accurate data to assist the users in their functions? The user is the judge, not the designer of the system. For example, is a 24-hour delay in reporting inventory status satisfactory? Is a 24-hour delay in responding to customer inquiry a livable situation? Which computerized systems generate reports that still require extensive manual support? For example, we recently reviewed a general ledger system that required manual preparation of the balance sheet and the profit-and-loss statement. On top of that, each entry was printed on a monthly basis—they practically needed a wheelbarrow to transport the December ledger to the accounting department.

Which systems still use punched card files instead of tape, disk, or diskette? Which systems run in obsolete languages, like AUTOCODER or

SPS?* Are there systems that run in emulation mode, indicating that they may not be the most effective? And what about new systems? Is there sufficient capacity to add new applications, or has data processing submitted a request for more equipment, including more core memory, tape drives, or disks? When these conditions exist, it is time to evaluate the entire data processing operation bearing in mind the possibility of the new minicomputer. If none of these conditions exists, we would be very much surprised and a little leary too.

Again, it is healthy to do a data processing audit followed by a request for a proposal. At this time, the availability of new low-cost computing power makes this audit important. Chapter 11 details the method for preparing a request for proposal. It is a case study of how one medium-size firm achieved savings in excess of $200,000 in data processing costs alone through cost displacement.

The Large-Scale Operation. The problem in the Fortune 500 companies is quite different. Yet more and more department heads and division managers are evaluating the economics of their own computer for either the division as a whole or for a specific application. If there is a large corporate centralized computer center, it most likely assesses the division with a data processing service charge. The use of a low-cost computer should be evaluated against this type of charge. This will be more difficult for two simple reasons. First, the total cost to the corporation may be higher with a large mainframe running along with a decentralized minicomputer. Second, our experience has been that the centralized data processing department will fight hard to prevent this from occurring and, as we pointed out before, it most likely will have the computer manufacturer's support.

Still, dedicated managers with profit-and-loss responsibility should accept this cost-oriented challenge. Three northern New York-based firms we know of have justified minicomputers along with a mainframe. In two instances, the minicomputer is used for very specific applications. The central computer facilities, in both cases, could not compete with the minicomputer in responding to the user's requirements, in terms of cost or the time needed to get the application "on the air." In the third instance, a Houston-based division bucked the establishment and installed an on-line manufacturing system with all accounting and information systems. The division selected a minicomputer that costs less than $4,000 per month and will be owned outright after five years.

Another Fortune 500 company spends $11 million a year on two large-

---

* AUTOCODER and SPS were the original programming languages used to instruct the IBM 1401 series of computers back in the early days of data processing. These languages were replaced by simpler languages, such as COBOL and RPG.

scale mainframes. At a recent Data Processing Management Association (DPMA) meeting, the controller told stories of increased staff and of implementation horrors that stunned the audience. It is possible that some relief could be attained through intelligent analysis of the use of minicomputers.

One manufacturing concern in Tennessee with whom we work closely uses a minicomputer from Digital Equipment Company that processes thousands of transactions daily at a rate of 6 cents per transaction. The system is dedicated and on-line. The corporate mainframe fought it all the way, but couldn't project less than 12 cents per transaction in batch mode. Because of the corporation's location, reports would be received two to three days after the fact. Even so, they fought so vehemently against the minicomputer that more than a year was lost in debate.

So even the largest Fortune 500 company can show the potential for cost displacement with one or a series of minicomputers. Citibank is one example of a company that seriously evaluated cost. Citibank installed a great number of minicomputers to handle such tiresome and costly manual functions as loan processing and demand-deposit accounting. Citibank officials have computerized (minicomputer, that is) functions that account for more than 5,000 positions and $80 million over five years. At the same time, responsiveness has reportedly improved. So the cost audit and zero-base budget may be equally rewarding for the Fortune 500 company.

Cost-Effectiveness

The only real criterion for using data processing at all comes down to cost-effectiveness. If tasks can be performed manually in a quick, easy, and accurate manner, an expensive computer is not required. But as organizations grow in size and complexity, the use of computers becomes feasible and desirable. Cost-effectiveness, on the other hand, depends on the circumstances, the company's requirements, and the computer selected. Our experience has shown that the new-generation computer is by far the most cost-effective solution for the small and the very largest corporations.

In speed, reliability, and manipulation of data, the new generation of computers runs circles around the older batch-processing machines, and at drastically lower costs. A recent study performed by the British Bureau of Standards showed results that must have been embarrassing to many mainframe vendors. Five of the tested machines were in the new generation. In comparing the costs, the IBM 360/40, at more than $18,000 a month, did not even qualify. The new Data General Eclipse was timed equally as fast as the expensive IBM 360/50, and the Eclipse can be leased for less than $4,000 per month.

Because of the new, smaller integrated circuitry, the new-generation computer has established a remarkable record of maintenance-free reliability. According to a recent study in the *Harvard Business Review*, the new-generation computer is substantially more reliable than the third-generation machines and has a much longer mean time before failure (MTBF) rate, the industry standard for measuring performance. This reliability, in itself, generates cost savings and lowers the frustration level of the users.

The new-generation computer is simpler in concept than the older computer. Its simplified operating system, job control, and programming ease can be converted directly into cost savings. Furthermore, unlike many batch-processing units, the new-generation computer can perform many tasks simultaneously. New reports and new tools for analysis are available within minutes thanks to the powerful report writer features of the new generation (for example, the QUERY* language developed by Hewlett-Packard for non-programmer use). ADDAPT simply makes sense—dollars and cents.

One major manufacturer raised its prices in the latter part of 1976. It was the same old story. But did you know that the cost of minicomputers made by the largest manufacturer, Digital Equipment Corporation, has decreased by an average of 17 percent each year for the past five years? Did you know that another minicomputer manufacturer, Hewlett-Packard, announced a new, more powerful line of computers in 1976, at a lower price than the earlier models? These computers mean real savings to those who will evaluate them.

RESISTANCE TO CHANGE

In an attempt to make distributed data and processing a reality, management may face prejudices and resentment. Although it means challenging marketing strategies, experience shows the validity of this new approach. Experience proved the obvious, that information processing should, and must, be in the hands of the user.

The major advantages may not be realized immediately. A reduction in data processing costs of 45 percent is important, but the vast new data base available to planners, the timeliness of data, and the concentration of responsibilities are the real payoff areas. But, of course, the transition is not a simple one.

The transition from batch to on-line processing may be accomplished

*QUERY is a computer programming language for the layman. This simple, English-language instruction or command allows the nonprogrammer to extract information from the computer as well as print reports to satisfy unique information needs.

only after considerable frustration. The technology is available at reasonable costs, and the cost-effectiveness can be proved, but the real challenge is people—to convince and develop their trust and their support.

Even when present conditions are clearly unfavorable, the idea of change, the end of the evolutionary process, comes up against attack and resistance. The past, plainly in the interest of a few, was in several of our experiences supported beyond any rational arguments. Fear and selfish motivations persisted long after concrete proof had established that a change was essential for any progress to be made. The treasurer of one small company grew wary. He challenged us: "What you say is impossible—a contradiction, in fact. We cannot get better systems and more power at lower costs. To increase power, we must upgrade, from my experience." This view is indicative of the old generation that has fostered our evolutionary growth era. Can this generation of managers evaluate a new alternative *objectively?*

In yet another but related incident, when we first began to explore the potential for competitive hardware, the entire data processing staff did not take the suggestion seriously. The data processing manager wrote, "In response to your suggestions, our staff is not interested in pursuing the use of minicomputers. They have informed me that small-computer experience such as you propose will not be particularly impressive on their résumés!" Incredible, yet this naive, sincere statement reflected the inner concerns of a staff trained in only one way of thinking. Without a doubt, ignorance of a new approach had ruled out acceptance of change.

It is our aim to prepare management for the unavoidable, as the data processing staff may be neither objective nor receptive to any proposal of change from a large-scale computer to decentralized, distributed processing. In the first place, this approach represents a very real threat to the technical staff because a smaller, decentralized system logically requires fewer people. It eliminates the need for a large central computer center. To the smart technician, it will be further apparent that a good systems design, a comprehensive information data base, and a powerful user report-generation capability may well reduce a large systems programming and analysis staff. Job preservation is a strong motive for resistance to change.

We can anticipate the reaction to any proposed changes of this nature. But we want to present an alternative, one that will not mean elimination of the existing professional staff yet will allow for new technical expertise to implement a distributed processing system.

Many data processing professionals are genuinely concerned about falling behind. They believe that in the long run their job security rests with being knowledgeable of the predominant computer system manufactured by

IBM, and the predominant language, COBOL. The organization must still recognize that *people* are unquestionably the key element in the success of data processing, people, not hardware. Your information system is no better than the people who design and use it.

There is a job to do: to educate employee viewpoints to company needs and problems while respecting their ingrained long-term need for security. "To hell with your résumé," is a short-sighted approach, however tempting.

SUMMARY

The marketing strategy of evolutionary-growth computers is obsolete. As part of the mystery, promises are made for new power, speed, and capability that will result in an effective data processing system but are often unfulfilled.

The new-generation computer makes it possible for management to challenge the evolution. This book is written to put management in a position to control its data processing resources. We recognize that challenge and the resistance that must be faced if our recommendations are followed. But as you will see, the benefits far outweigh any temporary resistance that will be encountered. Management can no longer afford to abdicate its role.

For computer costs and the effectiveness of systems are management's responsibility. They have always been his, and his unwitting abdication of this responsibility has had serious implications. This matter can no longer be delegated to the data processing manager. Let us end that era once and for all.

The process called ADDAPT, distributed data and processing, involves a point of view that is gaining popularity among many objective leaders in the field of data processing. We intend to challenge management to reevaluate its data processing posture, to join the new generation, and to develop acceptance among the users and the data processing professionals.

In evaluating its present data processing situation, managers should consider the three benefits of a *distributed system*. First, it is a system of minicomputers that provides interactive conversation through video terminals. By interactive conversation, we mean that through programmed control the computers guide the user through each step of data entry, at the same time validating the data and permitting immediate correction of errors (see Chapter 7). Interactive conversation instantly eliminates the need for many clerical steps, while accelerating the entry, accuracy, and timeliness of all computer-maintained information.

Second, managers should evaluate the benefits of integrated data bases of information (collections of data libraries) for the organization as an entity. An integrated data base is a library of information maintained on the computer that provides information for more than one system. Each data base, no longer categorized as payroll, accounts payable, or inventory control, reflects the information needs of the organization. Each data base may be simultaneously updated by users who are familiar with, and responsible for, the data. The existence of this organization of information prevents duplication of data, provides standardization, reduces processing and maintenance costs, and provides faster and more meaningful access to, and reporting of, data.

Finally, managers should evaluate the benefits of multiprocessing capability. Different applications and transactions from the same or different organizational units can be processed simultaneously. Thus, the application of cash, the placement of a purchase order, the payment of a bill, and the acceptance of a new employee may be overlapped and processed concurrently. Time is money. To waste it in data processing is costly.

The concept we call ADDAPT encompasses these three benefits: interactive conversation, integrative data bases, and multiprocessing capability. These are ideas whose time has come. And we have come a long way.

3

The Evolution of the Computer
An Unofficial History

It all started with ENIAC (the Electrical Numerical Integrator and Calculator), the first real computer, which was developed at the Moore School of the University of Pennsylvania in the early 1940s. ENIAC weighed more than 30 tons, literally took up rooms, and contained nearly 19,000 valves. This tribute to the ingenuity of humankind was conceived by Dr. John W. Mauchly and engineered by Dr. J. Presper Eckert. ENIAC was a decimal machine that operated on the basis of tens and used the valves for the electronic pulse-switching function.

CALCULATOR OR COMPUTER?

Some might mistakenly think of the earlier work at the U.S. Bureau of the Census as computing. It is true that in the 1890 census, Dr. Herman Hollerith devised a machine and a coding system that could read holes punched in cards that represented data, and could then sort and count them. This was the first successful unit record processor. But it was a sophisticated calculator, not a computer. Computers solve complex mathematical equations rapidly and repeatedly. Early calculators had the capability of counting. But it was Hollerith who developed the card so many people now refer to as the IBM card. It is really the Hollerith card, invented by Herman Hollerith.

The ENIAC was a major development, designed to make advanced calculations and to work out ballistics tables for the U.S. Army in its war efforts. This early computer was, in fact, financed by the Army. It is considered an advanced computer because it incorporated the ability to program or store problem calculations, was completely electronic, and had no moving parts. Its limitations, other than size, of course, were evident—to process only one program or problem at a time or to switch from one problem to another was a major effort. You speak of your valve jobs!

While ENIAC was being developed here, the British were also working on computers in their war effort. At the Department of Communications of the British Foreign Office, Alan Turing developed the rudimentary concepts of stored programs, using paper-tape recorders. This work then inspired Professor M. H. A. Newman of Cambridge to develop the well-known Colossus series of computers that first became operational in December 1943. Although the control mechanism worked on the principle of an exterior, plug-in systems design, data was entered from punched paper tape, and stored programs were used to convey instructions through the valve concept. Many people worked on the new computer concepts at the time. Even now, a small credit war rages in the United States and England. We don't want to get into that battle.

In the early 1940s, Dr. Norbert Weiner, of the Massachusetts Institute of Technology, developed the theory of *cybernetics*. Cybernetics is the study of human control functions and of the mechanical and electrical systems designed to replace them. Dr. Weiner was interested in using computers to emulate human communication. His work established several of the basic principles of the modern computer. And it was these very principles that took our society from the lowly calculator to the sophisticated computer.

Prior to the application of these principles, the computer was nothing more than a calculating machine. Dr. Weiner sought the means to shift the computing function away from the human and to the machine. It required the ability to perform multiple operations, make logical decisions on the basis of empirical evidence, and accomplish this without human intervention.

For the first time, the information and the program written to work on it could be accepted and stored in this computer simultaneously. Another advance was the adoption of the binary, or base 2, standard, rather than decimal arithmetic. This innovation of Dr. Weiner's established the basic architecture for modern computing, which has not changed significantly even today. His architectural design involves five concepts or principles that may seem elementary to us now, but they were revolutionary and ingenious at the time. These machines should:

1. Have a numerical central adding and multiplying apparatus (as opposed to differential analysis), using *registers* for execution.
2. Use electronic circuitry rather than gears or mechanical relays.
3. Use binary arithmetic (in accordance with the early policies of Bell Telephone Laboratories).
4. Not involve human intervention—programs should be loaded in the machine.

5. Contain a machine-loadable apparatus to store, read, and erase data, and be removed for storage of new data.

These features distinguished the computer from the calculator. Dr. Weiner's ideas changed the world of technology and laid the basis for the work of Dr. John von Neumann of the Institute of Advanced Study at Princeton University. Retained by the Moore School to advance the work on ENIAC, Dr. von Neumann published, in 1945, a report on the next successful U.S.-based computer, the EDVAC (Electronic Discrete Variable Automatic Computer).

But at the time EDVAC was just a concept, not the reality ENIAC was. In the interim, Harvard had developed another computer, similar to ENIAC, called the Harvard MK-1, a decimal machine designed by another American computer pioneer, Howard Aiken. It was built by a company called International Business Machines Corporation, IBM. Scientific computing had become a reality.

Dr. Eckert and Dr. Mauchly met again in August 1945, at the original site of ENIAC, the Moore School of the University of Pennsylvania. The subject was von Neumann's design of EDVAC. This was a critical conference, for although the principles of computing were clear, the design criteria were not. Dr. Jay Forrester, who represented the Massachusetts Institute of Technology, was also there. He and MIT would later develop the early Whirlwind Computer for the Navy. Dr. von Neumann had come to represent Princeton.

The early ideas of these men were open to patent, making it, indeed, a crucial period. Eckert and Mauchly had begun to realize the commercial applicability of these marvelous machines. Soon afterward, they resigned from their posts at the University of Pennsylvania and founded the first computer company per se. The commercial computer concept developed by these men was originally rejected by the IBM Corporation. IBM would concentrate on the concept of calculators because computers were not economically feasible, it was thought.

The Moore School conference was instrumental in firming up these early principles. More was on the way in the field of scientific computing. Using these same concepts Eckert and Mauchly formed their own company, the Eckert and Mauchly Computing Company (EMCC). The year was 1948—only 30 years ago—and there were no commercial computers available. Doesn't it seem incredible, considering how much of an impact computers have on our lives today? Eventually, EMCC was sold to the Remington Rand Corporation.

At the time, Remington Rand, with the new UNIVAC computers of

Eckert and Mauchly, was the only computer company in the world. Other companies, such as IBM, Honeywell, General Electric, and RCA, were not convinced of the commercial applicability and feasibility of computers. Each went its own way with its primary products outside computers. IBM, the current world leader by a substantial margin, concentrated on large-scale electrical calculators that used valves for the circuit-switching function. IBM also marketed complementary equipment, such as card sorters and card collaters. This was before 1950, for it was not until 1951 that IBM began to make its own computers.

THE COMPANIES

Remington Rand appears to have been the early leader in computers with its UNIVAC machines. These were the machines and concepts developed by Dr. Mauchly and Dr. Eckert. Remington Rand was an established company with a history going back to the early 1900s that had the product base to support the early developmental costs, which must have been considerable.

Herman Hollerith, mentioned earlier in connection with his work with the Bureau of the Census, had worked for a predecessor of IBM, the Computing Tabulating and Recording Company, back in the 1880s. So, Mr. Hollerith brought his Hollerith machines and his Hollerith cards to IBM. This is probably how IBM established its dominant lead in business machines. In the early days, IBM also dominated the card market and would lease its equipment only to those who would also use its cards. By leasing, IBM established a source of revenue that would carry it through the depression. Into the 1940s and up to the advent of commercial computers, IBM was the leader in business machines and calculators.

IBM also established a policy of price leadership during this time. Even today, IBM sets its prices above those of competitors and does it successfully. The reason IBM can set its own price structure at a high level is service. IBM realized back in the forties that other companies could also make computers and calculators—patents afforded only partial protection. By establishing itself as the leader in service, IBM was set off from the rest and was assured a future in the new world of computers.

Sperry-Rand sold the very first computer marketed in the United States. It was a UNIVAC machine designed by Mauchly and Eckert, and it was sold to the Bureau of the Census in 1950. IBM's entry came in 1951 when it produced the IBM 701, first of a series. It was sold to the federal government primarily for large mathematical computations and was IBM's contribution to ongoing defense efforts. By 1952, UNIVAC still had the upper hand with its more efficient computer.

While UNIVAC and IBM progressed through these early days with the first generation of computers, IBM remained dominant in the business calculator field. Continuing to produce more sophisticated calculators with designations such as 602s and 603s and later 402s, IBM had more than 5,000 installations by 1957. This provided a base for dominance in computers as well. IBM's strong marketing strategy moved customers up from calculators to their computer line.

THE NEW GENERATION

Survival in the early days depended on specialized marketing. UNIVAC concentrated on the military market, which ultimately led to on-line control systems. Then General Electric entered the field and headed off toward the banking and heavy paperwork industries. IBM put its considerable talent toward developing the business community. No single company has had more positive impact on industry in the area of data processing than IBM. IBM made commercial data processing a reality. IBM and UNIVAC wisely started with an understandable batch orientation, which modified existing manual systems with faster speeds and reasonable costs.

These differing approaches of UNIVAC, GE, and IBM can be seen even today. UNIVAC developed military systems with on-line terminals to support our national defense through command and control processing. The cost is high, but the market is the Pentagon where UNIVAC's 1100 series has accomplished a major penetration. The cost is so high that the current minicomputer companies can manufacture in a single month more computers than UNIVAC has ever made of the 1100 series. General Electric focused on the multiple-user banking market and evolved a timesharing environment. Although a limited market requiring heavy capital investments, GE remains the technical leader in timesharing systems and international communications. IBM went after the rest.

The impact of IBM was immediate, far exceeding that of any other company because of its realistic marketing approach and the vastness of its market. The 1960s saw a rush for computers that has been likened to the second Oklahoma land rush. In today's aftermath, IBM is the leader by a substantial percentage, as can be seen in Table 2.

Control Data didn't enter the race until 1966 and they concentrated almost entirely on the scientific market. Its penetration was significant because

Table 2. Mainframe computers.

Company	1975 Shipments* (millions)	Share of Market (%)
IBM	$6,500	65.5
Honeywell	760	7.6
Burroughs	710	7.1
Sperry (UNIVAC)	630	6.3
NCR	300	3.0
Control Data	265	2.7

*New production valued at purchase price.
SOURCE: "Minicomputers Challenge the Big Machines," *Business Week*, April 26, 1976.

of its high-quality, dependable products. Honeywell, Burroughs, RCA, and NCR had begun making computers during the late 1950s.

The rate of technological growth and new developments of the 1950s and 1960s was phenomenal. But the late 1960s through the 1970s saw new products in the large-scale computers market all but dry up. Even today, IBM markets the 370 series with virtual memory. But there is nothing new about virtual memory. It was actually offered by Burroughs during the early 1970s. As technology died down, several giant confrontations arose in this embattled industry, according to *Business Week*. Brutal showdowns were witnessed between IBM and GE, IBM and Control Data and RCA, and IBM and the European consortium of Siemens, Phillips, and Compagnie Internationale pour l'Informatique. In this country, GE and RCA withdrew from the computer business. The remaining companies continued to grow as the competition became more manageable.

Growth for the mainframe computers had come about through increased speeds and improved utilization of memory and its associated peripheral equipment, but a technical drought had developed in major new developments. It signaled the end of an era—one that had lasted for more than a quarter of a century and that had fostered scores of new products, each larger and more powerful than the last. The pattern was established: Plant an idea, expand it, and improve it, but don't change it! The buzz word became: compatibility—not change. The idea is to move up in power, speed, and ultimately, cost.

By 1970, computers were being marketed that could handle hundreds of millions of bytes (characters) of data with new disk-storage devices (and tapes) and millions of bytes of memory, while operating on multiple applications simultaneously. The costs of these large-scale computers were considerable, and although larger and costlier, they were basically the same old systems model, no different from the forerunners of the decade before.

A horse of a new color or, as a dear friend of ours used to say, "Same girl—new dress"? Everything had been done that could be done to advance the mainframe product line without making a radical change in processing philosophy. Was this the end of an era?

Mainframe manufacturers had invested heavily in the large-scale computers. A marketing strategy of evolutionary growth had been developed and was in place and working. So much momentum had been placed on expanding the existing products that the individual manufacturer was caught in an upward spiral. Furthermore, the mainframe manufacturers had (and still have) a mainframe problem: to protect and preserve existing product lines and a large customer rental base. Therefore, developing new products with improved capacity and at lower costs is fine and encouraged, but what about all those earlier customers who paid premium prices? And what if the new product flies in the face of compatibility? If a customer is made to evaluate a complete conversion to new systems, computers, and languages, it may well open the door to competitors and break the evolutionary process. Thus, the manufacturers, in fact, orchestrated the data processing phenomenon in American businesses, service organizations, and government.

One vice-president of systems for a large consulting firm in the Midwest recently described the situation matter of factly in an article in *Infosystems,* a leading data processing publication for management:

> Corporations must make changes in their computer systems in order to keep up with their business growth. Unfortunately, the data processing world is governed and tightly controlled by the manufacturers of EDP equipment and by the technicians that manage that equipment. The aim of the manufacturer is to sell equipment by offering planned technological advances. The sad truth of the matter is that computer changes in companies are often driven by technology without regard for the goals of the company or economic justification.*

The very sad truth, indeed. How did we get ourselves into this lamentable position? It can be understood if we travel quickly through the evolution of computers—what has become known as the computer generations. Let's begin with the unit record era and then move on to the first-generation computers.

*Robert C. Chomko, "ABC's of Improved Computer Performance," *Infosystems,* October 1976, pp. 50–51.

The first calculators in the commercial market, forerunners of computers, were the unit record processing machines. These machines derived their name from the way they functioned—one record at a time. Each record was recorded on an 80-column card, which became known throughout the world as an IBM card (but now you know that the real name is "Hollerith" card). Information was "keypunched" into specific, predefined columns on the 80-column card.

The calculator was programmed to read the card, to accumulate totals, and to print. Programming was achieved through "wired boards," which directed the electrical circuitry in making these simple mathematical operations of adding, subtracting, multiplying, and dividing. To run a program meant to plug in a board and stack the cards; the result was a printed report. Since there was no means of storing data (other than totals), systems were limited to the data on the card and its resulting totals.

Still, unit record equipment was a major improvement in the processing of large volumes of data, and it had several major impacts on the organization by creating a new entity and reducing so much to impersonal codes. The new unit record equipment consisted of several new machines:

□ A keypunch machine to code the card. A similar verifier read the card to validate the original entry. Interpreters printed the information on the cards for sight verification and reading.
□ Sorting machines to put the cards in order.
□ Collating machines to intermix two decks of cards that used like coding (such as a master payroll card and a detail weekly hours-worked card).
□ Calculating printers (such as IBM's 402–403 series), which printed reports from data on the cards.

There were also several new functions:

□ Wiring the boards for programming the unit record equipment.
□ Physically operating the equipment, loading paper and cards.
□ Coordinating different applications (scheduling to satisfy user requirements).
□ Designing and implementing new systems to take advantage of the new equipment.

These new machines and functions led to the creation of the data processing department, which reported primarily through the accounting organization but was held responsible for all applications. Staffing was a problem as we pointed out earlier, because relevant skills did not exist prior to the advent of these calculators. The manufacturer inevitably took a lead in personnel selection and, by agreement, in all user training on site and at the manufacturer's site, all of which seemed perfectly normal and desirable.

A new impersonalization was imposed on the users of data processing. The age of the number was entered, whether it was wanted or not. It started with the limited capability of the card and its 80 columns of data. Accounting (including payroll) and management reports were coordinated on punched cards through the new data processing department. There were employee cards, accounts payable cards, customer cards, inventory cards, exception cards, discount cards, and cards for all occasions or no occasions.

The cards were limited, of course, but codes, rather than long alphabetic descriptions, allowed for more data in 80 columns. It became necessary, therefore, to consider people and things according to numbers. Instead of using the conventional descriptive names of the past, employees were defined for the calculator by numbers, general ledger accounts by code, customers by numbers, and on and on. The punched card had brought on an entirely new philosophy. The actual had given way to the symbolic. At the same time, the machine became the dominant status symbol and few big companies failed to acquire one. Conversion to numbers was accepted and implemented with its impersonal implications because it was indeed the thing to do during the unit record era. More than 5,000 were installed by 1957, a significant marketing accomplishment.

Today many people look back nostalgically at unit record equipment, as we do. Once, in Fort Wayne, Indiana, the president of a large corporation asked us to help him gain control of a $5 million inventory of steel shipping containers. Where were those rascals? The problem was one of monitoring the reporting of shipments. We studied the problem for a week and decided we could put the system on the corporation's IBM 360/30 in three months. This was not acceptable. But, like many other companies, the corporation's 360/30 shared its workload with unit record equipment. The data processing department had moved to the third generation, but held tightly to the machines they understood better. We then recommended that they put the inventory control system on the unit record equipment in one week. We knew the steel containers followed a logical path from the initial contract, to placement at the customer's site, to loading, to shipping, and finally to receiving at the destination. We coded each move and through adding we could assure an even number 0 or 2 for each valid move. We then subtracted the location code from the previous move, which should always zero out, unless a move was made but not reported.

So, through adding and subtracting and looking for an even-number balance, the corporation could detect instances in which moves were going unreported. Corrective action was immediate by telegraph to our "around-the-world" agents. It all took one week and it did the job. All we had to do was wire several boards to add and subtract. Over the next year, the containers were traced down and the inventory regained. Most of the containers were in Viet Nam, serving as foxholes for the troops. The point was clear—unit record equipment had solved our problem in just one week because of its simplicity. The data processing staff had a more complex environment to work in. The era of long systems lead times and frustrated managers was upon us.

Optimism was high, nevertheless, in the early days of unit record processing, and the record will show that managers responded favorably to the recommendations of the manufacturer and their new data processing managers since the success of the operation seemed so important. Its uniqueness and great potential quickly made the data processing department a central new element in the organizational structure. It also became somewhat removed from the normal mode of company operations. The department was staffed by individuals who were dependent on the manufacturer for technical assistance, for all training, and, in many cases, for the recruitment of new personnel. The data processing manager developed a close relationship to the manufacturer, and out of pure necessity the manufacturer filled the void by providing essential support to the organization. At the time, IBM was the leader in providing competent technical support to industry. But, because of its antitrust problems, IBM is now forced to charge for its services, that is, to give separate prices for equipment and supporting services, a phenomenon known as "unbundling." Prior to its unbundling phase, IBM provided the very expert service that had put them at the top of the industry.

Other first-generation computers, which were introduced during this time period, were the large scientific computers discussed earlier—ENIAC, EDVAC, Colossus, and Whirlwind. They served the important function of developing the principles used today in the second- and third-generation computers. The first generation was made possible only through the large government grants both here and abroad. IBM's first-generation 700 series was developed through government grants. Several of the original twenty 701 systems were sold to industry, however. General Electric, for example, was an early user of IBM's 701 computers.

The vacuum-tube era, which followed in the late 1950s, is generally considered to have marked the advent of the second generation. It was during this generation that we saw that second Oklahoma land rush. Let's see what happened to the industry during this time and how it so greatly affected business data processing as we know it today.

THE VACUUM-TUBE ERA

The introduction of the vacuum tube to the mainframe technology ushered in the second-generation computers. This generation served to fortify the influence of the manufacturer on the business community. This was still necessary even in the early 1960s. The ever-expanding technology made it almost impossible to keep up with the changes and innovations while still running the day-to-day operations in a working environment. The manufacturer performed this critical function while the data processing manager struggled with new systems developments, new languages, and new capabilities.

The second generation significantly expanded the capability of the computer by providing a feasible means of storing data in memory. This new capability immediately made the unit record equipment and the large-scale calculators obsolete. The wired board was no longer necessary as programs (instructions) were written in a new symbolic language that could be processed by the computer to generate more sophisticated reports and at greatly increased speeds. In addition, the new machines were able to store historical information on auxiliary devices available for retrieval upon request. As we shall see in Chapter 8, a new breed of technician, the systems analyst, was assigned the task of applying scientific methods to produce those reports, upon request.

The capability of memory opened up a spectrum of possibilities that were not possible with unit record equipment. The move up to new computers was justifiable in many instances. The processing time alone was reduced by a factor of ten, which meant the user could easily process ten times more data. But was this important? The promise, at the time, was unlimited benefits, but the potential was not always realized. Why?

The hardware technology had clearly outstripped the software capability. In other words, although the computer had taken a giant step forward, without the supporting programs (software), they were technically crippled. How many companies had the rude awakening that hardware did not function unless we had the tools (software) and the trained staff to make it work? And again, the second generation represented a whole new technology that had to be learned. No educational background precisely fit the needs of the new technology. Once again, the burden was placed on the manufacturer to train and even recruit personnel. At this time, personnel aptitude tests had to be administered by the manufacturers. Out of necessity, the manufacturer evaluated the user's personnel and exerted a tremendous impact on hiring policy. When one of the authors got his first job with a Fortune 500 company, it was IBM that administered the aptitude test.

Another shortcoming in the second generation that prevented realization of the computer's potential was the "risk of conversion." The logic of the unit record—one record at a time—was carried over into the new generation. In many instances, entire systems were converted from the unit record equipment to the computer, in an attempt to shift as quickly as possible to the new machine. However, this effort failed to take advantage of the new capability.

We recall the frantic effort to use the manufacturer's software to speed the process of transferring data from cards to tape. We do not remember the same fervor for redesigning systems for the sophisticated new hardware. Unfortunately, the majority of conversions continued to use a good portion of the old because it was simpler to convert than to design. Today, many of those companies that made the conversion have early-generation systems operating on third-generation computers. And many organizations even held onto their unit record equipment, as in Fort Wayne, Indiana. The IBM 402 tabulator cranked along, sitting right beside the big mainframe. In another installation we know, the mainframe literally punched out cards to be processed on the unit record gear. The large-scale computer ran manufacturing operations, while the unit record equipment processed payroll and accounts payable. The computer was acting as a source of input to the unit record equipment. Then, during the second shift, this company leased out its large-scale computer. Was management occupying its role as director and protector of the assets? Effective data processing? Hardly!

The user organizations themselves were frequently ill-prepared to implement systems effectively. The computer was nothing more than a symbol of progressive management. If the organization could afford a computer during the prosperous early 1960s, it got one, even if it was unprepared to make it pay off. Furthermore, assistance from consulting firms was scarce and expensive. Programming, or software, houses were just beginning to be set up to meet the need. Service bureaus were also coming into being, but very slowly, and they were having their share of technical problems. We remember it well. The organization that opted for long-term potential had to put up with short-term pain, problems, and risks.

Finally, although the vacuum tube, second-generation computer went far beyond the large, often unreliable first-generation computing system, it was restricted in memory capacity, which normally consisted of 16,000 characters of main memory, was sensitive to temperature changes and electric current fluctuations, and was subject to sequential processing of large tape files. It could execute only one program at a time. In most cases, programs were loaded through decks of cards, a tedious and extremely time-consuming process, which made programming expensive. Memory restrictions made applications simple and repetitive in nature.

During the era of the second generation, the data processing department attained a strong position in the organization. New positions were created, which included the programmer and, as mentioned earlier, the systems analyst. The manufacturer became increasingly important as a source of essential support. For the first time, the manufacturer put on his marketing hat and guided the organization through a series of hardware evolutions to faster and larger computers within the same family. The early 1960s witnessed a terrible cost spiral that may finally come to a welcome end with the emergence of the minicomputer.

THE TRANSISTOR-ERA LOGIC

Transistorized circuits in the computer during the mid-1960s marked the culmination of the mainframe evolution. Again, the new technology made the previous technology obsolete. The restrictions on memory were dissolved as memory banks became available in a relatively compact chassis, the size of a standard refrigerator as compared to the suite-size ENIAC. Memory could be leased in increments of 8,000 to 16,000 *bytes,* a unit of electronically sensitized bits of data. Computers could be as large as 1 million bytes of core memory, as opposed to the 16K-character limit of the earlier machines. Execution speeds of the new computer were in the Space Age compared to its predecessor. This was the third-generation computer.

The third-generation system introduced an improved data-storing device, the random access disk, which revolutionized the industry. Data could now be written and read simultaneously and immediately without having to pass sequentially through large tape files. Data from any disk, in the multiple disk design, could be retrieved within fractions of a second. Disk systems were capable of storing millions of bytes of information. Programs could be stored and executed on these disks with far greater speed than had been possible when programs had to be read in by cards. Programs could now be called into the computer in seconds.

The major improvements over the second-generation system were reduced size and fantastic speed. The computer could now compute at previously unheard-of speeds for the commercial user. At the same time, the manufacturers announced that the second-generation computers would no longer be supported. Management, once again, was asked to convert to the newer, faster machines. The recommendations might have come directly from the data processing manager, but the encouragement was from outside. The alternative was not good in that the new generation was to be supported and the data processing staff was, by now, very dependent upon support (still true, in fact). In addition, new expectations were raised which in many cases were, again, unrealized. Why this time?

Even with the new disks, we still had to contend with the compatibility factor: The new computer could process data in the same sequential manner as the second-generation equipment. Feeling the pain of the last conversion, many data processing departments again shortcut the systems effort and converted sequential tape files to sequential disk files. And the special hardware forced the manufacturer to encourage companies to use old-function "emulation" programs with the new computer. We know of only a few installations that did not operate, for many years, under emulation. And the consultants became wealthy extricating clients from the horrors of data processing.

New languages were introduced that were designed to make the programmer's life easier. COBOL and RPG were the popular commercial languages supported by most manufacturers in an attempt to standardize. New software utility programs (such as card-to-disk and sorts) were introduced to ease the programming burden. These languages were powerful tools for the third-generation programmer and analyst. However, there was a serious trade-off: the ease of programming was achieved at the cost of efficiency. The savings gained by the new languages were expended in the cost of new memory required to take advantage of the so-called high-level languages.

The inefficiencies of the new languages were, simply stated, detrimental to effective data processing. More than ever, the need for large central data processing departments was set in concrete. The cost of computing was escalating rapidly. The more features the computer supported, the higher the operating costs. As computers became more sophisticated in the third generation, further job classifications were deemed essential. The old programmer became a systems programmer or an applications programmer. Systems managers came on the scene in an attempt to understand the new operating (software) systems that drove the computer. Data processing personnel costs grew dramatically, but in direct relation to the increased cost of the computer.

A very disturbing trend became apparent during the third-generation era. The manufacturer was making computers for data processing people rather than for the end user. The validity of this statement can be seen in the creation of high-level languages, utility programs, and job-control features, while perpetuating the need for a large central bottleneck, far removed from the end user. The disregard for the real needs of the user perpetuated by most mainframe companies signaled the end of an era.

A SHORT HISTORY COMPLETED

Early sales of computers in the second generation were not difficult to make. Many salespeople became rich during the halcyon years.

Industry sought assistance in the paperwork explosion, and the manufacturer responded with the potential answer. In the very earliest days, salespeople were primarily electrical engineers who seemed to be best suited for the new electrical machines. Their role encompassed sales, technical support, systems design, training, programming, and playing all-around nursemaid. But businessmen they were not.

As the industry moved into the third generation, marketing strategies and sales forces matured. During the mid- to late sixties, the one-piece band blossomed into an orchestra. Specialization became the byword. The successful computer manufacturer developed training experts, systems engineers for technical matters, and customer engineers for maintenance. The need to centralize all these disciplines into one electrical engineer vanished, and a new breed of salesperson emerged. A typical profile may have been a Wharton, Stanford, or Harvard MBA, clean-cut and aggressive. These were well-trained analysts, supported by a large base of technical support, who could communicate with the data processing staff and its management. For a short period, some manufacturers even enforced a dress code on their salespeople—the man in the gray flannel suit became a familiar face at their customer's location.

This new image was necessary because by this time the stakes were high. Third-generation computers were leased for $10,000 per month and higher, not including the staff costs, space, and supplies. Data processing had become "big business," and sales running into billions of dollars required real professionals who could be comfortable with the users' top management. An extensive sales training program was launched. Months of intensive training in technology and the psychology of sales were required before the first potential account could be attempted. A polished professional left those training sessions. Versed in organizational dynamics, cool under pressure, the computer salesperson and the most effective marketing organizations in the world had been structured. Salaries were supplemented by bonuses and, in at least one case, penalties were levied for loss of an established account.

Quite understandably, management was at a disadvantage in dealing with computer salespeople, who possessed the technical background to evaluate hardware proposals. Management's own data processing staff recommended the upgraded, new products as directed by the technical support of the salespeople. The arguments for increased capacity were logical and well presented by a business-oriented salesforce. Above all, data processing was remote, different: it was set off in the organization and, with the manufacturer, controlled its own destiny. Management soon abdicated its responsibility and would begin to pay the price. The data processing world was governed by the equipment manufacturer and the technicians assigned to manage the computer.

AS THE DUST SETTLES

Today, two inescapable truths emerge from the short history of data processing. In the first place, born originally of necessity, but later reared from a brilliant marketing strategy, the manufacturer's representative became an integral part of the data processing staff. As such, the representative greatly influenced the decision-making process of some organizations, especially as it pertained to new products and equipment. The manufacturers, somewhat sidetracked from their original goals, began to produce computers for the data processing staff, leaving the door open for a new generation of user-oriented computers. As we shall see, the founders of the minicomputers walked right through that door.

Second, a new marketing strategy was evolving. Although the early move from unit record equipment to the second-generation computers was understandable in most cases, incremental growth within the same family of computers during the second and third generations seems less justifiable. In most instances, the growth in costs and sophistication was not commensurate with the growth in effectiveness, as many wealthy consultants will attest. It further demonstrated management's abdication of its leadership role. It highlighted the need to justify cost increases against actual improvements, which could be measured, and to hold manufacturers to their commitments. This was not done.

FOURTH-GENERATION COMPUTERS

The real issue here is not the past. It is the future, as represented by the fourth-generation minicomputers and the advancement to distributed data and processing. Will management continue to be dominated by a philosophy that is not clearly in its best interest and by a series of computers designed for the data processing department? Or will management take charge and evaluate this new potential for computing power, which dollar for dollar surpasses the present power of the third-generation mainframe computers? This decision means breaking the relationship established between the data processing professional and the manufacturer and a return of the responsibility for data processing and systems to the user, which is really where it belongs.

4

The New-Generation Computers

Minicomputers are not new. Their origin is linked to the first-generation Whirlwind computer. Even the minicomputers were developed two decades ago in response to an identifiable need of the users. We will see how in this chapter. The first minicomputer was designed in 1957 and manufactured in 1966 by the newly created Digital Equipment Corporation and its founder, Kenneth H. Olsen. While at the Massachusetts Institute of Technology, Dr. Olsen, his brother, and several other engineers built the early Whirlwind computer in the Lincoln Laboratory.

The engineers' objective was to produce interactive computers that would improve communications between the end user and the computer. This was accomplished with the early minicomputer, which was designed for a single application—a dedicated processor. By simplifying its requirements, the engineers perfected its ability to respond. This opened up a whole new market.

A growth potential took shape. This potential may be attributed to three characteristics of the minicomputer that differentiated it from the mainframe. First, minicomputers can be designed to meet specific applications with quite diverse uses. For example, the minicomputer is ideal for monitoring processes, such as heart beats in the medical/professional industry and product flow in the paper industry. The minicomputer can act as a communications device or as a dedicated processor for a special application. At a Fortune 500 company located in Rochester, New York, it is designed for order entry where 24 clerks take doctor's orders over the telephone and place the order through a minicomputer manufactured by Data General fitted with a system configuration designed by a software firm named ULTIMACC of Maywood, N.J. Or the minicomputer can simply act as a front-end processor to a large mainframe. It can stand tall and alone, as shown in Figure 1.

Second, the demand for minicomputers is expanding simply because the minicomputer is powerful, reliable, and inexpensive. A brand new market of end users has been uncovered. It is the small business, which simply could not afford the large mainframe. But schools, universities, hospitals, and other nonprofit organizations are also beginning to realize the cost-effectiveness of the minicomputer. The research laboratory's scientists and engineers can benefit from the powerful and inexpensive minicomputer. And President Carter had a minicomputer in his airplane to show him the voting trends and statistics while he was on the campaign trail.

The minicomputer has also captured a market where reliability is of paramount concern. The minicomputer will operate effectively in environments where the mainframe fails. ROLM Corporation, for example, markets a minicomputer called the Ruggednova, which will operate in a temperature range of 6.5°–65.5°C (20°–150°F) while allowing rapid temperature fluctuations without failure. At the University of Rochester's Laser Energetics Laboratory, a Hewlett-Packard minicomputer must compute 72 hours before a result is produced; downtime is unacceptable in this environment.

Third, a unique marketing strategy using a new industrial concept called the original equipment manufacturer (OEM) has spawned a tremendous growth industry. Using imagination and scientific skill, the original

Figure 1. The new-generation computer.

equipment manufacturer has capitalized on the versatility and low cost of minicomputers to design new applications and use these powerful machines where only the mainframe previously squatted.

With the minicomputer's ability to handle complex applications reliably at reasonable costs, the OEM has opened up new markets and produced soaring sales for the manufacturers. Sales have soared. Digital Equipment projects a sales growth of 50 percent next year alone. This is staggering for a $900 million corporation. This growth will undoubtedly cut into the mainframe market where minicomputer penetration is certain. The only tangible deterrent to even greater sales and growth is the people part of the equation. The minicomputer is technically sound, as we shall see, but the human factor must be dealt with, as discussed later in this book. Management must be persuaded to analyze its present batch computer in light of the new development. We believe that an objective evaluation will hasten the realization of distributed processing, which will reveal the full potential of computers.

THE MINICOMPUTER—DIFFERENT THINGS TO DIFFERENT PEOPLE

Any operation that can be performed on a mainframe can also be performed on a minicomputer. Any differences that may be cited to set the minicomputer apart are architectural and do not minimize the computer's performance capability. All the buzz words that apply to the mainframe apply to the minicomputer as well. What is it that distinguishes the new generation from the old?

The Layman's Dilemma

To the layman, the difference between a mainframe computer and a minicomputer is large size and familiar names versus small size and obscure, new company names. Compared with an IBM 360/50 of the same memory capacity, the central processing unit (CPU) of a standard minicomputer is approximately one-tenth the size. The technical difference is the advanced technology in memory and logic circuitry. The new miniature's integrated circuitry permits complex operations to be placed on electronic chips, rather than large transistors, condensers, and all the circuitry between them. The integrated circuitry of the minicomputer combines many varied functions into one component.

But the layman must not equate small size with less power, for the opposite is true. Varian Data Machines markets 128,000 bytes of memory on one printed circuit board measuring 34 cm × 34 cm × 1 cm (14 in. × 14

Table 3. British government agency test, raw computation index.

System	Mainframe	Minicomputer	Instructions Per Second
CDC 6400	X		563,000
IBM 360/65	X		521,000
DG Eclipse		X	500,000
DEC 10		X	500,000
IBM 370/155	X		465,000
Honeywell 635	X		357,000
HP 2100		X	76,000
DG Nova 840		X	71,000
IBM 360/50	X		60,000

CDC   Control Data Corporation   DG   Data General Corporation
DEC   Digital Equipment Corporation HP   Hewlett-Packard

in. × ½ in.). This memory, semiconductor in design, attains speeds of 400 nanoseconds or less. The VD minicomputer has one of the fastest CPUs on the market today. The British government proved this point in a study of computing speeds, known as the benchmark test. The study compared the number of similar instructions that could be executed per second for several makes of mainframe and minicomputer. The results are shown in Table 3.

The performance rate is close, with the super Eclipse right up at the top. (Varian's V76 may be even faster.) Several minicomputers clearly outperformed the much-heralded IBM 360/50 at a fraction of the purchasing cost. There is an inverse relationship between small size in circuits and data paths and rapid performance. Over the next few years, millions of words of memory will be stored within the space of a very small cabinet.

But the layman shies away from the minicomputer, because it means dealing with new companies with unfamiliar names. Varian Data Machine manufactures the V70 series minicomputers from Irvine, California. Data General Corporation manufactures the Nova series and the Eclipse minicomputer in Southboro, Mass. Digital Equipment Corporation manufactures the PDP series and the DEC 10 and DEC 20 out of neighboring Maynard. And Hewlett-Packard makes the HP 3000 and its related minicomputers in northern California. Besides Hewlett-Packard, which is well known for its hand calculators, these companies are relatively unknown. Still other minicomputer manufacturers are General Automation, Interdata, and Prime Computers. Certainly they do not project the image of an IBM, Honeywell, or Burroughs. But the layman need not fear—these are strong, viable, sound companies in an expanding market.

The Technician's Acceptance

The technician finds an answer to our comparison question in modularity and reliability. The minicomputer is modular in that each function is uniquely contained in a specific printed circuit board. The frame of the computer merely houses shelves of the functionally printed circuit boards, which can be added or removed at will. The model number usually designates the number of shelves provided, such as DG's Nova 2/4 (model 2, four shelves) and Nova 2/10 (model 2, ten shelves).

Peripheral devices, also controlled through printed circuit boards on the minicomputer, may therefore be added or removed easily. Special hardware features can be attached, in modules, to the system as they are developed or determined to be needed. These features may include floating decimal arithemetic. The modularity of these features allows them, in the minicomputer, to function independently and concurrently, which greatly enhances the processing power and flexibility.

This has another advantage. Unlike the mainframe system, the modular design eases the problem of maintenance. If a printed circuit board is found defective, it is simply replaced (the "works-in-a-drawer" concept). This has the effect of minimizing downtime on the already reliable minicomputer. And the minicomputer design enhances reliability anyway; the central processing unit normally operates for months without trouble. In the larger mainframe, as the number of components increases, the greater is the need for interconnections and leads between parts. The greater this need, the greater the chance for problems. The minicomputer reduces this need for long interconnection, and the result is increased reliability.

A recent article in the *Harvard Business Review* by Gerald Burnett and Richard Nolan compared minicomputers to their big brothers. The authors maintained that "a minicomputer costs around $50,000 for a typical business application, and it can do a great deal of the work of computers costing $2,000,000. Stated another way, minicomputers cost approximately one-fortieth as much as large computers, but they can do a great deal more than one-fortieth of the work." * The authors state that one of the strong points of the minicomputer is its reliability. They reported that compared to other computers, the minicomputer's reliability was very high, because its relative simplicity required only a short time for repairs. The technical comparisons shown in Table 4 lend support to this concept of the minicomputer's reliability, which is what the technician is interested in.

* Gerald J. Burnett and Richard L. Nolan, "At Last, Major Roles for Minicomputers," *Harvard Business Review* (May/June 1975), p. 149.

Table 4. Technical comparisons of computers.

Factor	Large (IBM 370/168)	Medium (IBM 370/135)	Minicomputer (DEC PDP 11/45)
Reliability	High	High	Very High
Vendor support	Outstanding	Outstanding	Good
Purchase cost	Millions of dollars	Hundreds of thousands of dollars	Tens of thousands of dollars
Operating requirements	Considerable amount of specially prepared space and air conditioning; operators and well-trained systems programmers required	Same as large computer	One operator per shift, no special site preparation, good systems programmers required

SOURCE: Burnett and Nolan, "At Last, Major Roles for Minicomputers," *Harvard Business Review* (May/June 1975).

In the Programmer's Language

The programmer interprets the minicomputer's usefulness in terms of languages. Originally, the minicomputer offered only machine-oriented languages, such as an assembler and a limited FORTRAN capability. The programmer is concerned with whether the language capability is limited. But today this has changed, as the software has been developed and enhanced rapidly by the manufacturers.. The so-called machine-oriented languages are still more efficient, so the programmer may be urged (or persuaded) to write efficiently in FORTRAN or interactively in BASIC. Nevertheless, since 1975, the expansion in languages has been tremendous. Most of the major minicomputer companies now offer, or are developing, COBOL, RPG, and BASIC, the most widely used commercial languages available for any computer today.

In addition, new software features, such as information-retrieval capability and data base managers, are now available on most minicomputers. As we shall soon see, a data base manager is a manufacturer-developed software package designed to handle large data files efficiently. These software systems and languages are among the most sophisticated on the market today.

The standard techniques used with minicomputers are interactive programming and reduction of some of the monotonous time-consuming aspects of programming. The minicomputer is alive and on-line. The mainframe is busy elsewhere, and you must wait your turn to compile your program and, later, to test it. With the minicomputer, you simply sit down at your terminal, enter your program, edit it on-line, and test it as you progress. The computer guides the programmer through the process with such questions as: What program? What command? How do you define that item? This interactive (tête-à-tête) programming is estimated by an IBM representative to improve efficiency by 35 percent.

The minicomputer also permits routine programming to be shared with the user. We had a staff of programmers that concentrated on detail logic and data base design and left much of the report writing to the user. Standard information-retrieval software makes this a reality. Thus, the users become more involved. They are challenged to work with the computer, leaving the more esoteric issues, such as file designs, to the programmers. More on this later.

The Organization's Input and Control

The issue to the management of the user organization is with ease of operation and improved control. Unlike the mainframe and the large central data processing department, the minicomputer eliminates the need for dedicated operators, job-control specialists, systems programming specialists, and software managers for the operating system (software). As we shall see later, most minicomputer manufacturers don't even have to offer courses in operations. Anyone can be taught to turn the computer on and off. Besides, in most on-line environments, the computer runs continuously, 24 hours per day. Ease of operation is a certainty in this environment.

To the manager, the minicomputer means a terminal on his desk. Communications come directly from the user department to the computer through video terminals. These terminals are normally located in the user departments, and each user becomes responsible for the accuracy and timeliness of his data. Because data doesn't have to get filtered through a service department (central data processing), management and control of information processing is established with one unit, the user. Management sees the minicomputer for its timeliness and increased accuracy, while the user gains a sense of control over his systems and data needs. The job of managing is given back to the department manager. The accuracy of data is his responsibility, totally his. This is distributed processing which, by its very nature, should improve organizational efficiency and control.

The Controller's Concern—Cost

Perhaps the most important difference is cost, and this is the controller's concern. The minicomputer is a low-cost powerful processor that will do anything the mainframe can do and more, and at less cost. The minicomputer generally costs $100,000–$200,000 or $2,000–$4,000 per month rental, to the mainframe's $400,000 to $500,000—often millions.

Let us quote Fred Gruenberger, California State University, and David Babcock, also from California. They talk about the great cost of the large-scale computers compared to the minicomputers.

> The argument has been advanced for many years that the way to cheaper computation lies with even larger machines. It is certainly true that the cost of computing a given million instructions is less on a large machine than on a small one. But the net cost of delivering the results from those million executed instructions to the user may be enormous with the large machine.*

The reasons are simple, maintain Gruenberger and Bacock. First, there is an illogical pressure to put more systems on the large computers because of the heavy investment. This has led to a policy of establishing a flow of work to the computer which, by its very nature, is remote from the user. Second, the computer is heavily buffered from the users with red tape, complicated operating systems, and sophisticated communications devices. The one million instructions end up generating the execution of many million more instructions just to get this big computer to function properly, a kind of catch-22 situation. Finally, the net cost is greater because of the need for expert programmers to handle the increased complexity. Traditionally, these experts have cloaked their work in secrecy and made the work seem obscure and unintelligible to the user, a far cry from the minicomputer's interactive approach described earlier.

The minicomputer incorporates miniature circuitry. It can be manufactured on a mass production scale, and the manufacturing cost savings are passed on to the customer. Minicomputers are priced at a fair markup over manufacturing costs and not at the level the market will bear. The general-purpose minicomputer can therefore perform many functions at substantially reduced costs. Referring once again to the Burnett and Nolan article in the *Harvard Business Review,* the authors conclude that the purchasing and operational costs are the most significant advantages a minicomputer has over

---

*Fred Gruenberger and David Babcock, *Computing with Minicomputers* (Los Angeles: Melville Publishing Company, 1973), p. 214.

medium- and large-scale computers. This should make the controller happy—if only we can persuade him to evaluate one.

BETTER THAN THE MAINFRAME?

As we have seen, the minicomputer is different things to different people. It is compact in size, efficient in the way it uses languages, and interactive in programming; it provides return of control with ease of operation and renders significant cost savings. Above all, the minicomputer performs like the mainframe—it does everything the mainframe can, with sparkling new software. But the minicomputer can do one more thing. According to some experts in the field of data processing it outperforms supposedly comparable mainframe computers in execution speeds and cost effectiveness. On-line distributed processing is made feasible; this is impractical from a cost standpoint with the present batch-oriented mainframe computer.

Thus, the minicomputer has the potential to revolutionize data processing. It can decentralize information handling by placing responsibility for control, accuracy, and timeliness with the user department. It can break down the friction and finger-pointing that occur between the originator of data (the user) and the preparer of data (the data processing department). The minicomputer makes distributed data processing a reality because it is efficient, reasonably priced, and originally designed for this purpose.

The design characteristics of the minicomputer make it—not the mainframe—the vehicle for distributed processing. A short stroll through the technological pathway of the minicomputer will take the fear out of the new-generation computer.

MINICOMPUTER TECHNOLOGY

A minicomputer is a stored-program, digital computer that is suitable for specific and, recently, general-purpose applications and whose central processing unit, main memory, and minimal input/output devices cost less than $100,000.

According to *Datapro,* there are enough common elements in the minicomputer to come up with a reasonable general definition. Using their description, the typical minicomputer is a binary processor with a 16-bit word length. This is the number of bits (binary digits) that can be stored or retrieved from main storage during a single machine cycle. The mainframe, on the other hand, is a binary processor with an 8-bit byte and a 32-bit word length. The minicomputer data is addressed by the word, rather than the byte, for simplicity of design. In addition, the 16-bit word is more efficient in core utilization and execution, although it is more difficult for the programmer (unless a high-level language is used). The 16-bit word length neatly accommodates two 8-bit bytes and has proved an excellent balance of economy and performance.

A minicomputer employs integrated circuits that are housed in a small 48-centimeter (19-inch) rack. It weighs less than 227 kg (50 lb) and can fit easily in the trunk of your car (see Figure 2). The central processing unit (CPU) is about 48 centimeters (19 inches) wide, 25 cm × 53 cm (10 in. × 21 in.) deep, and looks like a stereo receiver (see Figure 3). It uses less than 500 watts of standard 115-volt electric power and requires no special air conditioning. In these times of energy consciousness, the minicomputer has a definite advantage over the mainframe computer in conserving scarce resources. It does not require the expensive subfloors to house miles of cable. It merely plugs into the wall and waits for instructions. Savings in space and site preparation should also be plugged into any cost justification for a minicomputer.

Figure 2. "It can fit easily into the trunk of your car."

Figure 3. "It looks like a stereo receiver."

The minicomputer is marketed in magnetic core or semiconductor memory, which is available in modules of 4,096 to 65,536 words. To compare this with the mainframe bytes, double the numbers (remember the 16-bit word is two 8-bit bytes) to 8,192 bytes and 131,072 bytes of memory. Multiple units may be incorporated into one computer system, so that memory for some minicomputers is contained in more than a million bytes. Speeds range from 300 nanoseconds up to 1.5 microseconds. Only the largest mainframes can begin to compete with the minicomputers in processing speeds. Parity checking and storage protection, validity checks, and protection from errant programs and programmers are necessary and available on the minicomputer. Minicomputers were designed to be interactive with the user, who works from an individual video display terminal.

Where does the minicomputer get its powerful interactive capability? Probably the real breakthrough in minicomputer technology is in its *interrupt system*. Unlike the batch mode, which processes one job at a time, the minicomputer's architecture provides an easy means of connecting multiple systems components, such as the user's terminals, which can be attached to the minicomputer. The interrupt feature can control the flow of data into and out of the computer from the external terminals.

The interrupt message informs the computer that a new user or a new program is being requested from the terminal. Your payroll person or an inventory analyst may be seeking information from the computer. Either request activates the interrupt system and tells the computer's memory to stop what it is doing, store the address of the next logical statement, and check on what that user is requesting. The interrupt system allows the computer to perform functions for the new user and return directly to the original program and at the exact point at which it was interrupted. This process is routine and functions with many terminals, printers, or card readers and it all takes place within nanoseconds, quicker than the eye can see.

Several (or many) external devices may be connected to the minicomputer to take advantage of its power. A line printer may be printing the latest balance sheet while several employees use terminals to add information or request answers. Each of these peripheral devices is channeled through an input/output concept referred to as a *bus*. The bus provides the path for data to travel from the user to the central processing unit for execution against programmed logic. The computer monitors the external devices through the bus structure, pulling in requests for data at amazingly fast speeds and servicing all users in priority sequence. When the processor polls the various devices and recognizes a request, it stores the device's specific and unique identifying address, transfers the data for processing, and returns to the unique address when the processing is completed.

This bus structure, which is typical for most minicomputers, is also considered a direct-access channel. It may accommodate as much as a million words per second. The power and capability of the minicomputer plus its communications hardware, called *multiplexers,* and selector channels for scheduling, allow it to talk to a great many terminals at the same time.

The typical complement of standard peripheral equipment includes teletypewriters, disk storage units, tape drives, card readers, paper tape readers, punches, and printers just as in the mainframes. But the minicomputer also has a large assortment of interfaces and controls for communications with multiple terminals, far more than the average mainframe has. Is there a difference? The list purchase price of the basic system, including 4,096 words (8,192 equivalent bytes, remember), is likely to be less than $5,000. A minicomputer is minipriced. Therein lies a major breakthrough. *Datapro* again:

> By all previous value norms in the computer field, it is a truly impressive package of computing power for the price.*

We, too, are truly impressed.

THE MINICOMPUTER IS USER-ORIENTED

How does the minicomputer correlate with the mainframe? In general, not at all. The design criteria for the minicomputer differed conceptually from those of the mainframe. Dr. Olson and his co-workers felt that a new direction was needed, not just a new machine. Interaction was the goal. The mainframe computer has traditionally been sold as a general-purpose computer, doing what it is programmed to do. Conversely, the minicomputer is a specialized unit that may be preprogrammed and, perhaps, dedicated to a specific purpose. It was specially designed to be conversational with the user, rather than being remote.

This concept can be seen in the new philosophy of software development: Minicomputer software is designed for the user in an interactive mode, rather than for the programmer in batch mode. All major minicomputer manufacturers presently offer software which provides new tools and support for the user. One example is data base management software now offered by all minicomputer manufacturers. Hewlett-Packard has stated that the primary objective of its data base manager is to reduce the programmer's effort; that is, the time and cost of writing programs merely to store and retrieve information. There are certain functions in data management which are repetitive, time-consuming, and error-prone, and if a programmer had to perform these functions every time he created a new program, it would be extremely inefficient and uneconomical. It has been so for years with only a breakthrough in recent times.

In the batch-mode mentality, continues the Hewlett-Packard representative, all data for particular applications had to accompany the applications

Reports on Minicomputers (Dehan, N.J.: Datapro Research Corporation, 1975), Technical Rept. MO7-100-101, p. 1.

DISTRIBUTED PROCESSING SYSTEMS

program. Thus data in the personnel file might be repeated in the skills file, the payroll file, and the medical file. When these files are combined into a common data base, redundant data is eliminated, storage costs are lower, and the data is internally consistent. The innovation is that the definition and control of information is independent of the applications. The common data base of logically connected files or items of data is then accessible to all users who have the security clearance. This simply translates into more efficient data processing, easier systems development, and lower programming costs. It is better organization of data.

The Hewlett-Packard minicomputer allows the user (not the programmer) to get at the data through a QUERY. This inquiry language allows the user to generate his own reports and retrieve information from his files quickly, efficiently, and in an on-line environment. This flexibility in the minicomputer again reduces the need for programming and places a powerful new tool in the hands of the user. Let's see how.

Normally, even the best systems analyst cannot anticipate the user's every future demand or unique request. The result is that a large percent of the analyst's and programmer's time is spent generating new reports and one-time requirements. An on-line minicomputer system provides an alternative. If the data is available on the data base, the inquiry language can be used to get at it on the terminal or with a user-formatted report. There are two features to the inquiry language:

Simple commands: There are usually fewer than 20 basic commands to get the data from the computer. They are common and simple commands, such as "find," which locates the data; "list," which sets forth the data in some order; "report," which prints the data; and some basic computing commands like add, subtract, multiply, and divide.

Data connectors: Data connectors simply spell out the relationship or range of data the user is interested in. There are only a few. They are "equal to" and "not equal to," "greater than" and "not greater than."

With a simple command, the data, and the data connector, users can find and report information quickly and without making a formal request to the centralized division of electronic data processing. You can "list" all employees with service "not less than" ten years, who have not been reviewed this year (that is, the last review was "greater than" 12 months). You can "report" all obsolete inventory which has not moved in 12 months and whose dollar value is "greater than" an expressed dollar amount. You can "find" all departments missing their annual budgets by searching for departments whose year-to-date totals are "not equal to" the year-to-date budgets. These simple techniques provide a degree of flexibility unavailable in most large-scale batch environments for two reasons:

□ The data files are not always available for use, as batch processing means one system at a time—your data file may not be the "one" when you want it.

□ Information is transmitted through scheduled reports. The on-line environment provides a desk-top terminal for access as the need arises.

To repeat, this flexibility reduces the need for detailed programming of every conceivable requirement. And the inquiry capability puts a powerful new tool in the hands of the user.

Another innovation sets the minicomputer apart from the mainframe and, again, was developed for improved efficiency. This is called "firmware" and means a set of internal subroutines which is hard-wired into the computer because of their frequent use. This firmware internally generates operational subroutines which relieve the programmer of coding requirements. A user who can type can begin to get results from the minicomputer with simple input and output specifications. In addition, the routines are always present in the computer for execution, and no memory capacity is used as the routines are embedded in the central processing unit. Only one copy of the routine need be present even when there are many programs using it. Saving core memory simply results in more users being able to utilize the computer at any one time and at greater speeds.

The industry and its marketing strategy also reveal the differences in philosophy between the minicomputer and the big brother mainframe. It is important to review these briefly to better understand the minicomputer itself.

THE INDUSTRY

Sales of minicomputers in 1976 reached the billion-dollar plateau led by Digital Equipment Corporation (DEC). Hewlett-Packard is the second-largest manufacturer, followed by Data General. Annual sales of four of the larger minicomputer manufacturers are impressive, as shown in Table 5.

Digital Equipment Corporation started the boom with the highly successful PDP-8 line in 1966. DEC now has 72,000 computers located throughout the world. Data General's president, Edson DeCastro, broke off from DEC over a disagreement on the best word length (he wanted 16 bits—now he's a hero) and founded his own minicomputer company. Its growth has been phenomenal, and it managed the unprecedented feat of delivering its six-thousandth computer less than four years after shipping its first com-

Table 5. Annual sales for minicomputers.

Company	1976 Estimated Sales (*millions*)
Digital Equipment Corporation	$936
Hewlett-Packard	456
Data General	161
General Automation	70.7

puter, the Nova, in February 1969. Its new Eclipse is a business-oriented computer, which competes head-on with the mainframes.

Growth of the leaders over the past five years has been impressive. Digital Equipment Corporation has grown from $146 million in sales to $936 million in the 1971–1976 period. During the same period, sales at Data General grew from $15 million to $161 million, and net earnings have kept pace.

The second rank of minicomputer manufacturers is made up of the aggressive, innovative young companies, such as General Automation, Varian Data Machines, Interdata, and Modular Computer Systems. Citicorp, one of the largest bank holding companies in the world, is committed to a program of minicomputers, using Interdata, to replace their costly mainframes. It is an interesting development to follow. Varian's excellent management and superior products should assure it a permanent place in the market, and the fact that it was recently acquired by Sperry (UNIVAC) should result in increased marketing and development.

Minicomputers are also built by divisions of well-established companies, such as General Telephone and Electronics, Lockheed, Raytheon, Texas Instruments, and Westinghouse. Honeywell, one of the earlier entrants in the field, is pushing forward in the commercial market and should become a strong competitor. There are also dozens of comparatively small and as-yet unproved companies whose survival will depend on their ability to back up their imaginative hardware ideas with effective marketing, production, software, and customer support. According to Datapro, more than 80 companies are now marketing minicomputers in this country.

The minicomputer company does tend to be small and innovative. Its existence, as in the case of Data General, reflects a new development (in this case, the 16-bit word), which was designed to improve efficiency and make interactive, user-oriented computers. These companies pursue a different marketing philosophy as well.

This marketing strategy of the minicomputer manufacturers is not difficult to analyze. Basically, there are three markets: the original equipment manufacturer (OEM), the sophisticated user, and the unsophisticated user. The OEM is a company with a full complement of engineers and data processing technicians. The manufacturer sells through the OEM who, in turn, will use the hardware with some of his systems or products for resale to the end user. ULTIMACC is an example of an original equipment manufacturer of unusual competence. Others include Comptek Research, Basic Four, and Quantum. Surprisingly, you may have thought these were manufacturers. Not so. They package their products from a variety of manufacturers to maximize efficiency at low, low prices.

Basic Four recently undertook an interesting marketing campaign that compared its system to the IBM System 32. Basic Four showed that its system has more capacity, more speed, and a bigger terminal. IBM just doesn't stack up, says Basic Four. Basic Four is an OEM, not a manufacturer. It compiles a system using memory from Microdata, disks from Diablo, which is a subsidiary of Xerox, and printers from Centronics. This system is successfully sold to end users as a Basic Four with applications packages and a small price tag. Microdata, which supplies the memory, is now in competition with Basic Four, marketing its Reality system. That's progress, we assume.

The original equipment manufacturer is an important factor in the phenomenal growth of minicomputers. It provides end users with the technical support that is not provided by the manufacturer. In this regard, the OEM carefully checks out your system prior to delivery. In addition, he provides that essential software support and those applications packages which make the little guy perform. He warrants the hardware for 90 days and his applications software for an entire year. He works closely with the manufacturer and is, in fact, recommended to the end user. The OEM and the manufacturer provide users with a double buffer of safety. Neither is going to let the end user down; they will both put forth their considerable technical strengths and reputations on the success of the installation.

The Sophisticated User

The manufacturer historically marketed through OEMs because of the need for technical support, which the manufacturer was not prepared to provide. So the second market for minicomputers is a variation on the theme. It is the more sophisticated end user's data processing department that has the in-house capability to make it work. Again, the manufacturer does not need to provide support. This in-depth expertise negates the real need for an original equipment manufacturer or it may merely reduce the need to some extent. This market, then, is made up of knowledgeable technicians who will seek peripheral equipment, software, and limited manufacturer's support which will enable them to implement their own applications. A large corporation in the Fortune 500 ranks would be considered a sophisticated end user.

The Systems House as Middleman

The third market is the unsophisticated end user who wants a complete turnkey system installed. A turnkey system is designed and implemented completely by the middleman, a systems house. In this market, the systems house does not add its own systems or products as the OEM does, and herein lies the distinction. Here, the design for the end user is unique and may require no user involvement in the development. Training and learning the application remains with the user. The user does not want to be involved in the technical aspects of the computer, but prefers to concentrate on the design. Minicomputer manufacturers have put increased emphasis upon the end-user market, which is potentially far more lucrative. It is also far more costly to enter and support. The manufacturer also concentrates on the assistance of this middleman or systems house, which is a realistic approach for many end users.

The systems house is made up of systems analysts and software "experts." Normally, each has a particular area of expertise which it markets. For example, one may specialize in financial systems, while another may have considerable expertise in order entry. Each systems house, however, provides turnkey systems using minicomputers. For example, Interactive Information Systems in Cincinnati, Ohio, provides an on-line manufacturing system that may be the most sophisticated in this country. The system consists of a core design which is modified for the unique requirements of the end user. Once the system is operational, ITS provides support from Cincinnati, where it makes changes through a terminal tied to the user's minicomputer transmitting over a common telephone line. It is truly Space Age-effective. The ITS system user concentrates on the system, the accuracy of input, and the performance. ITS makes the computer modifications without ever entering an airplane. It really works. ULTIMACC also uses this technique, which it calls Remote System Diagnosis (RSD). RSD makes it possible to inspect a system at the user's site using a dial-up telephone line which links ULTIMACC to its user anywhere in the United States. Ask your mainframe supplier for its comparable service.

The current marketing trend is toward larger memory banks and higher-level languages. We know that several manufacturers consider COBOL essential from a marketing standpoint, although the technician will tell you it is inefficient. We would warn end users and manufacturers to avoid the same pitfalls that currently plague mainframes—first, building machines for the data processing staff, but not for the end user, and second, starting the spiraling hardware cost cycle to support inefficient software.

Minicomputer manufacturers haven't gotten to that point yet, but they must not forget the reason for their existence, remembering that the real breakthrough to feasible on-line applications at low costs came as a result of the minicomputer's efficiency. Let's not go through another unproductive era—we just ended one.

Minicomputer prices have continued to go down in response to continuing technological improvements and aggressive competition. Data General, Interdata, and Varian have introduced new minicomputers that are program compatible with their earlier models, but feature lower price tags with improved performance. Although the price cuts have continued, *Datapro* reports that there is no reason to believe that minicomputer prices have reached bottom. As we mentioned earlier, Digital Equipment Corporation has reduced its price by 17 percent for each of the last five years.

Running with this trend is a concurrent trend toward a class of super-minicomputers whose power and flexibility rival that of vastly more expensive large-scale computers. Examples are the Data General Eclipse, the Varian V76, the HP 3000, and the DEC PDP 11/70. Most of these systems feature large-scale storage capacities, fast semiconductor memory, advanced memory management facilities, multiprogramming operating systems, and other big computer software facilities at prices ranging from $150,000 and up. Very cost-effective, the large Eclipse may be purchased for $160,000, under $4,000 per month over five years. The trend may be to more size, but the costs will continue to decline.

ANSWERING THE NEEDS OF THE USER

The minicomputer may be today's most cost-effective computer. We have tried to describe some of its features and characteristics, such as its word length and capability in handling multiple terminals simultaneously. The arguments in this chapter draw support from *Datapro,* which maintains that the minicomputer is an impressive package of computing power.

The trend toward better BASIC and commercial FORTRAN marks the minicomputer's penetration into the business environment and the scientific market. But compared to IBM's impressive $6.7 billion domination, success has been minimal. The minicomputer compares favorably in every technical aspect to the more expensive mainframe. And, because of its unique ability to handle multiple terminals, the minicomputer permits distribution of input and places control of systems back with the user—not just for one application, as in a dedicated system, but alone, measuring up to all your informational requirements.

Recap. The minicomputer can handle anything the mainframe can. The basic features of the minicomputer have been summarized here in an attempt to make managers aware of a vast new alternative to continued cost escalation. Minicomputers have grown in size and sophistication while reducing costs. This trend will continue, and right now the minicomputer is ripe for evaluation for most any business.

One very large Fortune 500 company is currently evaluating minicomputers to process its voluminous purchase-order/accounts-payable system. After extensive testing and a benchmark analysis, this major manufacturing concern determined that a minicomputer could meet their requirements. What were they? This company required approximately 50 terminals to process 15,000 to 20,000 transactions in a 10-hour day. The minicomputer met the test. Only the very largest corporations require this volume; one must concede that the minicomputer is an alternative that has to be considered.

Prior to the last few years, minicomputers lacked sophisticated software and, as in mainframes, the hardware outstripped the software capabilities. This was true of mainframes in the early days of computers. It is no longer true, as all high-level languages are now available as well as sophisticated data base managers to simplify the maintenance and accessibility of data.

The cost-effectiveness and efficiency of the minicomputer mean sure savings and the end to spiraling data processing costs. But the real advantage is the present capacity to implement on-line systems at affordable rates. Chapter 6 describes distributed processing in terms of the recommendations we have made. At a recent American Management Associations conference, one diehard mainframe user said that theoretically, distributed systems could be implemented with his large mainframe. We agree in theory, but it cannot be accomplished within a reasonable time frame, with a reasonable degree of success, at a reasonable cost, without a minicomputer. The mainframe simply wasn't designed to do the job.

5

Applications of the Minicomputer

The growth in minicomputer applications has paralleled that of the industry itself. The reasons for the two growth patterns are related. First, the expansion of minicomputers and applications is in response to the flexibility and apparently unlimited potential of the computer itself. Second, the low cost of minicomputers makes new applications both feasible and justifiable. Third, and a direct outgrowth of the first two reasons, is the effect of a new private company called the original equipment manufacturer, the OEM. These imaginative engineers and computer scientists took the versatile, low-cost minicomputer and began to use it in areas where processing had depended on laborious manual operations or the elaborations of the mainframe.

With a strictly engineering approach, the OEMs launched the minicomputer into the processes of A-to-D conversion, monitoring and control of industrial applications, and communications. Many common commercial applications followed in a very natural progression.

The minicomputer seems bound to emerge as the leader in information processing as well as the inevitable explosion of distributed data processing. Developed by original equipment manufacturers, minicomputers have the properties of flexibility and low cost so critical in a multiple-computer environment. Also, work in the communications field, which characterized early uses, places minicomputers at the very heart of a distributed data processing network. And it all began with rather simple engineering applications.

ENGINEERING APPLICATIONS

Analog-to-Digital Conversion

Circa 1970: The hardware referred to as the minicomputer had important advantages over existing mainframe computers. Something like the early development of the mainframe had happened. The hardware had outstripped the software. The minicomputer could perform amazing feats, but there was little available expertise to tell it how to function. Unlike the time of the mainframe, the technical void would be filled by the original equipment manufacturers. Back in the mainframe era, this same vacuum, you will remember, was filled by the computer manufacturer with its technical sales force.

A similar situation exists today for the new microprocessor technology. The *microprocessor* is a memory module on a tiny chip of silicone—an electronic brain on a chip. A semiconductor memory, the microprocessor performs the arithmetic/logic operations in the minicomputer. If software can be added, the microprocessor becomes a very small computer. This microprocessor can now be used in such diverse but specialized applications as microwave ovens, traffic lights, and computer terminals.

The problem is that the hardware is five years ahead of the software. Today, few engineers understand the techniques needed to make microprocessors function. In 1970, when this was the case for minicomputers, it was the OEM that came to the fore, developing the software to make the hardware function. The void that had enticed the OEMs into the minicomputer market involved engineering applications, and OEMs are, after all, engineers and problem solvers.

Competition was wide open at the time. The mainframe manufacturers were busily occupied with second- and third-generation computers. With new commercial applications being developed at a rapid pace, as pointed out in Chapter 4, developing a computer to make analog-to-digital conversions must have been a very low priority for the mainframe computer manufacturers during those halcyon years of data processing. The mainframe marketing strategy focused instead on supplying the total computing capability for stand-alone processing of the organization's information needs. This need for engineering set the stage for the emergence of the OEMs as well as the prosperity of the minicomputer manufacturer.

The first and simplest engineering use of minicomputers was probably to make analog-to-digital conversions. The applications in power plants, counters on machinery, and electrical analog signals are too numerous to list. But to give you one example, analog computers have been used to control airplanes in flight for years. The analog computer records changes in wind speed and direction and in altitude pressure. But it can only record these changes—it cannot analyze the data or communicate it effectively to the pilot, navigator, or ground crew. The analog data has to be collected, converted, and analyzed, all of which can be accomplished by the minicomputer, for the presentation of alternatives to the crew. The miniaturized, compact minicomputer can easily be located on board the aircraft, so the conversion and analysis can be made on the spot.

Analog-to-digital conversion was a natural application of the OEM and the minicomputer. Each application was defined, programmed, and implemented almost entirely by the OEM whose own software routines and customized modifications became known as "turnkey" applications. The user lacked the expertise (remember the technical void). As a rule, the user did not see the point in spending time to learn a technique for a one-time specialized application. So the market for turnkey engineering services continued to grow. Supported by a staff of electrical engineers, systems designers, and programming specialists, the original equipment manufacturer possessed all that was needed to develop and support a new engineering product base for the end user.

This product base quite naturally expanded into the next phase of engineering applications, that of monitoring and control. It is logical to assume that the OEM efforts in power plants, manufacturing environments, and utilities made them aware of the potential for using minicomputers for more advanced applications. And again, the competition from mainframe manufacturers, with the possible exception of Honeywell, was limited in the engineering application. Once again, the minicomputer was modified and customized for a very specific purpose.

Monitoring and Control Applications

There are many examples of minicomputers in monitoring and control applications. For example, the minicomputer was recently used to test a new propulsion system. A high-speed ground transportation vehicle with speeds of up to 250 miles per hour was tested with a minicomputer manufactured by Varian Data Machines by the Department of Transportation in Washington, D.C. The goal was to establish the practicality of a new method of propulsion that would reduce the friction between the rail and the wheel.

The minicomputer was a Varian 620 that had only 8,000 bytes of core memory. Set up to accept telemetered data at a rate of 64,000 bytes per second, the data was calibrated and converted into engineering terms, which enabled the investigators to determine the performance characteristics of the new propulsion technique.*

The Cardiovascular-Renal Research Laboratory of Howard University

*Ronald Jurgin, "Minicomputer Applications in the Seventies," edited by Fred F. Coury, *A Practical Guide to Minicomputer Applications* (New York: Institute of Electrical and Electronics Engineers, 1972), p. 152.

used a Hewlett-Packard 2100 series minicomputer to monitor heart pressure in dogs. Using implanted sensors, "the investigators measured, monitored, and recorded the primary cardiac variables of physical dimensions, pressures, flow rate, ECG, and heart rate of conscious dogs, acquiring the data under computer control." * The computer permitted this data to be instantly recorded, analyzed, and printed.

What had begun with the development of simple analog-to-digital monitors had quickly evolved into complex process-control systems. Original equipment manufacturers build automatic testing equipment for such companies as Kodak, complete with thousands of printed circuit (PC) boards, which interface a maze of complex testing requirements. It is not uncommon for large companies and government institutions to issue procurements of several million dollars on the development of highly sophisticated, minicomputer-based monitoring and process-control systems. It is currently in vogue for local government authorities to consider replacing sewer and water-pump operations with process-control monitors and switching systems. Communities and power authorities are considering the use of power monitors in those areas of the country that are susceptible to huge swings in power requirements, such as New York City and Chicago. The purpose of these systems will be to monitor the power-consumption levels, to determine the times when reserves would be most needed (peak load), and to allocate power resources as economically as possible, while maintaining the highest possible service level. Projects like this one are taking place all over the country and will have established a standard by 1980.

Another energy-related application of minicomputers is process controls in industry. A PDP 8/S minicomputer manufactured by Digital Equipment Corporation will control refueling operations of a large nuclear generating station near Denver. A major requirement for this minicomputer was a fail-safe design that would prevent inadvertent errors on the part of an operator. The minicomputer had to maximize efficiency during the refueling process to reduce the time required for completion, because no electrical power is generated during this period. Studies had shown that a manual monitoring process would be subject to human error and would create other problems. The answer was the superdependable minicomputer manufactured by Digital Equipment Corporation.

Minicomputers are used extensively in the paper industry where there is a complex, continuous process. The minicomputer is used for one purpose—to improve the quality of the final product. Moisture content, pulp condition, felt condition, and weight must be monitored. Otherwise the delicate bal-

*Jurgin, p. 160.

ance needed to produce quality and strength of the paper might be upset. The need for automation stems from the need to reduce imbalances.

The computer receives measurements of quality-definable variables and performs highly complex analyses of, for example, nonlinear calibrations characteristics . . . for different paper grades. Production rates, fiber consumption per produced reel, and means and variances of quality-defining variables can be prepared regularly for management. The computer can calculate, on-line, the true cross-directional profiles of, say, . . . weight . . . and moisture.*

The minicomputer provides the technology for control in this environment. Variances are immediately reported on-line for corrective action.

The need for rapid transit systems opened up the issue of the feasibility of a totally automated transportation system using minicomputer technology. Houston has implemented one of these systems. Las Vegas was in the final stages of contract negotiations for the first personal rapid transit system in the country when a referendum voted the project down. The personal rapid transit system consisted of compact four-passenger rail cars that could be programmed to take a small group to a specific location, such as a casino or hotel. The project was estimated to be in excess of $200 million dollars in all.

Projects like the Las Vegas project are not simple design applications. The proposal effort alone cost more than $40,000 and required the teaming of three high-technology companies. The prime contractor held responsibility for the manufacturing and functioning of the cars, the major subcontractor handled the sensors and microprocessors within the cars, and the third subcontractor was responsible for the command and control system (which included the guidance and surveillance systems). The technical proposal on the command and control systems alone ran more than 400 pages in length and drew on the resources of engineers, mathematicians, and software specialists alike. It was the work of a skillful original equipment manufacturer.

The final proposal to this complex and sophisticated central computer control-processing network consisted of three 64K-byte, 400-nanosecond minicomputers, two of which would operate back to back, at all times and in full redundancy, to ensure 100 percent operational status. The remaining auxiliary processor was designed to continuously monitor all the functions of

*E. B. Dahlin, "Interactive Control of Paper Machines," in *Minicomputers: Hardware, Software and Applications,* edited by James D. Schaeffler and Ronald H. Temple (New York: Institute of Electrical and Electronics Engineers, 1972), pp. 248–253.

the primary processor. If a failure were detected, all systems and functions would automatically switch over to the auxiliary processor and the third processor would become the auxiliary.

The vast complexity of this operation was to be driven entirely by a Data General minicomputer, with all dispatching functions, all monitoring functions, all signal sensing totally guided and controlled by this simple minicomputer. Incidentally, this application marked the inception of a new minicomputer company called Tandem, which opened its doors for business in the latter part of 1975. Unlike its predecessors, Tandem offers a dual computer with all the operating system and compiler features to make it acceptable to the OEM and systems house communities. The two minicomputers back each other up for total reliability.

We can expect more of these kinds of safety-lock design applications in the years to come. Tandem represents the ongoing progress in minicomputer technology, which opens doors to even more applications. This new company's system eliminates downtime. It is a nonstop system, because the software reassigns the work of one processor to the other if failures occur. This will create new horizons in the monitoring of human functions, failsafe transportation systems, and probably a whole new realm of applications in communications.

Communications

Minicomputers have been vital in the field of communications. The primary use is in the area of data concentration. A number of low-speed input devices, such as teletype and human-interfaced terminals, can be connected to a minicomputer. The data is amassed, accumulated, or "concentrated" before it is transferred to another, presumably larger, computer (either a minicomputer or a mainframe) for processing.

A second communications technique, which will be discussed more fully in Chapter 6, is to effect communications between two or more computers. A third communications application of minicomputers is to attach peripheral devices, such as terminals and printers, to the minicomputer, which then becomes a remote batch data-entry station for a larger central computer site.

You are probably most familiar with point-of-sales applications. In these applications, the sales clerk has a small (usually green) terminal at our favorite department stores. The clerk uses the terminal to both verify credit and check the status of customer charge accounts. The clerk simply keys in the customer's account number and within seconds either good news is conveyed by a green light, or bad news is represented by an unfriendly red light.

In this transaction, an inquiry is being made into the customer's status. The account number is transmitted to the minicomputer, which is probably located somewhere in the department store. This account number, along with other account numbers being queried, is then transmitted with a unique request code over dedicated communications lines (perhaps a common telephone line) to the central host computer. The host, too, may be a minicomputer which is now powerful enough to act as a host, as we shall see. The host computer then locates and retrieves the record of the customer's credit and account from its data base. It determines the status and whether or not the transaction should be made. This advice is then transmitted back to the sales clerk in the form of an activated green or bad-news red light. All this is accomplished within seconds of the request.

The minicomputer and its specialized software provide the ability to perform this credit check on-line. The various green terminals are attached to a single communications line or cable. The only difference between this type of terminal-processing application and the more familiar batch application is the removal of the application programs (the credit-checking logic) from the minicomputer, which is located at the source of data entry (for example, the department store) and the incorporation of these programs at the centralized host's location. Since central checking is economical in this application, the host is provided with a vast data base of your credit information. It is therefore a true host computer serviced by a terminal-processing communications network.

A related communications system is in effect at the Food Fair Store in Baldwin Hills, California. Similar systems may be found everywhere. This engineering application ties the cash register directly to a minicomputer. Each item is color-coded and numbered. Meats and vegetables are stamped with the weight and price per pound. The checker simply enters on the cash register the color code, code number, and quantity.

The minicomputer computes prices and sales taxes. The customer is provided with a list of all items purchased. A communications interface device (called a *multiplexer*) identifies the exact cash register and forwards this identification to a dedicated minicomputer. The minicomputer accepts the data, identifies the source, stores the data, and performs the necessary calculations. It also edits the data for invalid transactions. Using regular telephone lines, the computer transfers the data back to the cash register through the multiplexer. The advantages of the minicomputer are that it relieves the checker of computations, maintains accurate inventories, and

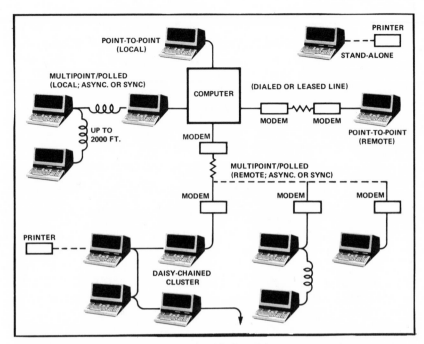

Figure 4. Terminal processing systems with the minicomputer.

analyzes store-wide customer buying habits. All this is accomplished primarily with a Honeywell minicomputer on only 16,000 bytes of memory.*

Another frequently used application of minicomputers as communications handlers is in manufacturing data handling. This concept of on-line data capture is used to collect information at the source, where the responsibility lies (see Figure 4). The sources of information would include:

1. *Shipping dock for receiving raw materials and shipping finished goods.* A terminal located at a shipping dock can immediately update inventory records that reflect shipments and receipts. A small printer can prepare shipping papers, packing instructions, and address stencils.

2. *Manufacturing operating departments where products are produced or assembled.* A terminal can be used to record the progress or completion of a manufacturing order. Shop floor monitoring and control of work in process are facilitated by timely input of status data from the source of the activity.

---

* Jurgin, pp. 165–167.

3. *Timekeeping where employees record hours on the job.* A terminal can transmit labor information, including manufacturing order number, quantities produced, and time required. This information is vital for engineering standards and cost accounting.

The minicomputer literally polls or canvasses the various terminals to see if data has been input. If so, the data is accepted and edited. If the data is valid it is stored in the minicomputer, where it awaits transmission to the host. For example, an order may be completed and the operator, using a local terminal, may enter the order number, the quantity produced, and the scrap. The computer polls the terminal, edits the data for validity, and sends back an electronic pulse to indicate acceptance (green light) or error (red light). This polling, acceptance, and editing requires only seconds of an operator's time and microseconds of computer processing.

Other related applications may be running concurrently, as the polling occurs when the processor is free. The minicomputer acts as a concentrator of data and as a single source of manufacturing information for the host. If it didn't, the host would be faced with many individual devices vying for its communications resources. Moreover, only edited data is transmitted to the host so the editing feature does not have to be performed again.

For communications applications the minicomputer is simply performing some major time-consuming functions formerly centralized at the site of the host. It consolidates, edits, and formats data for larger processing programs. In data processing parlance, the minicomputer is "off-loading" the host. This reduces the need for larger and more complex operating systems, more communications interfaces, and what would eventually amount to a big increase in computer memory and costs, which has been our message all along.

In a sense, the minicomputer acts as a terminal for transmitting the data to the host. Savings in communications costs can be substantial for those who evaluate the properties, performance, and cost of the minicomputer.

COMMERCIAL APPLICATIONS

To a somewhat lesser degree, the growth in commercial applications may also be attributed to the imaginative original equipment manufacturers. In this area, the more specialized systems house, with its packaged programs, played a larger role in its development. Over the past five to seven years, a number of commercially available systems were designed for the minicomputer: on-line customer order/entry systems, payroll and accounting systems, general ledgers, and manufacturing systems. The minicomputer sales force will identify sources of applications programs in their sales effort. In the case study described in Chapter 10, the very existence of a manufacturing package proved a deciding factor in selecting a dedicated minicomputer. But even today applications packages for minicomputers are not overly abundant.

Development of custom applications packages remains primarily with the user or with a turnkey system developed by an outside systems house or an OEM. Yet in some very specialized areas, original equipment manufacturers have developed small systems for the small user. These systems, currently designed and marketed by Wang Laboratories, Basic Four, Microdata, and Comptek Research, represent the entrance of minicomputers into the commercial world of data processing. It is the evolutionary process of moving from one market—scientific—into the next area of potential economic reward—commercial. Let us examine two small users, doctors (or dentists) and lawyers.

The Professions

The Doctor. The independent doctor (or small clinic of doctors) normally cannot afford the luxury of a large computer. Nor do doctors want the aggravation and expense of a data processing department. Yet each has information needs that include the basic accounting requirements of accounts payable, customer billing, payroll, and general bookkeeping. Tax preparation is also important, and that makes the need for automation real. That need is being filled by several original equipment manufacturers and systems houses.

For the doctor who decides to use the service, a system that uses terminals is proposed. A terminal is installed in the doctor's office and he or she is given access to a timesharing system, which consists of fully programmed bookkeeping and medical applications in an on-line mode. The doctor and staff are supplied a phone number and sign-on password to gain access to the system. Thereafter, all pertinent record information is relayed over phone lines into a central timesharing computer, which is usually, but not necessarily, located within the same city. Processing takes place on-line, and batch payroll and receivable information reports are mailed or delivered on a scheduled basis. From these humble beginnings, some systems houses and OEMs have developed small stand-alone systems that do not require any in-house technical expertise to process the accounting applications. From this base, other innovators have branched out to meet the need of small systems users like the lawyer.

The Lawyer. At first, law firms tended to be concerned about exposing their files to an off-premise timesharing organization. They generally preferred the security of an in-house system, and several prominent OEM companies capitalized on the new commercial requirement. The most popular systems consist of several terminals linked to a small minicomputer, where information is kept on small cartridge disks. Lawyers want to record the time they spend on client matters to arrive at a basis for billing. The volume is usually significant and indicates the need for data processing. For example, a medium-size law firm of 20 lawyers may generate approximately 2,000 to 3,000 transactions per day as each lawyer records his or her time in minutes and hours.

A new development in data processing grew out of this unique application for lawyers. It is called word processing.

Word Processing

Word processing takes on many forms from the magnetic tape selectric typewriter (MT/ST) manufactured by IBM and introduced in 1964 to the total computerized text-editing word processing systems recently announced by Digital Equipment Corp. From a systems point of view, word processing encompasses systems in which a mechanical typewriter captures keystrokes on magnetic tape, which allows an operator to back up and correct errors easily. A minicomputer stores letters and documents on a disk file for retrieval and editing.

The minicomputer greatly expands the usefulness of word processing for lawyers. Standard documents, such as rental agreements, wills, standard contracts, and mortgage papers, can be stored on a disk file. To produce a legal document, the operator inputs only the variable information, such as name, beneficiary, and dollar amounts, after which the system is activated to produce a complete legal document.

Because the operator, or typist, can locate and retrieve each word and line of a document, errors can be corrected rapidly and in a one-time operation. The old line or word is simply deleted, and the new line or word added. The minicomputer's stored-memory capabilities allows operators to search and find paragraphs, merge new data into the paragraph, make some tabulations and charts, reformat letters and documents, and perform any other text-editing features.

The growth in word processing stems directly from the potential savings in clerical time and cost from "automatic" typing. The minicomputer makes word processing affordable and desirable for information processing. Today, the word processing industry is projected to be a $2 billion market by 1980. Almost all minicomputer companies are represented in the field in one way or another.

There are several reasons for the impact of minicomputers on word processing. For openers, speed. A minicomputer-based word processing system can type at a rate of 500 words per minute, as opposed to the automatic-output typewriter rate of approximately 150 wpm. Flexibility and versatility are also increased with the minicomputer. For example, the system can search an entire document for a single error and correct that error wherever it appears—this process is known as global search and insert.

Automatic page numbering is another feature of the minicomputer-based word processing system. With the addition of inexpensive computer memory to a word processing system, that can handle numbering and limited storage, plus the fact that some marketed word processing systems provide accounting subsystems, the minicomputer can function as a complete administrative package for the lawyer.

OEMs in Today's Commercial Market

With the doctors and lawyers representing only one market for minicomputers, the interest in small-scale computing power began to grow. While the majority of OEMs concentrated on the development of scientific monitoring and control systems, from 1968 to 1972, it would seem today that the shift has been made to commercial systems. In addition, many software houses that previously made their livelihood from providing contract-programming services on the large-scale computers are now engaging their efforts in becoming proficient in minicomputer software and systems applications. They are finding it increasingly apparent that, among applications currently operating on large-scale computer systems, only a few cannot operate on a minicomputer system and, more importantly, at one-fourth (or less) the cost. A well-designed on-line system is easier to program, smaller, less complicated, and faster in execution on a minicomputer than on a medium-size mainframe.

One software house that used to promote only the very large-scale data processing systems is now learning the operations of the Data General Eclipse, a Prime computer, and a Basic Four. Several months ago in New York City we observed a Varian V76 computer in the room adjacent to a Hewlett-Packard HP 3000. (The HP 3000 is shown in Figures 5 and 6. Compare with the small computers in Figures 2 and 3.)

These systems represented developmental projects. As each project approached its target date, it was moved out the door as a completed system,

Figure 5. The minimum-configuration HP 3000 Series I with system console.

Figure 6. Typical 3000 Series II augmented with multiple terminals, disks, and so forth.

DISTRIBUTED PROCESSING SYSTEMS

with hardware and software integrated into one turnkey system. The Varian computer was shipped to Kansas City, where it was to be used as a data acquisition concentrator supporting more than 100 terminals; the HP 3000 computer, on the other hand, was to act as a dedicated on-line order/entry system. The same systems house was expecting a Data General Eclipse to arrive momentarily for yet another turnkey application. This expertise in developing systems is the trend in low-cost computing potential.

Mini/Maxi Processing

Still another trend has developed over the past two or three years—the mini/maxi concept. The minicomputer does the interactive on-line processing, which allows a large-scale computer to perform batch and large-volume processing requirements. This is similar to the terminal processing systems we described earlier for retail stores and warehouse operations. But there is one difference. This concept is an advancement in the evolutionary growth of minicomputers as the minicomputer takes on a much bigger role in the total system. It becomes much more than a small concentrator of data with only 32,000 bytes of memory. Its significance in the total data processing scheme is enhanced and increased. Let us briefly identify three examples of the mini/maxi concept in the emerging history of minicomputers. The first example is an accounts payable application that will support 32 terminals and a data base of 90,000 vendors for a large Fortune 500 company. The successful minicomputer processor will have the following systems requirements:

□ *Response time* (the time between entering data and getting a response from the minicomputer) of 3 seconds or less.
□ *On-line capability* to edit all data update a live on-line data base.
□ *Immediate responsiveness* to any and all applications programs in the total system.
□ *Accommodation to concurrent use,* in this case 32 users and terminals.

All these requirements would seem to add up to one very big computer.

The purpose of this particular application was to "off-load" the vendor file from an overworked mainframe that was costing the company a bundle. The system must be able to add new vendors, inquire into the status of existing vendors, and make changes in the vendor file. The system also has to record such activity as receipt of orders and overdue payments.

The challenge this company faced was to accomplish this large task not with a conventional mainframe, but with a dedicated minicomputer to lower total data processing costs. After processing the daily workload, a magnetic tape of transactions was to be generated by the minicomputer, which would subsequently update the larger host computer, which operates best in the batch mode. After receiving the information on magnetic tape, the host would proceed to calculate payments and generate vouchers and other reports for a total accounts payable system. Several minicomputers met this requirement, and the system was implemented. It represented the classic mini/maxi concept, as the minicomputer flexed its muscles at a Fortune 500 company and won it over.

As with the terminal processing systems, the principle of mini/maxi processing is to off-load the mainframe. But in this case, the power and size of the so-called minicomputer permits it to handle a greater taskload and more complexity. In the shared environment, the minicomputer is normally reserved for the more complex on-line and interactive aspects of large systems. Batch processing is left to the mainframe.

This concept is true of the second example of mini/maxi processing— the vast California-based Bank of America. This application is for on-line tellers at 1,000 branches who have to inquire into customer savings and checking accounts as well as update files from the teller window. When the system is completed in late 1978, there will be more than 10,000 on-line terminals handling more than 10 million accounts. The system will consist of two clusters of minicomputers, one located in Los Angeles and one in San Francisco.

The bank selected General Automation minicomputers. Although there are a total of 20 minicomputers in the system, total cost savings of $14.6 million are projected. The cost of the minicomputers is an estimated $4 million, in contrast to the $18.6 million it would cost for mainframes to do the same job. In the near future, batch processing for posting of deposits will be handled by six mainframes at the two locations with information fed by the minicomputers. In the long run, even this step will be eliminated.

The advantages to the system are many. A teller can now "access" a customer record directly instead of having to telephone the customer's branch for the required information. The use of two computer centers with separate clusters provides a failsafe backup. Static data, such as address changes and new accounts, will also be on-line and edited in the interactive mode. Elaborate communications links have been established using modems* and common telephone lines. Future plans are to use General Au-

---

* Modem is an acronym for MOdulator-DEModulator. The modem holds the telephone and makes the connection.

DISTRIBUTED PROCESSING SYSTEMS

tomation minicomputers in the East for international links. If this comes to pass, the Bank of America may well have the largest real-time computer network in the world.*

The trend at the Bank of America takes off with the mini/maxi concept but is apparently progressing toward something else. The same is true in another example of the mini/maxi concept, that of a large manufacturer of instrumentation devices. They have developed a manufacturing system that allows the user to input data in an on-line environment while processing some information on a large mainframe. The system is now marketed throughout the United States.

The inventory control module is on-line and functions exclusively on the minicomputer. A current inventory master file contains all information on inventory status, including on-hand balances, work in process, and on-order balances. Other information, such as lead times, descriptions, lot sizes, and usage history, is also maintained on this file. Thus, using a powerful minicomputer (PDP 11/70) from Digital Equipment Corporation (and more recently, an HP 3000 minicomputer from Hewlett-Packard), users can update files as transactions occur. Users may also inquire at any time into the inventory status.

A routing file and work center file are also maintained on the minicomputers. Manufacturing orders are traceable throughout the plant by means of terminals and the powerful minicomputers. For heavy processing, a larger mainframe was originally included in the design. The bill of materials and product structure files are maintained on a mainframe for the extensive process-bound materials requirements planning module. The manufacturing orders are exploded backward to determine which raw materials are needed to complete the original order. Then, in a time-phased report, the company schedules raw materials purchases. This is known as materials requirements planning. The maxi performs this time-consuming function in the batch mode.

This is a perfect example of the mini/maxi concept, showing information retrieval on-line and large processing programs in batch. But as the minicomputer has grown in power and sophistication, it too has become a qualified candidate for all types of processing. The California-based Bank of America and certain manufacturing companies that use manufacturing packages similar to the one described earlier seem to be headed in that direction. Why, then, can't the minicomputer do the on-line inquiry as well as the heavy processing? Why not?

*Neil Kelley, "Bank of America Goes Distributive," *Infosystems,* March 1977, pp. 46–48.

As minicomputers increase in size and become faster and more powerful, the need for a mini/maxi approach becomes less apparent. As in the case of the manufacturing system we described, there now appears to be no need to flip-flop from one system to another. The bill-of-materials explosions, the manufacturing "recipe," and all other "maxi" functions can be handled quite adequately on the large-scale minicomputers currently on the market. Perhaps the term "minicomputer" is completely wrong for these new larger models. Can 2 million bytes of memory and a capacity for 800 million bytes of auxiliary memory really be considered "mini"? Can a processing speed of 250 to 400 nanoseconds be considered mini? These new computers can perform tasks that were once relegated only to mainframes. The manufacturing system described earlier has been reprogrammed to function entirely on an HP 3000 minicomputer. The process—and its success—are described in the Chapter 11 case study.

This conversion of an entire manufacturing system was possible within a reasonable period of time, as the minicomputer requires no auxiliary or add-on software packages to support multitasking, multiprogramming, or terminal management. These sophisticated features, which are essential to on-line processing, are built into the basic operating systems of the minicomputers. In addition, the larger minicomputers are designed to operate with the virtual memory technique now touted by the mainframe manufacturers.

Not only can the modern minicomputers support the same sophisticated operating systems and data base managers of the mainframes, it has also eliminated much of the burden, overhead, and unwarranted mystique. Even the junior programmer may now feel more at home in the less complex environment—remember, the data base manager is a software package designed to control files and relieve the programmer of this highly technical responsibility.

The historical development of the minicomputer's applications is leading us to a new era in data processing applications—the era of *distributed processing systems*. Considering the flexibility, low costs, and communications applications of the minicomputer, distributed systems have become feasible. Minicomputers open up new opportunities for on-line manufacturing systems and customer order/entry systems. Batch operations, such as payroll processing, can be handled easily with the added benefit of on-line inquiry into personnel data bases.

For those organizations that would like to move into the world of real-time on-line processing, the answer may well be a stand-alone minicomputer that supports multiple applications accessible through multiple terminals. For with existing sophisticated terminal monitors, multiprogramming operating systems, and powerful data base managers, we can think of no applications that operate on a mainframe that cannot operate as effectively on the large minicomputers.

Where will applications for the minicomputer go from here? They will evolve toward those areas in which the cost of mainframes is now prohibitive. Minicomputers will lead the evolution to distributed processing and return computing power to the hands of the people.

6

Automatic Distributed Data
And Processing Technique

According to the limited information available on the subject, the concept of distributed processing probably originated in 1968, when Drs. Edward Bennett and Joseph Spiegel founded a company called Viatron. Their objective was to put an inexpensive Viatron terminal on every employee's desk. The Viatron terminal rented for $39 per month. The terminal was likened to the way the early typewriter got its start. An expensive piece of equipment, the first one purchased had to be kept in a centralized location, with clerks using it on a scheduled basis. Then, as the price went down, a typewriter was placed on every desk. This is probably an accurate picture of how we wound up with distributed typing. The advantages in time and efficiency were obvious. The same is true for computing power.

The idea of a terminal at every desk or in every department popularized the term distributed processing. By 1973, distributed processing became narrowly defined to mean processing of data at remote locations with expensive telecommunications networks linking multiple computers.

It is true that the concept of distributed processing can become very complex with message switching and communications networks. Certainly, what we are trying to do is to provide the stepping stone and path to the more esoteric network systems. There are steps that can be taken today to improve the effectiveness of the computer and the computing process. These steps can make distributed processing a reality in the imperfect world of communications, and they can literally propel your organization to unrealized benefits from data processing.

THREE TYPES OF DISTRIBUTION

There are several different concepts of distributed data and processing. One of the simplest, yet most effective, methods is referred to as *the star con-*

cept. This concept involves having a central data base on a singular computer that many terminals have access to. Communication is limited to multiple cables that connect the computer to various departments in the organization. Its effectiveness arises from the fact that it shifts responsibility for data and the data base to the user. It is also economical, as it requires only one computer with no communications problems. Today, the computer hardware and software are available from the minicomputer manufacturers at a very reasonable cost.

The star concept is illustrated in Figure 7. The computer and data base include the computer, the disk mass storage units, tape drives for historical storage of each transaction, and the printer. Furthermore, it houses the data base for all applications, which are accessible by means of the terminals. One of these user terminals may be located at a remote location with a tie-in to the computer through a common telephone line and the device called a modem, which holds the telephone and makes the connection with the

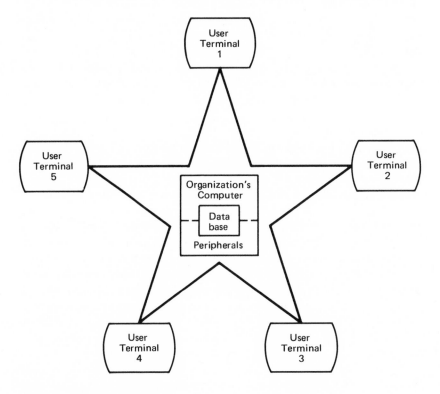

Figure 7. The star concept.

leased wire. It is as simple and effective as picking up a telephone, dialing a designated number, and going on-line.

A second type of distribution, *hierarchical distribution,* is slightly more sophisticated, but just as feasible today. One or more remote locations have their own minicomputers, files, printers, and tapes. These locations communicate to the central processor over leased telephone lines and transmit summary data, such as sales, expenses, inventory balance, or other data needed at the central location. This creates a hierarchy of users from the subsidiary up to the corporate, or main, office. As the number of users at remote locations increases, a small traffic-cop, memory-only computer may be required, as we will point out subsequently.

The *ring distributed network,* the most complex type of distribution, is a series of autonomous computers that communicate with each other continuously. These sophisticated communications are now available through two minicomputer manufacturers, Hewlett-Packard and Digital Equipment Corporation (DECNET). The ring distributed network is in the evolutionary stage and is useful only in the very largest of organizations, such as the federal government, the military establishments, and the very largest Fortune 500 companies.

Our emphasis is on the star and hierarchical types of distribution because they exist in a form that is both practical and realistic for today's data processing users, even at the entry level. The precise nature of the system and the exact hardware depend, of course, on the overall processing requirements and philosophy of a given organization. These considerations can only be made by management, hence our plea that control over data processing be returned to management.

Whether star or hierarchical, distributed processing is on-line data processing with systems controlled by the end user. The data is distributed through terminals, and the process timing and requirements are decentralized. This technique, referred to as ADDAPT (Automated Distributed Data And Processing Technique) is a function of need and available software. On the other hand, the location of hardware is simply a matter of economics on the basis of time and cost of data communication, workload, and any other relevant economic factor that has an impact on the profit or service level.

Distributed data and processing may be as simple as resource sharing with the star concept, whereby several users share the computer's components, such as the memory, disks, tapes, and printers. They also share applications programs that act on their unique files of information.

Or distributed data and processing may use the slightly more complex idea of a hierarchical structure in which remote locations have their own minicomputers but transmit summary data home if it works toward the benefit of the whole. Each concept has its own key elements that should be reviewed for a better understanding of the not-so-mysterious concept of distributed processing.

KEY ELEMENTS IN THE SYSTEM

Paramount to distributed processing is on-line accessibility to a computer. Whether the computer is actually located at the user's site or is located at a distant site is irrelevant, except for the economics involved. However, this is not the same as remote batch entry, such as the IBM 2740 terminal, where data is entered, batched, and transmitted for processing. The missing link, for true distributed processing, is the direct on-line access to a computer. The interactive editing and interactive retrieval of data are missing in remote batch processing, in which data is manipulated unnecessarily and unproductively from key to tape or tape to diskette at the remote site, only to be repeated in reverse at the computer site before any results can be made available.

In contrast to batch processing, distributed processing is on-line, alive, and interactive. It returns systems control to the user and eliminates the need for a large, centralized data processing function, even though the computer may have a central site. Remote entry of data is merely a short step above the mailing of manually transcribed documents to be processed centrally by the large data processing group.

Certain key elements in true distributed processing are necessary to satisfy the on-line function. They are data entry, local editing, data base access, and communications. These, then, are basically software considerations.

Data Entry

Data entry in distributed processing means that the information is entered into the computer by the system's user. Payroll input is made by the payroll department, personnel transactions by the personnel department. The bank clerk enters his or her own transactions as does the airline reservations clerk.

Data entry at the user level has all the advantages we have discussed. It concentrates responsibility with the people who understand the system and its requirements. Several processing steps and data handling functions are reduced, which then cuts down on errors and shortens the time period in which systems are kept current and valid. Above all, it permits improved editing.

Local Editing

The second key element in distributed processing, then, is local editing. As information is fed into the computer, the computer checks its validity. This is *not* the batch environment in which we would experience the cycle illustrated in Figure 8.

The batch-edit cycle may take days. It is inefficient. Distributed processing cuts through the inefficient tie-ups by establishing an interactive process between computer and the user. Again, the computer checks and reports the validity of the data that is fed into it. The computer can be programmed to prevent erroneous data from entering the system or merely to flag it as an error. In either case, the person most familiar with the data

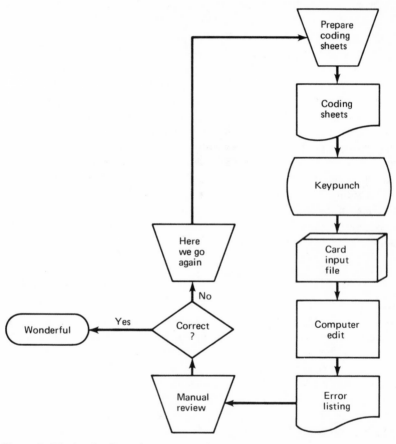

Figure 8. The batch-edit cycle.

DISTRIBUTED PROCESSING SYSTEMS

makes the decision on the basis of the data already stored in the computer and reported to him or her.

What we mean when we say that the editing is "live" is that the user can compare new information with that on the computer using a video display device—a terminal, as shown in Figure 9.

The general ledger clerk enters the account number and the interactive computer asks, "Do you mean cash on hand?" If so, the account is debited or credited and the general ledger is made current. The editing takes place when the computer asks its question. This differs from the batch environment in which the clerk submits the data, and if it is a valid account, the ledger is updated. The same principle holds true for personnel files, manufacturing data bases, and any other on-line data. It constitutes a critical difference in information processing, as the informed user becomes the source of editing and correcting errors with improved accuracy being the result.

Data Base Access

A third feature of distributed processing is data base access and management. Here, too, distributed processing of data is a unique departure from the currently dominant method of data processing, batch processing. Distributing data to the users with terminal access provides the opportunity to have information on-line for all applications at the same time. The real-time environment allows swapping of transactions by multiple users with multiple systems. This is not a new type of processing—timesharing systems have been available for years. The breakthrough is the technological advances in minicomputer hardware and software, which now make file access and distributed processing economically feasible.

The concept is simple. Large disk capacity, large memory, and sophisticated operating systems provide the technical clout to allow users access to any data base as required. The user does not have to wait until a designated hour to input a general ledger transaction or update someone's personnel file. In fact, the general ledger is on the computer along with the personnel file. At their terminals, users simply request the information needed, analyze it, review it, and perhaps update it, and results are available

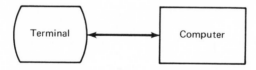

Figure 9. The interactive cycle.

to the user immediately. It looks something like the diagram shown in Figure 10.

What is important here? There are several concepts: First, each user can access any of the data in the computer, through one of the six terminals, unless confidentiality is invoked and security words are issued to limit access. Aside from the case of confidentiality, each of five data bases of information is resident on the computer in massive disk files. Each is available for review, analysis, and active transactions. Second, because each data base is available, any terminal can access it. For example, terminal I can get to the manufacturing data base with its product structures and quantities on hand. Terminal I can also access the customer order/entry data base with customer history, ship-to addresses, and sales information. The general ledger department can use terminal I for posting to the general ledger, and personnel may use it to update an employee's record. Besides the obvious

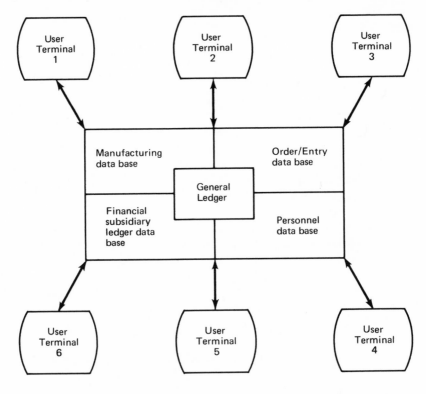

Figure 10. The general ledger transaction.

convenience and flexibility, the chief advantage is that the computer data is available and "in phase" with the department or system user. Distributed processing makes this kind of data access possible.

The centralized data processing function in a batch environment is illustrated in Figure 11. Each system is unique, with only one system in the online mode. Sales is batch-oriented, as is manufacturing. Transactions in the plant are updated once at the end of the day. Inventory status is available only once on the basis of the activity from the day before. Files do not "talk" to each other or share data except as cards (disk or tape) are punched out and held in the queue until the related system is ready for processing. Timeliness and data access are missing in this nondistributed batch environment.

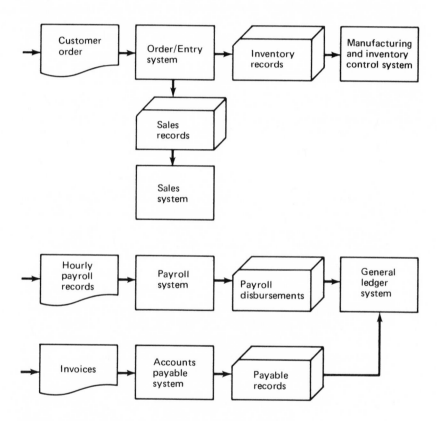

Figure 11. The centralized, nonintegrated batch system.

Communications

The final key element in distributed processing is communications. Communications is essential because distributed processing moves data and data processing to the users, whether they are at remote locations or are department heads in offices that flank the computer room. This is the concept of automated distributed data and processing technique about which we have spoken. The data is available to the remote user. Why not the processing of data?

Communications may consist of nothing more than an extended cable that ties the user to the computer or a leased telephone line connecting a subsidiary organization in another town and state to a shared computer. Management's primary consideration in the area of communications is how much time is being spent unproductively in transferring data. For example, a manufacturing firm with a remote subsidiary may be accumulating data at the subsidiary and then transmitting it over leased lines. At the centralized computer site, the information is recorded on diskettes. The diskette is then read and the information reformatted on tape for processing by the large mainframe.

Too much time and expense spent on unproductive data handling and communications may justify a real-time distributed network. These considerations should be part of a larger study of short- and long-range organizational needs. If distributed processing seems appropriate and cost-effective, as illustrated in the following section, management must begin to analyze communications from a "macro" point of view. Specifically:

1. The hardware system (minicomputer) and its terminals must be capable of operating in a local, remote environment. The terminals must be designed for use several thousands of feet from the computer via cables. The terminals must also have direct access to the computer from a distant location by means of telephone lines.

2. The computer system must be *multitasking*—the remote user must have access to the computer as required; local users must have the same access when their requirements dictate it.

Without these two features, management will limit its capability to expand and to realize the benefits of distributed processing. Let us review distributed processing and its various alternatives.

ADDAPT

Figure 12 illustrates the concept of the Automated Distributed Data And Processing Technique, showing two alternatives: resource in the star mode

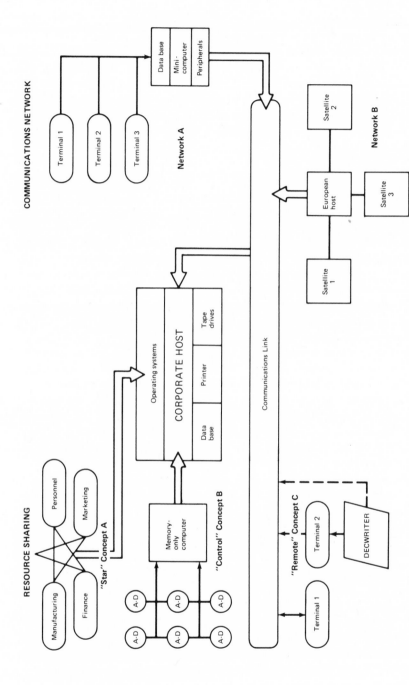

Figure 12. Two forms of distributed processing with centralized computer.

of sharing and communications networks in the hierarchical form. The AD-DAPT concept, which is feasible with minicomputers, gives the user many options according to what best suits his particular needs. For example, in the star concept, local resource sharing (A) may take the form of multiple terminals distributed to various end-user departments, such as manufacturing, finance, personnel, and marketing. Each terminal accesses the same data bases simultaneously, so that personnel adds a new employee while manufacturing orders a product, and each department is in control of its own destiny.

Remote resource sharing (B) is a hypothetical Southern subsidiary in the star mode, which communicates to the host computer on terminals over voice-grade telephone lines at no additional cost. The subsidiary benefits from the accounts payable, the general ledger, and the payroll applications systems. They have their own data base, which uses the computer's extensive disk capacity. They may have a DECwriter (made by Digital Equipment Corporation) tied to one terminal for reports, paychecks, accounts payable checks, and printing of the general ledger. The volume is low. Control resource sharing (C) monitors production machinery with analog-to-digital (A-to-D) converter attachments. Using a memory-only minicomputer, manufacturing communicates with the host computer to monitor performance, signal downtime, and control the equipment.

The communications network brings us to the hierarchy. It consists of remote computers at distant sites, which communicate over the network to the host. Communications network (A) is a larger national subsidiary where the volume of transactions justifies its own satellite computer, three terminals, a fast printer, and a disk storage device. Accounting data and sales data are transmitted daily to the host for consolidated statements, which are available the day of final close-out. The host is able to display sales daily to the corporate controller on his terminal. A profit-and-loss statement could be reviewed daily for this subsidiary—cash position, too, as a matter of fact. Any data that is of a confidential nature, and which should not be accessible to corporate personnel, is handled by means of security passwords on the satellite computer. Thus payroll data may be inaccessible to anyone but the payroll department and the president of the subsidiary.

Communications network (B) in Figure 12 is a theoretical European cluster. Here the European host minicomputer communicates with several subsidiaries (another cluster) and their satellite minicomputers, which have their own peripheral equipment, including disks, printers, and terminals. The host minicomputer is the central controller for all satellites. Summary sales and accounting information captured by the satellite throughout the day is transmitted to the host for long-term storage and consolidation. The host has a large disk capacity that eliminates the need for large data bases at each subsidiary. Inquiry and management requests take place by means of various cathode ray tube terminals at the subsidiaries, which often results in interesting interactive displays. All data is updated on a real-time basis at the completion of each business cycle, known as a *session*. A series of general ledger entries or a group of line items in a sales transaction would constitute a session.

Information in the communications network (B) is entered at the subsidiary on terminals that connect with the satellite minicomputer for editing and summarization. Incidentally, the editing and consolidation application programs should be identical for each subsidiary in order to reduce total applications development costs. A servicing request is then made to the host minicomputer to receive updated information for posting to the central data base. The satellite can continue its normal operational functions, retaining the data in its queue until the host is ready for transmission. The summary data is then transferred and the task completed.

The design philosophy incorporated into this approach is to maintain an on-line backup of all current information with a long-term (years) copy in the host data base and a temporary (one-year) copy in each satellite's storage. At the same time, the subsidiary can use the detail data for accounting, detail sales reporting, manufacturing, or personnel. The satellites, all as compatible as possible and standing alone, supply the subsidiaries with low-cost in-house computing power. Thus, the satellites summarize and communicate daily with the European host, which in turn can communicate by satellite with the corporate host. A multinational U.S. corporation consolidates daily European sales in its European headquarters and at day's end, transmits all sales to the United States. It is effective, inexpensive, and available for all multinationals.

As the workload on the corporate host increases, a memory-only police system may be installed to control the traffic back to the host. This is called front-ending and is not a complex procedure. The software now exists to make front-ending economically feasible. The real issue is the need for information from the various subsidiaries, not the technical ability of a minicomputer in a hierarchical distributed processing environment.

THE COMMON LINK

What do each of these variations have in common? First, they put control of the system and the data in the hands of the end user. The user should be responsible for the original systems design, the training, and the operation.

As such, in each of the variations, the responsibility to get the correct data into the system as it is received rests solely with the end user who understands his system and his data. He should design the system in the same manner as he originally designed the manual systems. In essence, he has his own minicomputer to work with. Not having to worry about file designs, the user must specify his needs in terms of input forms and data, calculations, effect on the various data bases, and reports and displays.

The processor operates in his department through the terminals. He shares with others in an on-line environment. Each of these systems shares the concept of sharing.

RESOURCE SHARING

Ultimately, distributed processing is resource sharing. The resources are the various devices, data base files, and applications programs. Sharing is neither a mystery nor a gesture of generosity. It is necessary to achieve accurate data, timely reporting, and cost savings. As we have said all along, it makes no sense to duplicate data and then multiprocess it repeatedly in a batch mode.

Device sharing. The multiple use of terminals, disk drives, tapes, and memory results in cost savings. One 50-million-byte disk, in an efficient environment, can house a world of information. Why not segregate a section for a subsidiary in the South? The terminals are multifunctional, which means any terminal can access any system and throughput is improved at peak load. It also means a smoothing of peak loads through daily updates, rather than a batch mass entry. Device sharing, then, is an integral part of distributed processing and is the most flexible approach. As we once told a development team, let your imaginations soar, but keep our costs down to earth.

Data base sharing. Sharing terminal users may have access to the same data base of information at the same time. For example, the personnel and payroll departments both use the personnel data base. Personnel uses it for career planning, salary reviews, and equal opportunity reporting, while payroll uses it to generate checks and keep salary history. But it is one file, and it is shared by the individual users as they need it. Figure 13 illustrates both terminals and data base sharing.

Applications program sharing. Like subroutines are shared between systems and users. In a communications network, each individual satellite should share common systems for general ledger, for example. In our experience, the subsidiary with on-line terminals uses the host payroll, accounts

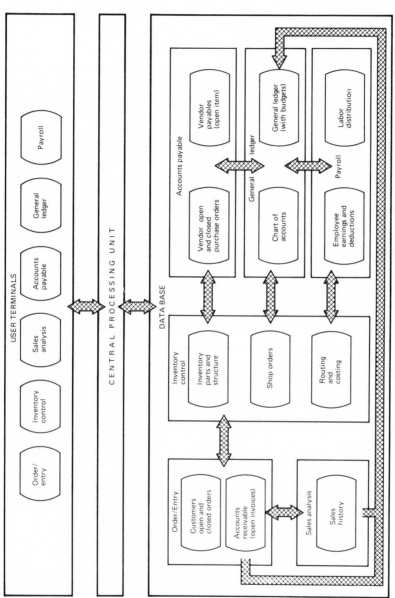

Figure 13. Proposed system for data base sharing.

payable, and general ledger programs; it can use the manufacturing system and customer order entry as well. This is applications program sharing, which means sharing technology as well as the real costs savings.

In another company's experience, several independent subsidiaries were planning to implement computer systems; no two computer systems were the same. In Italy it was Olivetti, England wanted Honeywell, and Australia wanted magnetic ledgers. The German subsidiary wanted a system in which programming changes were made with a soldering iron. Since we were rusty on welding techniques, we recommended a holding pattern. The problem was complicated because each request was for the same applications systems, including cost accounting, payroll, general ledger, and manufacturing, but the hardware reflected nationalism and the local sales effort.

The solution, in this case, is to use the distributed processing concept of shared applications systems. The cost of designing, programming, and testing like systems at each subsidiary is prohibitive. With each subsidiary designing its own systems, the result would be incompatible systems. So good ideas and techniques are lost. To incorporate different methods of data transmission is foolish. The inefficiency should be obvious. Under the diverse recommendations, data would be stored in diskettes in one location, cards in another, magnetic ledger cards in Australia, and on a soldering iron, we assume, in Germany. This approach would be disastrous in any reasonable attempt to consolidate reports and information.

BENEFITS TO DISTRIBUTED PROCESSING

Most experts agree that distributed processing provides an avenue for efficiency and responsiveness. It absolutely reduces data redundancy and its associated inconsistency. Questions of systems integrity also favor the distributed approach, observes a Honeywell project leader on their distributed data base systems. It is a very cost-effective means of processing data, reports *Computer Decisions,* an industry-wide magazine.

There are several reasons for the growing popularity of distributed processing. Equipment costs have come down considerably, and minicomputers offer a shorter implementation period. Consequently, the implementation cost is much lower. Once installed, minicomputer systems have lower operating costs. Site preparation costs are also lower. The *Computer Decisions* article further reveals that low-cost computers as hosts or talking to low-cost hosts via communications networks will have a considerable impact on our approach to current information processing.

All this is true. The impact of distributed processing will be felt through interactive conversations with the minicomputer, integrated data bases, and multiprocessing.

RECOMMENDATIONS FOR DISTRIBUTED PROCESSING

In order to realize the benefits of a truly responsive computer network, we recommend use of a system of minicomputers that provides for interactive conversation through video terminals. This is far superior to the batch mode, which so many users are accustomed to—the same batch mode that causes long queues and shifting priorities. DEC reports that users interact with the computer through a variety of terminals: high-speed cathode ray tube terminals for extremely fast response when a hard copy report is not necessary; the 170-character per second DECwriter for printed copy; or the industry workhorse Teletype for low initial cost. Although users control their activity through such terminals, resource sharing also gives them access to, and control over, minicomputer peripherals, such as card readers, line printers, paper tape devices, disks, and tape units. Thus, users have interactive terminals for ease of use and operational efficiency along with resource sharing for high performance and large system effectiveness.

Interactive conversation greatly improves accuracy because the data is edited at the precise moment the user enters it into the system. Experience shows that the shorter the delay between a transaction and error detection, the easier and more effective is the correction. We hope that's not a generality, but it is logical. Certainly, it is true that interactive communications speed up the data processing. Batch processing is normally overnight and with errors it may be 48 hours later.

Interactive conversation eases the training effort because the user is guided through each transaction in a question-and-answer mode. Let's pay a bill: (1) Hit the terminal start key, (2) identify yourself for security reasons, (3) ask for accounts payable, and (4) you are ready.

None of this is complicated. In the example shown in Figure 14, the minicomputer verified the vendor name and invoice number. It validated the account number and displayed its name (building material) on the screen for visual approval. It considered the logic of the data, and it calculated the 10 percent discount. It was also able to cut a check, update an accounts payable register, close an outstanding invoice, and make the appropriate entry on the general ledger. The user and the minicomputer were communicating up a storm.

While accelerating the entry of data, interactive conversations eliminate the need for keypunching, batching, and submitting data to a central com-

The Computer Asks	The User Responds
Which payable transaction?	Pay/Bill
Who is vendor?	Barrett Division
What is invoice number?	12345
What is item?	Roofing material
What account classification?	112-3432
Payment due?	9-13-77
Amount?	$3,176.25
Discount?	10%
Continue or end?	End

Figure 14. Paying a bill in the question/answer mode.

puter facility. This means not only savings in time, but in costs as well. Excessive handling of data is unnecesarily costly for the organization. How many keypunch operators must be employed to support a large data processing department? These remote data entry clerks may be more productive elsewhere—they are not needed when the user controls his own input. We strongly recommend interactive conversations with on-line terminals. Remember, it works for programmers, too, in developing new systems.

Integrated Data Bases

Integrated data bases of information for the organization as a total entity are recommended for effective distribution of data and processing. An integrated data base is the organization of information in a file structure which represents the total information requirements of the user. All files are on-line and accessible. Transactions are processed against all relevant files, not one at a time, as in batch processing. Such file integration is enhanced by a data base manager technique.

Data base managers, which are software packages for controlling files, are written to reduce the time and cost of writing programs. The data base manager provides one uniform method for handling all the users' files, and it simplifies access through a structured, defined organization of data. Remember, the minicomputer operates in a real-time, on-line environment. Many users are working with the minicomputer at the same time, and a single transaction, as discussed earlier, affects many files. In this environment, the minicomputer must have a data base management system to control in-

DISTRIBUTED PROCESSING SYSTEMS

Table 6. Data base managers marketed on minicomputers.

Manufacturer	Computer	Data Base Manager	Supplier
Data General	Eclipse	INFOS	Data General
DEC	PDP-11	Product 3	ELS Systems Eng.
Interdata	7/16, 7/32	Product 3	ELS Systems Eng.
Data General	Nova series	Product 3	ELS Systems Eng.
Hewlett-Packard	HP 2100, HP 3000	IMAGE	Hewlett-Packard
Varian	V70 series	TOTAL	CINCOM

tegrated files. In most minicomputers today, all management functions are available in the software for the on-line systems. This means that the minicomputer is more efficient, easier to use, and easier to maintain than the large mainframe.

Today, most major minicomputers either have developed their own data base managers or have suppliers who have developed data base managers for them, as shown in Table 6.

Management can see from this table that the minicomputer has some sparkling new software to complement its impressive hardware. Table 6 shows that minicomputers support sophisticated file software, which is essential for managing data in a distributed processing environment.

With this new sophistication, integrated data bases are a reality. The data should now be organized to reflect the organization, rather than separate systems, such as payroll and personnel. This has a tremendous impact on systems design. Contrary to discrete and individualized batch systems, information needs in the new generation are defined by transactions. After all, the organization is a complex interaction of people and transactions. People are hired, accounting entries are made, budgets are produced, bills are paid, personnel are paid, sales are made and recorded, and shipments are received. In the past, each of these was considered a separate system, as shown in Table 7. Remember?

In the batch mode, each system stands separate and alone, and data is processed in sequence, one at a time. This is necessary because all the master data (the data base) is not accessible at the same time. The instruction to "Load payroll," to data processing people, means to mount the payroll file and process timecards against it. As we have shown, correlated (or exactly the same) data may be duplicated in other files elsewhere in separate systems.

The concept of integrated data bases, which we recommend as an integral part of distributed processing, allows the users to look at the organiza-

Table 7. The old-generation batch systems approach.

Transaction	System
People are hired	Personnel
Accounting entries are made	General ledger
Budgets are produced	Production control
Bills are paid	Accounts payable
People are paid	Payroll
Sales are made	Accounts receivable
Sales are recorded	Sales analysis
Shipments are received	Inventory control

tion as a whole. It is a total organization approach that examines transactions as they affect data bases of information. This approach maximizes what the machine can do. Each transaction is analyzed as to what data bases it affects, regardless of the systems. Is this the real transactional analysis? It is possible for three reasons:

□ The integration of data bases provides the opportunity to define systems to include the relationship between various functions rather than segment each in a unique batch process.

□ All data bases can be maintained on-line at a reasonable cost.

□ All data is edited at once in an interactive interchange between the user and the machine and only good data is allowed to update data bases.

In contrast to the batch systems approach, the transaction is defined as it interacts with all related data bases. The data bases reflect the organization's need for information on, for example, personnel, financial matters, and manufacturing management, and each transaction is applied to all integrated data bases at the same time.

The transaction to record the hiring of a new employee shown in Table 8 involves the personnel file and the financial file for this person's salary, and for its incorporation into the departmental budget. When one transaction is entered into the computer it updates all integrated files at once and editing is made on-line. All files are clean and accurate, and the computer is functioning as an information processor.

Multiprocessing/Multitasking

A multiprocessing or multitasking capability is also recommended for distributed processing. Multiprocessing simply means that multiple transactions

Table 8. Integrated data bases and transactional analysis.

Transaction	Personnel					Financial			Manufacturing			
	Name	EEOC	Salary	Pension	History	Account	Debit	Credit	Inventory	Shop Floor	BOM	History
People are hired	X	X	X	X	X	X	X					
Accounting entries are made						X	X	X				
Widgets are produced						X	X	X	X	X	X	X
Bills are paid						X	X					
People are paid	X		X	X	X	X	X					
Sales are made						X		X	X			X
Sales are recorded						X		X				X
Shipments are received						X	X		X			X

X represents the information required to complete the transaction.

with different objectives from different end users can be processed simultaneously. This is similar to the argument just described and is possible for the same reasons. The minicomputer has the capacity to hold all files on-line at one time with multiple terminals to allow access to the information. In our transactional analysis (see Table 8), all eight transactions may be entered simultaneously for editing, updating, and processing. Thus, in one part of our organization a shipment is recorded, while in personnel we prepare to add a new employee to the organization. Why should one of these transactions have to get in a queue behind the other? Why should one employee have to wait to get his or her answer from the computer, while another employee is higher in the queue? We are not convinced that a sales transaction is more important that a production order, or vice versa. Nor should you be. It's all irrelevant with multiprocessing minicomputers.

Multiprocessing allows each terminal to be prepared to accept user input, submit it to the minicomputer, and generate the results in a display or report, as required. Not to belabor the point, the benefit of this approach over large-scale batch processing is *time*. Time wasted is costly, and now it is even unnecessary.

ADDAPT RECAPPED

From the Viatron concept of a terminal on every desk in the star concept, to the sophisticated communications hierarchical network of several minicomputers, distributed processing is an exciting approach. Its usefulness resides in software and functional systems rather than the location of hardware, which is a function of economics and workload. Its impact is to return data preparation and control to the user and reduce user dependence on a large central data processing department. It means direct access to a computer after disqualifying the remote batch data entry concept. Management will want to know that multitasking and remote communications are available in any system they select.

Although there are several variations to the theme, the common link for all distributed systems is resource sharing: the economic sharing of peripheral devices, computer files, and application programs. This means the end user has access to a powerful computer with sophisticated peripherals, which he shares with other end users. It is a power and timeliness he has never known, and at a low, affordable price. It is the basis for our recommendations for a revolutionary shift to minicomputers and an end to the evolutionary spiraling costs.

Minicomputers are critical to distributed processing today because of their cost and architecture. Mainframes are simply too expensive and were

DISTRIBUTED PROCESSING SYSTEMS

not designed for distributed processing; they were designed for batch processing, at which they excel.

Minicomputers were designed to operate with terminals and time-sharing. These two features are essential for effective processing at remote location or even different departments. Otherwise, everyone would just sit at a terminal and wonder when his turn would come, perhaps for hours. The minicomputer was designed with operating systems for interactive conversation with users; it is this environment which has made distributed processing feasible. Mainframes, on the other hand, require special new software to allow them to do what the minicomputer does naturally by design. And the extra software is very costly indeed.

The low cost of a minicomputer makes it feasible to place one at a remote location for even a small workload. Transmission by telephone lines is available and, if the host computer is sick, the distributed minicomputer continues to work at its own pace.

This is a timely recommendation and there is strong support behind it. A recent study by a firm named Gnostic Concepts in Menlo Park reported that the market for distributed computing systems will exceed $5.6 billion by 1980, in the United States alone. According to the study, this will represent nearly 37 percent of the total computer hardware shipment value. The main increase will be in factory data-collection systems, point of sales, banking with automated tellers, and control systems.

As another example, C. W. Spangle, president of Honeywell Information Systems, recently spoke on "The Expanding Role of Minicomputers." He observed that distributed processing is the trend of the future because it is becoming less expensive to add new small systems for upgrading. Distributed systems may be more modular and easily expandable. The systems more nearly follow the pattern of the organization itself—our position with regard to the computer as being "in phase." Other advantages over a large central department are better response time, higher systems availability, and enhanced throughput.

But Spangle's speech ended with a rather disarming and somber observation: "Distributed processing will not come easily." Why? Because it is not a better idea? No, "Because it is so different from the centralized system. It is inevitable that there will be some resistance by centralized organizations to a decentralized structure."

SO LET'S MOVE FORWARD

All along, we have been hinting about resistance to change. The resistance may be heard the loudest from the data processing environment, but it will also be heard from end users who are unfamiliar with computers and the new terminals that will begin to appear. And some middle managers will also resist as a result of pressures from data processing technicians and the cold, hard fact that we are asking them to manage where they have never managed before.

We must address these issues, which are organizational and psychological in nature. They bear no relationship to the technical aspects of minicomputers, distributed processing, and communications among computer systems. These are the tough issues. To address them, we will discuss first the implications for the long-standing and entrenched department of data processing. For this is the unit that will be affected most directly from an organizational point of view. We will show how sensitivities can be preserved and the effect of overall change minimized.

The remainder of this book deals directly with resistance to change from data processing professionals, end users, and middle management itself. The final chapter presents a case study aimed at bringing all the parties together in a real-life situation where one company implemented a distributed processing system and encountered some of the very resistance of which we now speak.

7

Distributed Processing and Organizational Design

The traditional data processing organization is centralized for some very valid reasons. In the earlier days of data processing, only about twenty years ago, computers operated in the batch mode. Then, too, the early computers were expensive and required special technical skills. It was not feasible to place an expensive computer and a well-trained technical staff in each division, functional area, or department.

Nor would it have been desirable, because coordination of systems would have been a problem. Systems development would have been difficult at best. This issue remains today, even with distributed processing. What is no longer an issue, however, is the need to return systems and data to the user.

The issue, from an organizational point of view, is one of centralizing versus decentralizing the data processing function. This issue can only be discussed with a full understanding of the makeup of the data processing function. For the data processing function is neither a single-purpose nor a single-minded organization. It is a three-headed entity that requires diverse skills and disciplines. The organization chart shown in Figure 15 illustrates the point. Our experience has taught us that certain basic elements should remain centralized, but that major processing improvements result from returning other skills to the user departments and organizations. We believe that the best of both worlds is attainable.

MAJOR FUNCTIONS

Data Control

The centralized data processing organization must be scheduled. The average data processing center has many systems applications, which will be

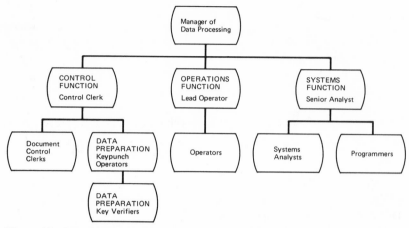

Figure 15. Organization chart for the department of data processing.

processed during the day, week, or month. These applications, which must be scheduled to run on the computer, include some of the following:

☐ The organizational payroll must be run semimonthly or weekly. This requires collecting and preparing timecards and labor reporting information.

At years end, W2 forms must be scheduled. Quarterly 941 forms must also be scheduled for the computer.

☐ Monthly accounting records and the general ledger must be scheduled. This means that the daily journal entries, or the government-oriented obligations and finding entries, must be prepaid for the computer.

☐ Manufacturing plans and inventory balances must be scheduled to provide manufacturing planners and purchasing agents with information on available inventory levels.

☐ Many miscellaneous applications, such as asset records, cash-flow reports, bank balances, and personnel reports, must be scheduled into the busy computer.

To coordinate this effort, the typical data processing centers normally have a data entry and data control function. Headed by a central control clerk, this function schedules the receipt of source documents from the individual departments or subsidiaries. The well-organized control function normally has a calendar of expected source documents with a special month-end closing schedule. Source documents are logged in and scheduled for preparation of data.

Data preparation is the process of preparing the source data and transposing it from the written word to some computer-readable format. The most common format in use today is the punched card invented by Mr. Hollerith before the turn of the century. Other methods that are becoming popular include keying the data directly to magnetic tape, called key-to-tape, and keying the data directly to disk storage, or key-to-disk. In any of these circumstances, a staff of keypunch operators or data entry clerks is required. Normally, these operators report to the central data processing manager through the data entry control function.

A related function is key verification. In this instance, the source data is re-keyed to verify the accuracy of the original keypunch effort. Generally, a red light flashes to indicate a discrepancy between the original keypunch card and the attempt at verification. By all rules of logic, verification is an expensive, time-consuming, and wasteful effort. But no one will deny that key verification is essential in a centralized data processing organization.

Operations

The second major function in a data processing function is operations, which differs drastically from the data entry function. Operations means "running" the computer. The people who perform this task are called operators. In a large organization, there may be many operators, and for those computer departments that have more than 8 hours of daily processing, there will be second- and third-shift operators.

The basic function of an operator is to run batch systems on a set, scheduled basis. To "run" a system, such as the weekly payroll, the computer must be turned on and loaded with the payroll programs, which tell the computer how to run the payroll. This program may be loaded from punched cards, magnetic tape, or the disk, the most conventional methods. Historical files must be mounted on tape drives, or disk drives, to be accessed by the computer programs. In this example, the permanent historical files would be the year-to-date payroll records filed by employee. Now the system is almost ready.

The operator finally loads in the current data needed for preparing the payroll. In this case, the current data would be the hours worked during the week by employees. Normally, this is loaded through punched cards, or magnetic tape. The operator is responsible for putting the blank paychecks in the printer. Later he will be responsible for removing the checks and putting in the preprinted forms for the payroll journal.

After the payroll system has been run, all files that are now updated are stored for the next week's processing. Cards are "boxed" and stored, and the operator is ready to run the next scheduled system. In more sophisticated environments, the operator may "stream" multiple systems in a running sequence called a "job stream." The operations group is responsible for loading several systems with their files and new information while letting the computer call in each system, execute it, go on to the next system, and so on, until the job stream is complete. The operators in this environment control the processing of sequential systems through a job-control language technique referred to simply as the JCL.

The operations function has other functions that are important to the central data processing organization. One very important function is the control over all computer files. Extensive labeling of the tape and disk files is

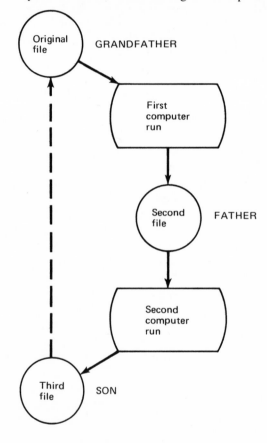

Figure 16. The grandfather concept.

DISTRIBUTED PROCESSING SYSTEMS

necessary in order to maintain the identity of the various systems files, including the general ledger and payroll. We will never forget one large chemicals company, which used a small minicomputer to control the tape files of its massive batch-system mainframe. Tapes were stored in vaults that encompassed room after room of tape files.

The operations function is normally responsible as well for "backup" files, kept as a protection measure should one of the current files be lost or destroyed. The most widely accepted method is the son–father–grandfather concept used in batch environments. The current file is updated by new data; the newly created file is called the son. The old file becomes the father. Somewhere in the file room is another, older file, which is the grandfather. It looks something like the scheme shown in Figure 16. This is a major responsibility and makes operations a vital function indeed.

Still other functions of operations include the scheduling and coordination of preventive maintenance by the manufacturers. Operations is responsible for the environment in which the computer functions, including the temperature and humidity. Finally, operations maintains a record or "log" of jobs run during the shift and the time required for processing. This log is later used to analyze scheduling and running times and can be a source of information for billing users for computer time used.

Systems

The last organizational component in this troika is the systems function. It is here that the impact of distributed processing will be felt most and will be contested hotly for years ahead. For it is here that the glamour and so-called professionalism of data processing rests.

The systems function is normally headed by a senior analyst or a manager of systems and programming. In larger organizations, the systems and the programming functions may be separate, which inevitably causes communications problems of some magnitude. Regardless, the team of systems analysts is made up of the professionals who design, program, and implement systems for the user departments. The systems analyst must be quite a remarkable person for he or she must understand the user's systems and design a system for the computer that will solve some obscure but ubiquitous problem, while at the same time improving the user's destiny. The systems analyst must then program that design for the computer and make it work. Then, as we will discuss later, the same person must turn into a teacher and educate the user in this new system.

The demand for systems analysts in the job market remains strong. A talented systems analyst can make a major contribution to his or her organization, whereas a charlatan can raise havoc, and it is often difficult to distinguish between the two until it is too late. The problem is easy to understand. The systems analyst is a technician who understands the electronic computer, its capabilities and its limitations. A technician who can make the computer work through some technical programming languages called COBOL, FORTRAN, APL, PL-1, BASIC, or RPG, the systems analyst is not familiar with the user's needs and systems requirements. We place systems analysts in the untenable position of designing something to which they have had very limited exposure.

HOW IS PROFIT AFFECTED?

Theoreticians have argued for years for one or the other—that is, for a centralized data processing function versus a decentralized one. In a later chapter, we explore the argument for centralization as put forth by data processing professionals. There are advantages and disadvantages to each. Furthermore, the real decision is heavily weighted by the particular circumstances of the individual organization. The real decision should be what works most effectively to improve the information processing and, in the profitmaking organization, what structure affects the bottom line most significantly. Too often, this is overlooked by managers who are not managing data processing. Let's look at some of the theoretical considerations in the issue of organizational structure, and then let us put them in perspective. Three issues in this decision are always the cost of the computer, the cost of software development, and responsiveness.

Hardware Costs

One computer is less expensive than two. Logically, the total costs of hardware seem to favor the centralized data processing structure. In fact, as we've pointed out previously, there is not much sense in placing multiple computers where one will handle the workload. We are proponents, remember, of "sharing."

The argument for centralization is also a historical one because of the high cost of computers and the technical support required. The current argument is for the "unit cost of computing." The proponents of centralized data processing contend that centralization results in a lower cost per transaction. This has led to the utilization of the computer 24 hours a day; it is the "fill it to capacity" syndrome, which we ridiculed earlier.

One counterargument is vulnerability. If the entire corporation with all its divisions is dependent on one computer, the corporation would be seriously affected if its single computer were to become inoperable for an extended period of time. This, of course, depends on how heavily the corporation depends on its central computer.

Software Development Costs

No one should argue this point. A centralized or shared effort is essential, as it costs too much to develop similar systems for each of similar divisions in an organization. It is inefficient, too, and really not very smart. We remember a rather inept systems analyst in one multidivisional company who designed a fancy accounts payable system for a remote subsidiary (using a rather crude means to transmit the data), while the corporation processed its accounts payable transactions on unit record equipment. When the new enlightened management woke up, the corporate accounts payable system had to be completely redesigned, as the subsidiary's system had such limited capability.

In this case, just a little common sense, or a heavier dose of management, could have reduced the development effort by one-half as the larger corporate requirements would easily satisfy the remote subsidiary's requirements. Duplication of effort in systems development is expensive and must be dealt with if decentralization is to be effective. Can we share here too?

As a corollary to this argument, a centralized system allows for better control of the technical staff, which is critical in a data processing environment. As we pointed out earlier, good analysts are in demand, and this rather valuable resource is not infinite. Effective data processing and profit-line impact will depend on the best utilization of the systems function in the data processing environment. On the surface, this would clearly tend to favor a centralized function. Here analysts could work together on technical problems without recreating the wheel for each new system. In addition, more overall direction of the systems effort can be generated from a central corporate department, where goals and objectives can be translated into systems priorities.

Responsiveness

Few will argue this either. Responsiveness means time, and time is money. Responsiveness to user needs is most often enhanced by decentralization. Working at the user level, more effort will be generated directly to his needs rather than be dissipated through the multiple requests for multiple systems by multiple competing interests, these interests being either different departments, different functions, or different subsidiaries or divisions. The decentralized function also allows the user to deal more directly with the data processing entity rather than requiring that he sort through an organizational structure he does not understand, or deal with persons not totally familiar to him. This is especially true of the very large organizations and even the smaller ones that have a multidivisional structure.

Responsiveness in a large central organization is almost always an issue. It is more than the time lag in submitting source data, keypunching it, verifying it, scheduling it, and then running it. It is more than the aggravation of error listings that must be corrected and resubmitted to the lengthy process. The argument is really that data processing technicians are trying to solve business problems which they simply do not understand, and time is lost. Responsiveness in a central data processing function is a deep-seated problem.

There are corollary issues here too. Frequently, animosity develops between the user departments and the central data processing department. In other cases, the cost of the service is a bone of contention because the central data processing function is expensive. For example, a manufacturing firm in Tennessee can process its requirements for one-half the cost quoted by the corporation's central data processing staff, that is, 6 cents per transaction, as opposed to 12 cents per transaction. The reason is the large main memory, disk capacity, tape drives, supplies, environmental equipment, and staff required to run the central data processing department. And it is the user who pays.

Animosity does not do much to improve the responsiveness of the central data processing entity. Setting users back in charge of their data processing destiny does improve responsiveness, however, for the reasons developed in the first chapter of this book. The question here is how to do it. Then, if it can be accomplished, how will it affect our three cost issues—hardware, software, and responsiveness?

DISTRIBUTING THE FUNCTIONS

The answer may well be to distribute certain of the data processing functions, but not the entity per se. Data processing professionals maintain that you cannot set up separate departments throughout the organization, as it would be too costly and inefficient, and control over systems would be lost. Let us agree with them in theory that there should be control over the data processing function, so that everyone is not randomly doing his own thing to the detriment of the organization as a whole. The controlling factor should be top management. Let's call him the president or director of information systems, who reports directly to the president. Let's review the three functions of data processing ever so briefly.

□ *Data entry and control:* Schedules and completes the data preparation by changing the written word to a computer-readable mode.
□ *Operations:* Schedules and runs the various systems on the computer.
□ *Systems:* Designs, programs, and implements user's systems on the computer.

Data Entry

In a distributed environment, data entry should be returned to the user. Source documents should be designed such that the user department, using on-line video display terminals, assumes full responsibility for putting all its information into the computer. With the responsibility for data inputting goes the responsibility for its timeliness and accuracy. This will mean taking the first important step toward on-line processing and an important step away from the old-generation batch mentality. It is a giant step.

The general ledger clerk will now enter her/his own journal entries and, as we discussed earlier, the computer will edit and verify the account number, the valid dollar limits, the date, and any other relevant information. The payroll clerk will now enter employee hours or labor distribution hours directly when the information becomes available. The manufacturing planner or the warehouse supervisor will now tell the computer that a shipment has arrived in a certain quantity against an established purchase order.

The middleman (the data processing entry clerk) is eliminated from the equation forever. This means savings in time and the total data processing budget. And this cost has not been transferred to the user, as you will see.

Operations

In a distributed environment, operations must remain with the computer, as in a centralized environment. Although the function changes dramatically, there is still a need for someone to maintain that piece of hardware. In a central batch environment, the principle function of operations was scheduling and running different applications. In the distributed environments, files remain on-line, and new data is entered as it becomes available. Thus, the scheduling function is unnecessary with the exception of any batch-produced reports.

Even in an on-line system, some batch reporting will surely remain. For example, the printing of paychecks, W2 forms, and payroll registers is processed in the batch mode. Similarly, the general ledger printout occurs at one point in time. Logically, weekly or daily production schedules are printed at one time. The operations function can assume the responsiblity for any reports that remain in the batch mode. Our experience dictates that this is not a major, but it is an essential, function. The biggest problem seems to be the special forms, such as invoices, paychecks, accounts payable checks, and bills of lading or shipping papers. In the latter instance, a small printer may be dedicated to printing these documents inexpensively, if the volume justifies it.

No, the major function of operations is not scheduling in a distributed environment. We would contend that the major function is to "police" the computer and the users. The new responsibility is to upgrade routine operations, and it justifies a new title: the systems manager. The systems manager stays with the computer.

In policing the computer, an important consideration in distributed processing is security. Payroll data is normally considered confidential. Not everyone should have access to other employees' salary. Other confidential information may be resident in the general ledger or in customer sales records. In addition to confidentiality, certain information should be available only to designated departments; for example, inventory balances should be available to planners and purchasing agents, but not to the payroll department.

One of the key responsibilities of the policeman, therefore, is maintaining security through *passwords*. In our new on-line environment, a user. signs on in the morning by typing HELLO. The user then requests the system by name, such as, PAYROLL. The computer will ask for the password, which unlocks the payroll data base. If the user does not know the password, that ends the processing. If the user enters the correct password, processing may begin. Incidentally, this new computer can be programmed *not* to display the password on the video display terminal, so that no one can look over a user's shoulder and steal his or her password.

The systems manager assigns passwords, controls access to the system, and periodically changes passwords. The systems manager can also lock out users from the various systems. He can assign only one specific terminal to a specific function, such as payroll, and then closely guard the use of that terminal.

The systems manager is also responsible for backing up the system. Each transaction in an on-line environment is "logged" on tape or disk. In the event of any malfunctions, it is the systems manager's responsibility to "bring the system up" or, simply stated, start it up again and get the system back in use. Normally, the logging tape is listed daily as an audit trail for all transactions. This, too, remains a centralized function associated with the computer itself. Maintaining a tape library and historical audit reports is the responsibility of the systems manager.

The final and undoubtedly the most important function of the systems manager is the maintenance of the organization's data base. We have discussed data bases before, but now it takes on organizational implications. Figure 17 illustrates a data base for a manufacturing concern. Actually, the data base consists of a set of functional data bases. The heart of the data base as a manufacturing concern is the manufacturing data base, which consists of the inventory master, product structure, work center, and routing files or data sets. Other functional data bases include payroll, accounts payable, sales, and order entry. Each of these functional data bases transfers information into the general ledger data base. All together, these functional data bases make up the organization's total data base. (See the discussion in Chapter 9 on the relevance of the data base to its users.)

The importance of the data base cannot be overstated. The systems manager is responsible for the integrity of the entire data base, its security, and the efficiency and speed of obtaining data from it. On the other hand, he is not responsible for its content; that responsibility rests with the user. The integrity of the data base means that information from the data base remains

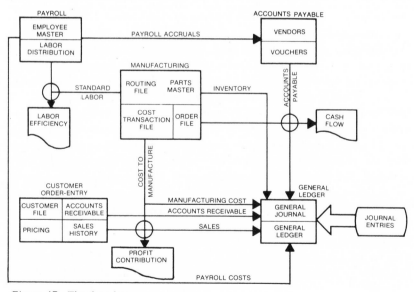

Figure 17. The data base.

that in an on-line environment, these files are always on the computer and are being accessed by many users simultaneously. The systems software, including the data base manager software we discussed earlier, is employed to keep the data bases synchronized. The systems manager must be knowledgeable in the technical aspects of the software and is therefore responsible for the integrity of the data base.

Because the data base is for the use of many end users, its maintenance rests logically with the hardware and not with the multiple users. Furthermore, it is a rather technical position that requires special training and a knowledge of the hardware rather than the user application. It should remain with the hardware. Finally, the systems manager "reorganizes" the data base periodically to better utilize the physical space on the disk files so that access time is minimized. This is a routine function for the systems manager. Maintenance and the physical environmental considerations remain with the hardware, even in a distributed system.

Systems and Programming

The systems and programming functions in a distributed environment should be returned to the user. It has simply not been effective as a centralized function. Analysts never really come to grips with user problems. However, some central control and coordination is needed. Otherwise, the software development costs will be prohibitive and inefficiencies in using the computer will surely follow. Again, this coordination and control must come from top management—it is simply too important.

There are at least two reasonable alternatives for achieving decentralization while assuring control and coordination of the systems effort. One alternative is used by one of the largest banking institutions in the world, Citicorp, which is the corporate entity of New York's Citibank (formerly First National City Bank). Citicorp is a strong advocate of minicomputers and distributed processing. This corporation uses a variety of minicomputers and distributes them to each major function and organizational entity, which justifies the requirement for computing capability. According to one vice-president, John Olson, the first step was to decentralize the systems function and assign systems analysts directly to the user departments.

This step greatly strengthens the inadequate systems support at the end-user level. The analyst is an employee of the user department and is therefore responsible to it for his performance and the effectiveness of systems he designs. As a major part of his training, the analyst learns the user's systems, his problems, and his opportunities for improvements using the computer.

After the indoctrination of the analyst and the decentralization of the function, Citicorp distributed minicomputers to the various functions and began phasing out the large central data processing department. A coordinating committee of top vice-presidents was set up to coordinate all the systems efforts and assure continuity within the overall objectives of the bank. But this committee does not operate at the detail systems level of the so-called systems planning committees, which produced such dismal results in the 1960s. Rather, it is a high-level steering committee set up to avoid duplication of effort and share new ideas to promote the most efficient processing of information for the corporation. This committee exemplifies the process of returning data processing to management, leaving the technical details to the analyst and putting both in the proper perspective.

An example of Citicorp's use of minicomputers is reported by Citibank, New York City's largest bank. The application is simple: an on-line system that allows clerical personnel to respond to customer requests for their account status. The system, which will replace a manual system of return phone calls and letters, will allow immediate access to customer accounts for more than 2,400 correspondent banks. The control is centralized, but each of the correspondent banks will access its own files through video display terminals. The system includes a minicomputer built by Microform Data Systems. The system will allow a customer service representative to retrieve a customer's account number and his account balance while the customer is waiting on the telephone.

It is a powerful and inexpensive use of a distributed process that epitomizes responsiveness. According to the latest information on the corporation, Citicorp will continue to decentralize, using minicomputers located at the distributed locations of users for still more applications.

A second alternative to distributing the system's function may be more acceptable. In this approach, which was implemented by a medium-size manufacturing firm, the systems analysts report to a manager of data processing in the corporate headquarters, but are assigned permanently to the end-user departments. This gives the analyst a straight-line reporting relationship to his manager and a dotted-line relationship to the end user. Figure 18 illustrates this approach. Here, the centralized data processing relates only to the hardware.

Organizationally, only the coordination of systems and the systems management function remains an entity. The systems analysts are assigned to the specific function of controlling their systems absolutely through video terminals. In a larger environment, each function may justify its own hardware, in which case the same relationship between central and distributed functions prevails.

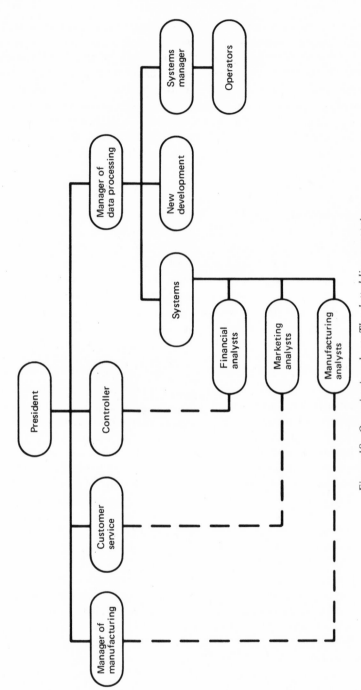

Figure 18. Organization chart: The dotted-line concept.

In Figure 18 the analysts are located in the data processing department. Their key function, however, is with the user, as we shall see:

The financial analysts are responsible to the controller for all financial systems, including payroll, general ledger, accounts payable, and monthly profit-and-loss reporting. These analysts are familiar with the computer programs and the user's systems.

The marketing analysts are responsible to customer service and the marketing operation for the customer order/entry system. They are also responsible for the sales and marketing reporting and they, in fact, designed and programmed both.

The manufacturing analysts are responsible for the inventory and production control systems at this manufacturing concern. These analysts work with the manager of production and inventory control and have become familiar with the manufacturing function, as well as the sophisticated on-line system that supports the manufacturing requirements.

In a dynamic environment with ever-increasing systems requirements that fall outside the principal departments (marketing, finance, and manufacturing), a separate analysis may be established and termed "new developments." Under the direction of the manager who reports directly to the president, this group will handle special systems requests. In the case of this manufacturing concern, this group provided the key to implementing new systems in subsidiaries and making whatever minor customizations were required to fit in a diverse division.

THE COST-EFFECTIVENESS OF CENTRALIZED DATA PROCESSING

This organizational change will not come easily. It will be resisted. As we concluded in Chapter 6, distributed processing itself will not be welcomed by some because it represents a break with the traditional central data processing department. It raises the planning function to the level of top management and leaves the technical considerations to the more specialized data processing manager and his trimmer staff. How will such a change affect costs and responsiveness to user demands?

The Cost of Hardware

Distributed data and processing is an idea whose time has come because for the first time it is cost-effective with the new minicomputer, which also happens to be mini-priced. The logical argument that centralization reduces the overall cost of hardware is now questionable and even suspect. The large

overhead factor in a centralized data processing setup makes this an expensive alternative. No generalities can be made here, for each organization has unique requirements and unique organizational structures. Each must evaluate its own potential for minicomputers and distributed processing.

But certain facts remain. A large centralized computer requires much more sophisticated software, such as operating systems, data base managers, and communications interfaces. It requires massive memory. Figure 19 is an example of memory utilization in a real environment. The two memory maps (as they are called) show that the two computer systems are configured with similar capacities of 192,000 to 196,000 bytes. But the large mainframe on the left has so much software that it has only 75,000 bytes for use by the applications program, as shown in the unshaded areas.

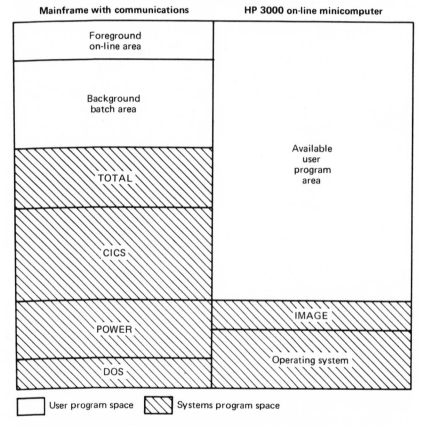

Figure 19. Memory utilization in a real environment: mainframe vs. on-line mini-computer.

The newer minicomputer technology is more efficient and simpler in concept. In a prototypical system we evaluated, the usable core was 132,000 of the 196,000 total bytes. The minicomputer memory was dynamically allocated to each user on the basis of the amount of memory required to process each application. The mainframe, on the other hand, was configured to run one job at a time in the batch partition (54,000 bytes), regardless of how much memory was actually required.

The result is obvious inefficiency and the need for more and more memory. In addition, the mainframe and the typical central data processing organization normally translate all systems programs into COBOL, which is not a memory-efficient language. Again, more memory is required with more overhead, more cost. Although COBOL is available, the minicomputer is usually programmed in the more efficient FORTRAN, or the interactive BASIC languages. In the same experience reflected in the memory maps (Figure 19), the 192,000-byte mainframe could not support even one more on-line application. Because of its design, the minicomputer supported five major applications on-line. The cost of the minicomputer was roughly 25 percent of the mainframe.

There are other overhead considerations which, in many cases, negate the argument that centralization reduces the total cost of hardware. The central large-scale mainframe requires special raised floors for special electrical wiring as well as special temperatures with air conditioners and dehumidifiers. But most importantly, it requires a specially trained, expensive staff of technicians.

As a result, some companies are now finding that it is cost-effective to replace mainframes with several minicomputers, or at a minimum to shift major functions from the mainframe to a minicomputer. In each case, the minicomputer is distributed to the end user. One example is Lowe's Department Stores, a large chain of retail stores in the Southeastern United States. Lowe's replaced a central data processing department with multiple Eclipse minicomputers manufactured by Data General Corporation. We previously cited several manufacturing firms that have dedicated manufacturing and order/entry systems operating right at the user's location, as opposed to the central mainframe.

The Cost of Software

The second argument for centralized data processing is equally suspect today. In the first place, it applies only to multidivisional environments. For the single government or private organization, this is not an issue. But in the multidivisional company, if management blindly agrees to the design of dissimilar systems for multiple locations, it would indeed be costly. This danger exists with distributed processing, as responsibility is also distributed. In larger organizations, the position of corporate information systems takes the responsibility for preventing duplication of effort, beginning with a *corporate computer plan.*

The corporate computer plan defines the long- and short-range objectives for information processing in the corporation (or organization) as a whole. The plan defines the hardware requirements for the multiple divisions and sets up a schedule for implementation with responsibilities clearly defined. This plan should consider only what can benefit the organization and, in the profitmaking sector, the bottom-line effect of the computer. It should be an objective evaluation of the organization's needs, rather than its present situation. Most importantly, the plan should set up a schedule for software or systems development. These steps plus a close monitoring of the plan will preclude duplication of effort.

A good example of a corporate plan with control over software development costs is the Kodak Corporation in Rochester, New York. Here the corporation was originally responsible for designing and programming the major systems, which would be identical in its worldwide divisions. The systems were implemented under corporate control in each division. Software is identical and is written for one model computer. Each division is autonomous from a data processing point of view and has its own systems staff. Kodak maintains a staff of analysts in Rochester to monitor modifications submitted by the divisions, establish a communications link between divisions, and document all major systems. It works and reduces the total software development costs for Kodak.

In a single computer operation, where we recommend distributing data entry and systems expertise to the user departments, the cost of software does not differ in the distributed scheme. In fact, the on-line aspect of the minicomputer reduces the cost of systems development. As noted earlier, some maintain that interactive programming improves programming efficiency by up to 35 percent. We agree. Interactive programming operates much the same as interactive conversation between the user and the computer. The programmer makes changes to his program using the terminal. Once the change is made, it is compiled and tested directly from the terminal.

Compare this simplicity with the central mainframe environment: Program changes are made on coding sheets. The coding sheets are keypunched and run in a batch mode with other program changes. A listing, similar to an edit listing, advises the programmer of any errors he has made. He then corrects the errors and resubmits the change for another listing. When the programmer has a "clean" compilation, he can test his system changes. Thirty-five percent is probably a conservative estimate. So the idea that software costs are less in a large-scale central data processing organization is subject to analysis by the enlightened manager.

Responsiveness

In many instances, distributed processing is organizationally sound. Whether it uses shared resources or the network of remote computers, the Automated Distributed Data And Processing Technique (ADDAPT) is a concept in phase with the times. The arguments against it, such as hardware and software costs, must now be challenged. In smaller organizations, the idea of placing a terminal at every desk makes very good sense. Even in the largest of organizations, the potential benefit of breaking down the large central data processing organization is real. Certain functions can be processed more efficiently by the user. This has been proved in many Fortune 500 companies that took the initiative to decentralize.

The principal reason is responsiveness. Central processing, with its multiple demands, cannot respond as rapidly to user requests as the user can with his data processing system under his direct control. Remembering that three of the key elements in distributed processing are local data entry, local data editing, and data base access, management—including data processing management—must try to put these elements into effect, with responsiveness and profit improvement the potential benefits.

Here's another example: A small, concerned company in Pennsylvania took analysts from the user departments and trained them in the concepts of programming. Management wanted to decentralize its new data processing department. This was attained to the benefit of the organization as a whole.

The same can be attained with the newer, simpler computers, which put new tools in the hands of the users. Such tools as flexible data base managers and inquiry languages allow users to get to the information on the data base without needing assistance from a technical programmer.

The challenge is to create an environment in data processing that breaks down the language problems and the communications gap that exist between data processing professionals and the end users. The job content of the systems analysts needs to be redefined so that new emphasis is placed on data management and systems integration, with an end toward getting away from their role as one-time report generators, trouble-shooters, maintenance programmers, and interpreters of the end users' daily problems. The result will be more effective interpretation of valuable resources and increased responsiveness to user demands and needs.

8

Distributed Processing and the Data Processing Professional

These are difficult times for the data processing manager and his organization of systems specialists. There is a growing trend toward distributed processing and decentralization. His function and his department will change. American Management Associations has initiated a new, three-day seminar directed toward this very subject. The topic of this seminar? "The Crisis in EDP Organization: The Impact of Minis, Data Bases, and Distributed Systems." The three most advanced concepts in electronic data processing—minicomputers, data bases, and distributed processing—have generated a crisis in the data processing organization to which there has been rather strong reaction.

This crisis cannot be ignored, as minicomputers, data bases, and distributed processing are here to stay. The crisis comes from the fear of decentralization and loss of control by a central data processing department. Ironically, the move to distributed processing grew out of user frustration. The inefficiencies, long queues of requests, and poor responsiveness to needs that have historically characterized centralized data processing organizations stimulated the need for change.

The change is inevitable because it is sound and logical. Advances in computing power and communications make it technically feasible. The objective is to make data processing more effective by "putting the action where the people are." It is not a change for change's sake nor a deliberate attempt to decentralize or diminish responsibilities. The new capability makes it feasible to centralize some functions, whereas others can, and should, be redistributed to the users. At the same time, security, quality control, and development costs must be monitored and controlled from a central, but high level of, management perspective. The proposed change means only that centralized functions of data processing will be different.

What we fear, however, is that this change will come ever so slowly and for all the wrong reasons. It will not come in a reasoned and timely manner, because it will be resisted. It may not be resisted rationally, but because it represents a threat to those who control data processing. These people are not management but the data processing professional and the computer manufacturer. Alarming as it may seem, a positive move toward effective data processing may be held back because of the current makeup of the industry and the fact that management does not now control the data processing function.

Effective data processing may not even be achievable at a reasonable cost with the conventional centralized data processing department as it now exists and with the current philosophical makeup of the technical staff. We observed earlier that the computer manufacturer and the data processing staff perpetuate a kind of conspiracy in maintaining the organizational status quo. In recommending that management control the data processing function, we present a means to persuade and convince the data processing professional.

THE ORGANIZATIONAL STRONGHOLD

The data processing department affects every functional area of an organization. In the private sector the computer is used to process information needed for production scheduling and inventory control. The computer generates paychecks, prepares the general ledger, and processes other accounting systems, such as accounts payable and accounts receivable. Marketing information is formulated on the computer as well. Forecasting customer requirements is one of the more sophisticated uses of the computer. Data processing has wide-ranging capability and responsibility, but this advantage presents the problem of a logical station. Should the data processing staff report to the accountant? The production manager? The marketing vice-president, or the vice-president of administration? Two realities will emerge, no matter who becomes responsible for data processing:

□ The unit that controls the data processing group serves to gain the most.
□ The data processing group is located far from the majority of the units or users who depend on it for their information lifeline.

What you get is organizational confusion. The data processing department achieves an interesting independence, even from the unit it reports to. It is unique and physically remote from those departments outside its reporting responsibility, yet within its sphere of influence.

At the same time, the centralized data processing department takes on a great deal of responsibility. Few other disciplines with a technical base have the potential to affect the total organization to quite the degree of the data processing department. Users are very much in the hands of the systems analysts when it comes to new information requirements—even more so when it comes to priorities and schedules. Our experience as consultants has brought us in contact with the ever-looming queues of requests for data processing services as new reports and new systems are needed to keep pace with expanding needs for information.

This responsibility is not well located in any one particular organizational unit. This technical service organization, with so much influence, sets priorities for users on the basis of incomplete knowledge. This group usually does not have access to the overall organizational goals and strategies with their short- and long-term alternatives. Furthermore, the organization expects the technical staff to operate from a level of business understanding it does not possess. From its remote perspective, the department and its staff are expected to know what only the user can master.

Just as a sequential computer is quite literally out of phase with the daily operations of the organization, the department in its centralized seclusion is out of sync. The learning cycle itself results in changes so that the analyst never really catches up. By the time the department's staff has studied a given application, the needs have shifted. And because of the complexity of systems design and implementation, the learning time for resolving information needs grows and grows.

Most companies acquiesce to the queues and the long systems lead times as a normal cost of "doing business" with the computer. The more progressive companies try to bridge the gap between the data processing department and the end users; to these companies, the queues are intolerable. A common bridging technique, promoted by several CPA firms, is to establish a management overview committee. The committee, staffed by the middle management of user departments and members of the data processing staff, is sometimes referred to as a *systems planning committee* or some similar name.

The purpose is clear: to help data processing personnel evaluate user requirements and set priorities consistent with overall organizational priorities. In addition, the systems planning committee is set up to educate management to the complexities of computers. Clear purposes yes, but in execution the committee is not always effective. These are the major drawbacks:

1. Time restraints allow these committees to handle only the large requests for such services as major new systems. Small changes, alterations, and maintenance requirements are the problems of the data processing man-

ager. Yet the small changes are generally the cause of the bottlenecks. They are what take up most of the available time.

2. Meetings tend to get bogged down in technical minutia, no matter how hard laymen try to retain the management overview perspective.

3. The early enthusiasm for management participation inevitably wanes after nine months to a year. Apathy then sets in. Meetings are scheduled less frequently and the committee loses whatever effectiveness it may have had.

So much for the idea of involving management in setting up priorities for systems work and scheduling data processing tasks and staffs—excellent in theory, but so often unworkable in practice. The queues remain. The management committee may have failed, but it was clear that this committee was set up to solve a very real problem, a problem of confusion and failure to communicate.

The systems planning committee may in some instances have an early impact, but it is not the answer to a very complex problem. It is a forced answer at best, without a good fit. And when it inevitably gets bogged down, the only remaining component is the remote data processing department, once again setting the priorities for the organization as a whole. It has been experienced many times before. Ask any computer salesman: This unique unit will not actively seek to change its independent status. It is secure in its position within the organization. Most systems were designed here; all data is processed through here. All documentation, if any, rests here. What is the incentive for change?

PROFILE OF THE PROFESSIONAL

The problem is manifest in the lack of responsiveness to user requirements and to the information needs of the organization as a whole. In addition to the communications gap, the systems analyst has another problem: the newness of the discipline. The end user, as we have said, understands the application, but not the machine. Meanwhile, his processing needs have been translated into obtuse systems diagrams buzz-worded into computer specifications and programmed in COBOL or RPG or Swahili, as illustrated in Figure 20. He cannot communicate well with the data processing analyst, who launches into an imperfect implementation scheme better known as the systems process. Several major steps must be followed in order to take a system from concept to reality. Here, the following major tasks are performed at a minimum by the systems analyst in an effort to satisfy the end user's requirements:

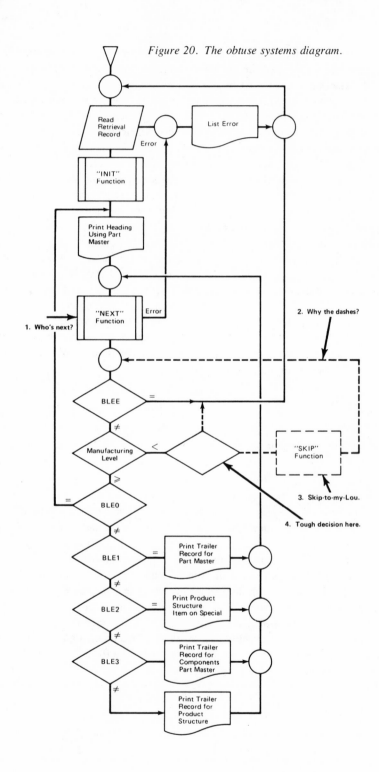

Figure 20. The obtuse systems diagram.

□ *Present System.* The analyst first tries to understand the present system, including manual processing steps, normal application logic, and all exceptions to the norm.

□ **Systems Requirements.** The analyst documents the requirements *of the user.* He answers the question of what the user needs in terms of information, reports, and other outputs.

□ *Detail Systems Design.* The analyst designs a computer-based batch system intended to meet those systems requirements and conform to the present system if necessary. Don't forget those exceptions, please.

□ *Programming Specifications.* In this step, the analyst goes into his isolation booth and prepares to tell the computer what to do. The analyst or a programmer (or both) then translates the specifications into a machine-readable language, which will guide the machine in accomplishing the task, a step called programming.

□ *Systems Test.* Now, our analyst tests all programs based on his understanding of the user's requirements. More progressive departments have the user play a major role in this task, as they will request user buy-off or acceptance. All too often, user involvement is shortcut.

□ *User Training.* The multitalented analyst turns teacher to train the user in the system that he, the analyst, designed.

It is easy to appreciate that this may be a long process. Figure 21 shows the complexity and overlapping of steps. The idea is to avoid shortcutting, as failure to communicate at any step will result in misunderstandings and disappointments. Yet one person or group of analysts is assigned to perform these tasks and make the system work.

Deepening Security

In a dynamic, frequently changing system, reliance on a single analyst is dangerous. Changes are made, documentation is neglected, and the security of the analyst deepens. Patches are added, routines are deleted, and the audit trail back to the user requirements is lost. Customized routines, which are seldom done in the same way by two different analysts, further reduce the ability to train anyone else in a specific system. The end user may become the end loser in terms of time and effectiveness.

Historically, the systems analyst has assumed a major responsibility to maintain his new system after implementing it with the systems process. He is asked to master a specific area of the organization, say accounting or manufacturing, and yet in all likelihood, he has never entered a debit or controlled a widget. But, he is asked to communicate with the user of a dis-

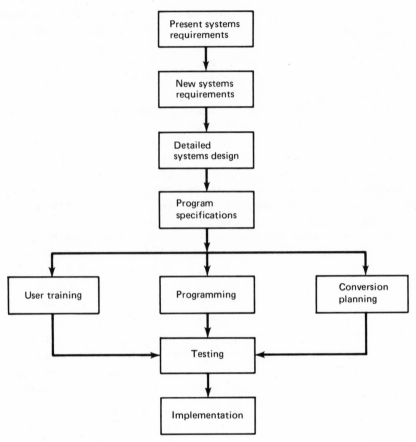

Figure 21. Phases of a systems study.

cipline he does not understand. And, as a result of it all, he ends up with almost complete control over the processing of data for the organization. He is required to perform to exacting standards without error. Will he succeed? Only time will tell, unfortunately.

Don't Rock That Boat!

Some data processing professionals become comfortable in this environment. They find themselves in a position of security born out of their technical knowledge, their systems awareness, and the very large responsibilities management has bestowed upon them. Users depend on the analysts for even their most minor systems requirements. The manufacturer befriends the analyst in an attempt to retain that account, since it is the analyst who has longevity throughout the lengthy systems process. Heck, why rock this boat?

In the preface to this book, we wrote of the manufacturer and a conspiracy to perpetuate jobs and promote an escalation in hardware sophistication and, inevitably, costs. The manufacturer is in a position to provide technical support, whereas the analyst has already established his permanence in the company. With such support going for the analyst, the idea of changing to a new concept, a new computer, a new vendor, a new way of thinking is "unthinkable." In what other area of an organization does the vendor establish such a close working relationship with the staff to the point where he can directly effect decision making? Management must acknowledge the potential for a relationship that is clearly in the best interest of the analyst's job security and the manufacturer who wants to *protect* the account and, eventually, sales. Who is acting for the benefit of the organization? Where is management?

Enter the Minicomputer

The minicomputer appears to have the real potential to end this relationship. Will the analyst or the manufacturer embrace this new concept? It is doubtful. The analyst's strength lies in the knowledge of and control over systems. With a minicomputer, as discussed in Chapter 4, and again in Chapter 6, the concept changes from batch processing of discrete and independent systems to on-line systems, which translates into new systems and more user involvement. The centralization of knowledge is clearly diffused, and the focal point of data processing shifts toward the end user.

Second, the minicomputer is a new technology and a new way of thinking. Batch processing is undesirable on the new-generation computer and is, in fact, unwanted. This new technology affects all aspects of data processing:

□ Input of data on terminals, instead of cards, means a new way of organizing systems.

□ Interactive processing eliminates the error (editing) cycle and changes the processing cycle. Job queues and job-control libraries are also eliminated.

□ Reporting, and large volumes of paper, are replaced by video display terminals. Reports serve to support or back up these displays.

□ Programming languages change from high-level COBOL to more interactive BASIC or more efficient FORTRAN. (Hewlett-Packard, Data

General, Digital Equipment Corporation, and Varian Data Machines now support COBOL, but this is a marketing necessity, not an enhancement to their computers.)

These vast changes in technology may not be welcomed by analysts who are not familiar with them. The security blanket becomes threadbare. Fear of losing one's job provides a strong incentive to resist change. And changing computers represents insecurity. This change strikes right at the heart of the analyst's security, which is his knowledge of systems and the systems process.

A Warning to Management

Systems analysts have been in demand since their function began. The analyst can afford to be "on the look" and turnover in data processing is common. One irreverent personnel director we know refers to systems analysts as gypsies. The gypsy treasures his résumé as a critical document; he may feel he requires big mainframe experience in order to be marketable. Without doubt, there are more IBM 360/40 computers installed than HP 3000 computers. Management can predict that the data processing staff will resist any change they feel will not enhance their résumés. Remember, we warned you. One analyst actually put in writing that minicomputer experience was not consistent with his career objectives!

For each of these reasons, the data processing professional, including the data processing manager, will not lead the charge to distributed processing and minicomputers in your organization. This was borne out vividly as we recently made a presentation before the American Management Associations' seminar on the Crisis in EDP Management. After discussing the implementation of a minicomputer system, we asked who would resist this idea most vehemently: Management? Users? Data processing? The response was unanimous: data processing! What was the audience mix? One-third management and two-thirds data processing managers. You know they will resist, and they know it too.

THE MANUFACTURER'S POSITION

The mainframe manufacturer will not attempt to persuade his customer to change. Other than Honeywell and NCR, and soon Burroughs, competitive minicomputers are not manufactured by mainframe vendors. IBM is in a difficult position because of its leadership position. To replace a $13,000-per-month machine with a $5,000-per-month equivalent machine is not exactly a palatable idea. Only recently did IBM introduce a minicomputer, but it is limited in capability and competes only with the lower end of the minicomputers spectrum. IBM must protect its large base of rental equipment and cannot be expected to launch an aggressive program that could result in its own demise.

Even to allow a minicomputer to share the workload is not a pleasant prospect—this opens doors. As we described, the manufacturer provides technical support and maintains his real role in your organization through the data processing department. The minicomputer substantially reduces this need for resident technical support on an ongoing basis. The minicomputer is not complex in operation. Most minicomputer manufacturers don't even conduct a training course for operators. The operating system is easy to understand. There is no scheduling of jobs, no complicated systems generation (we are putting this in for the data processing folks who will not concede that the minicomputer is simple to operate), no computer operators, no job-control language. The minicomputer just runs, and runs, and runs.

This has long been a goal of organization leaders. Again, the technical expertise should be returned to the organization where it belongs, rather than remain with the manufacturer. No mainframe manufacturer will break down your door to urge this change or a change from the evolutionary growth pattern he markets. In fact, you will have a battle on your hands when you recommend a new look at data processing. According to Cullinane Corp., a large and successful developer of sophisticated software, some manufacturers attack when they sense the loss of a sale. In a Spring 1976 edition of *The Wall Street Journal,* Cullinane wrote that even your data processing manager can't beat the odds:

> The problem your data processing manager has is that when he starts to select a competitive product (in computer software, incidentally), the computer manufacturer will often go over his head to upper management to question his decision. This creates problems for him and, ultimately, for your company because the manufacturer can cost you a fortune, virtually millions of dollars, in computer costs, a fortune in personnel costs, and take forever to develop new systems.

We agree, having had the same experience on more than one occasion.

The Computer Lessors Association, Inc., which competes with the mainframe manufacturers, also agrees. They tried to tell management the same thing in their book, *The Intelligent Guide to Computer Selection,* published in 1975. The Association states that data processing professionals and the manufacturer "have tended to create and maintain an élite status for computer operations . . . a belief that these operations are essentially unique and shouldn't be forced into the company mold. This is nonsense."* Furthermore:

The manufacturer's salesmen are in constant contact with them [the data processing managers]. The typical manager is well aware that such salesmen have gone over the head of his counterparts [remember Cullinane!] who had the temerity to recommend someone else's equipment. . . . When this happens often enough, a manager loses his taste for trying to save the company money. There's another thing to consider. It is *safer* for a manager to follow the manufacturer's recommendations and simply pass them along for management's approval . . . to recommend an alternative calls for strong management talent and guts. It's only a matter of time until such a manager will make a mistake, and he fears that the vendor will quickly trumpet the mistake to company management.

In moving to distributed processing and away from a larger mainframe, the manufacturer told one company's management that they would be the laughing stock of town. It's a small town, but they swallowed hard.

THE INEVITABLE CRISIS

This all adds up to a crisis in the data processing organization. The ideas of responsive systems, now seemingly realistic and cost-justifiable with minicomputers, represent a threat to security. The traditional data processing organization which has been so unresponsive in the past is faced with the potential for a new responsiveness, which never really existed before. Management, if in charge, has new tools to challenge the status quo. But perhaps management does not have to fight the entrenched organization of data processing.

Today's managers must react, for they can no longer feel secure in the belief that the central computer staffed by technicians is best for the organization, or that it is even workable. Robert B. White, executive vice-president of Citibank, says it well:

We end up grasping for technical solutions to what are fundamentally business problems. That is why the large-scale computer really doesn't work. Driven by technical realities, its capabilities are comprehensible only to technical people. And they are not running our business.

It was against this background that the minicomputer manufacturers made their

* Computer Lessors Association, Inc., *The Intelligent Guide to Computer Selection*, Computer Lessors Association, Inc., Washington, D.C., 1975, p. 53.

entry into the marketplace. Unable to penetrate the technical barrier guarded by the data processing fraternity, the minicomputer manufacturers went around them. They went directly to the manufacturing segments of the business and they delivered an extremely simple message: We have machines that can replace your labor and increase your productivity and profits and that can do it fast. They were eminently successful.

Although fun (to some) to consider, to launch a full revolution is certainly not a desirable course of action for the inquisitive manager. A better approach would be to arouse the interest of the technical staff in order to initiate an objective look into the potential for distributed processing. This may well be possible if we can first break down some of the inherent biases of the data processing manager and eliminate the issue of security. Gaining the support or the present data processing staff is, in fact, possible.

GAINING SUPPORT

Although we believe that the principal issue is security, other factors are involved in gaining the support of the technical staff: state-of-the-art technology, the challenge of change, the fear of visibility, and the relationship with the manufacturer. Let us discuss each of these with the full realization that every organization is different. We draw only upon our experiences dealing with data processing people and their fear of distributed systems. We want to share them with you.

SECURITY

To the Systems Analyst

No computer system runs by itself. No computer can program itself or design its own systems. The minicomputer is no exception so that the systems analyst's fear of losing his job is simply unfounded. In fact, his job does change, however, and this should be explored with the data processing staff. In the first place, distributed processing de-emphasizes the entry at the user level. This means that the analyst may become much more valuable as he learns the user's application and the user's problems and needs.

The scope of his task in a specialized area is greatly expanded from the mundane small systems to the more global needs of the users. This is because of the shift from many smaller systems to the concept of information processing using data bases. The analyst should be assigned responsibility for functional areas, such as marketing information, manufacturing processes, or financial reporting. His task is to develop the data base of information that will best perform these functions.

Unlike the old days of batch processing, the analyst in the on-line environment must create an atmosphere for instant retrieval of data. His programming effort is to provide instantaneous retrieval of data from the data base and simultaneous display on the terminal for immediate access. He must design around the problems of redundant and repetitive reports which are infrequently used, and eliminate lengthy clerical procedures, which tend to bog down an efficient operation. His goal is the total information system and its effect on profits and service.

Unlike the old days of batch processing, the analyst should train users to be able to retrieve data without extensive programming effort. Through the use of information retrieval language such as QUERY, which we discussed earlier, users should be able to write their own routines for nonrecurring information needs. One-time reports requested from managers should be within the technical capabilities of the users who have been trained by the analyst. The analyst, in turn, has more time for the important informational assignments that result from long-term departmental goals. It is not at all unrealistic to say that the systems analyst becomes the information specialist and the end user's data base manager.

In a July 1976 research report from *Computerworld,* the trends for EDP spending and budgeting were summarized from a computer census questionnaire. *Computerworld* reported that total user spending for EDP products, services, and salaries will exceed $30 billion for the calendar year. The breakdown of these dollars, shown in Table 9, reflects the fact that 40 percent of the total dollars will be spent on hardware, while only 33 percent of the total dollars will be spent on salaries. It is doubtful that this total will be

Table 9. Distribution of U.S. users' EDP budgets for 1976.

EDP Products, Services, and Salaries	Percent
Hardware	40
Salaries	33
Outside services and software	14.5
Datacommunications	8.5
Supplies	4

Adapted from *Computerworld,* July 1976.

DISTRIBUTED PROCESSING SYSTEMS

reduced, but distributed processing and minicomputer technology will shift the percentages until the majority of dollars spent will be for salaries. This is a favorable situation.

Distributed processing, for the first time in almost two decades, will open up the door for pouring more resources into brainpower than into mechanical devices. Hardware always outstrips the software, but it can now be challenged and changed. The result should be higher-level systems analysts with less mundane one-time systems requests and more impact on the organizations they serve. The challenge is there for those who will evaluate it objectively.

To the Data Processing Manager

The data processing manager is faced with a different problem. Distributed processing necessarily decentralizes certain functions such as data entry. It encourages users to depend less on a centralized department for routine reports and one-time information requests. It encourages self-sufficiency and, as such, may be considered a threat to the data processing manager. We have been through this before and know that it is real.

The answer to a data processing manager may well be a redefinition of the scope of his assignment. One absolute truth in distributed processing is that someone, or some organizational entity, must coordinate new systems development and maintain a high level of quality in systems work throughout the organization. Otherwise, duplications and inefficiencies result. This coordinating role may well become the new responsibility of the data processing manager. Standards and levels of quality may also be included in his expanded role, whereas for someone with lesser vision, merely maintaining the physical hardware may be his reduced role.

For the medium to large organization there is a need to expand data processing services to other departments, divisions, or subsidiaries. The expanded role of the data processing manager could encompass this organizational need. For during the first 25 years of computing with computers, most corporations and service organizations did not develop long-range plans for data processing. Now may well be the time to do just that. With the new capabilities for several computers and communications networks between them, the potential for a worldwide or organization-wide plan is limitless. No better time exists than now to transfer ideas and share developmental efforts with compatible computer hardware.

Of course, it is true that every organization differs with respect to its needs for data processing and data processing professionals. But it is equally true that two positions emerge from the expanded capabilities of distributed systems. The first is the operations manager, and the second is an organizational overseer to plan, expand, and control the development and quality of the systems effort. The current data processing manager can expand his scope within the organization far beyond the day-to-day operation's problems. The issue of his security depends on his scope and perspective and management's ability to articulate it.

VISIBILITY

Some resistance to change may result from a fear of visibility in the data processing department. Whether or not the fear is real is only hypothetical, but visibility is a fact. The data processing manager's job has never been an easy one with its hardware failures and midnight phone calls from frustrated operators. But on-line systems add a whole new dimension to the problem. When an on-line system fails, a great many people in the organization will know.

Visibility results from the fact that many users are connected directly to the computer. When it fails, they must wait. When they must wait, they will call. Unless it is a major hardware failure, the wait is brief, but the awareness of a problem is total. The issue of systems reliability is therefore important, and the need for good backup procedures is essential, as we have discussed. It is an issue that should not become a major factor in the decision to go on-line, but it is an issue that must be clearly explored with the data processing manager. If his fear of visibility is high, he will never promote a change to distributed processing and on-line accessibility to data. The wrong man may be in charge.

TECHNICAL ADVANCEMENT

By this time, you have begun to see that on-line data processing and distributed systems are inevitable. On-line technology is the state of the art. In breaking down the resistance to change, we urge managers to promote this knowledge among their staff of data processing professionals. To move toward on-line systems will do far more for them than just strengthen their technical capabilities. To remain with a batch environment is a short-range approach.

In fact, there is a mainframe syndrome among data processing professionals. IBM, as we pointed out earlier, has more than 67 percent of the computer market with the second manufacturer holding less than 10 percent.

But, fortunately, other manufacturers have excellent products too. Unfortunately, most data processing professionals are unable to evaluate computer hardware, and too frequently are caught up in the mainframe syndrome. It is management's challenge to open his eyes to other potential manufacturers and products.

Mainframe manufacturers, including IBM, are not the leaders in distributed processing. The true professional should be able to evaluate these new minicomputers and realize their huge potential. It should whet his appetite and stir his sense of challenge. To make the move from batch processing to on-line processing is exciting and a clear step forward technically. Specifically, the analyst must be made to realize that he is, under on-line processing, "closer" to the computer than ever before because he programs now interactively. This greatly improves his effectiveness.

Interactive programming is the process of inputting programs directly to the computer through a terminal. Editing of coding statements is instantaneous in much the same manner as data is edited in applications systems, which we have described. Batch programming, on the other hand, has the same limitations as batch data entry. The batch programmer codes onto coding sheets which are keypunched and processed on the computer, usually at night. The next day, the programmer normally receives his error listing, which must be corrected and resubmitted to the computer for rerunning. These "shots," as they are frequently called, are time-consuming, unproductive, and frustrating. Interactive programming is continuous and on-line. We said earlier that in a presentation we attended, an IBM spokesman stated that interactive programming can improve productivity by 35 percent. Our own experience corroborates that statement.

What's more, interactive programming and interactive systems are more challenging and produce greater rewards, in our experience. Management should be able to make the data processing professional aware of the potential benefits to him of leaving the batch environment behind. But we have seen so many instances where the ingrained mainframe syndrome is hard to break.

We have seen staffs undergo turnover in order to provide the types of responsiveness which managers must insist upon. We remind the reader that the ever-important résumé will deter some of your staff from making the change. Personnel changes may be necessary when the analyst will not objectively evaluate alternative hardware and the potential for distributed processing. In summary, management can gain the support of the data processing staff if it is willing to be professional and evaluate the options. But there will be those who will not take this trip.

Progress will come and distributed processing, in some form, will proliferate throughout the world of data processing. For we recently read that if the nationwide telephone systems had not progressed with new innovations and clerical reduction devices, the demand for service would require that every woman between the age of 20 to 50 years would have to be a telephone operator. The potential information explosion requires that we process data effectively and that we spread the workload or we are going to have a whole bunch of centralized keypunchers.

RESISTANCE TO CHANGE

The conclusion here may be that although there will be resistance to change from the technical staff, there are positive ways to encourage an objective evaluation of the potential for distributed processing. The need for good analysts does not end with distributed processing nor does the need for overall direction and supervision. And the state-of-the-art technology should whet the appetite of the true data processing professional.

But remember that three parties are involved in this trip. So far, we've discussed only the data processing professionals. What about the end users? They too must be supportive of change. The end users frequently complain of that damnable computer, but will change come any easier for them? For one thing, change does not affect them in terms of their position in the organization to the extent that it does in the case of data processing personnel. But change is change. Let's meet the ultimate user and try to understand his problems.

9

Distributed Processing and the End User

The data processing organization is not the only one affected by this new concept of computing. In this chapter, we will concentrate on the impact of distributed processing on the individual departments that will now share the computer through video terminals.

The impact of distributed processing is to shift a significant amount of responsibility from one central organization to several user organizations. With the shift in responsibility, it may be maintained by some that the only thing accomplished is a shift in the workload. In some cases, this may be true, but in most, it simply isn't so.

A second important change for the user in shifting the responsibility is the whole idea of scheduling staff time. In the past, schedules were largely dependent on the computer schedule. This concept changes in the distributed environment.

Finally, the responsibility for reporting results and coordinating documentation requirements shifts to the various users. Along with this third responsibility goes the whole spectrum of accuracy of data and timeliness of reporting. Once defined, the system's responsiveness also becomes an important function of the user organization, rather than the department of data processing, with its multiple demands and many masters. These new responsibilities must be sold to the user organizations, which may be skeptical at first. What impacts will these responsibilities have on the user?

SHIFTING WORKLOAD

For the past 25 years, the data processing department has been responsible for data entry. In this capacity, data processing employs a staff of keypunch operators. These guys and gals take handwritten coding documents and

139

keypunch the data into punched cards to be read by the computer. The question of shifting workload is a simple one: How was the source document prepared?

Systems are frequently designed for ease of data entry. This is logical because systems designers want to speed up this nonproductive process. They want to reduce the need to stop and make decisions on where to punch what data. For example, general ledger journal entries are transferred from source documents to coding sheets, which are formatted to facilitate keypunching. Look at the coding sheet format shown in Figure 22.

The idea is to transcribe from the source, such as a bank balance, a payroll expense, an accounts payable entry, or any other standard journal entry. This document is keypunched and verified.

Coding sheets are used in complex transactions (manufacturing), repetitive transactions (payroll), or diverse transactions (accounts payable). In the latter application, the source document is a vendor invoice, in which each vendor's invoice is different from the next vendor's. Invariably, keypunch operators are not required to search differing invoices to format the final punched card. For whatever reason, whenever coding sheets are required, distributing the data entry function to the user neither shifts nor increases the workload.

Simply stated, the time and effort required to make the transcription from source documents to coding sheets can be input directly into the computer through the terminal. Instead of taking the time to code, the clerk can use the terminal to format the data, to have the data edited, and to update the data base of information. What is remarkable is that all the information is in the computer and available for use, and two major bottleneck steps have been eliminated, keypunching and keyverifying.

If, on the other hand, source documents are keypunched directly, then it may be true that the workload has indeed been shifted from the central data processing department to the user. This increased workload in the user department must be handled by hiring additional personnel or by offsetting the additional work with some time-saving feature of the new system.

Account	Description	Debit	Credit
1 2 3 4 5	6 7 8 9 10 11 12 13 14 15	16 17 18 19 20	21 22 23 24 25
x x x x x	x x x x x x x x x x	x x x x x	x x x x x
x x x x x	x x x x x x x x x x	x x x x x	x x x x x

Figure 22. General ledger coding sheet.

There are two important points here. First, the overall time required to process the data in either case will be reduced because the verification step has been eliminated. Second, the issue of shifting workload is bound to arise. It should not be ignored or even treated lightly if a distributed system is to be accepted. The answer lies clearly in making the user aware of the potential workload shift and the overall reduction in clerical effort for the organization. It is called training.

SCHEDULING AND REPORTING

The second major impact on the user is scheduling of work. It is difficult at times to get away from the ingrained batch mentality. The month-end closing cycle is legendary. Accountants wait until the last working day before they start to close out the month. Standard journal entries, such as prepaid insurance and prepaid taxes, are coded onto those well-known data processing coding sheets. These are submitted to data processing and the following time-consuming cycle:

Data preparation
Edit listing
Corrected edit listing
Trial balance
General ledger
Profit-and-loss statement
Month-end closing

Then it's 10 to 15 days into the month before management gets the results.

The problem is scheduling and batch processing. General ledger accountants are geared to this schedule, and it is expected. The challenge is to break this cycle and convince users that the timeliness of data is a function of their schedule, not that of the computer. Data should be input in the most practical manner, as received, and as best benefits the organization's profit position. We have pointed out that the computer, which operates day and night, is ready to accept, edit, format, and even print.

In the case of the general ledger, the goal should be instant profit-and-loss status. As expenses are incurred, they can be recorded. Major payroll expenditures can update the general ledger file as incurred. Standard journal entries, such as the prepaid expenses we mentioned, should be input during the first month of the fiscal year for the entire fiscal year. With such timeliness, including sales transactions from the customer order/entry systems and cost of goods sold from manufacturing, a profit-and-loss statement is possible at any point in time. In a marginal or dynamic business, this may be as critical as it is attainable.

The problem now is one of education, rather than the limitations of a mechanical device. The reader should stop at this point and consider how this power will work to his advantage as information is scheduled on the basis of its availability and the natural cycle of the environment. The publisher will revel in the day-to-day sales status of any one of his books. The social caseworker would love to have an up-to-the-minute listing of available social services and job opportunities for a client. A businessman would love to monitor a sick subsidiary, and so on.

Surprisingly, the job of convincing the department heads that the staff does not have to be scheduled by the computer is a challenge. Breaking old habits does not come easily. And it is all the more reason why top management must dictate the products and systems for computing, taking this responsibility back into its domain. For management should set the schedule and pace on the basis of its needs to improve profits or provide services. Reporting cycles do not necessarily have to be daily, weekly, or monthly, but depend on the need for information.

The tendency is to hold to the past. We've always had our daily inventory status report, so we still want it. Even when one on-line manufacturing system displayed inventory balances as of the moment, one "old-timer" (of about 29 years of age) clung to his daily inventory status report for about one full day. Then he was charged for the paper and computer time and shown that it was obsolete by the time it was delivered.

The challenge is to educate the users in the new capabilities. To most, it will be clear. To others, it signals a shifting workload, more responsibility, disrupted schedules, and a change. Let's review one proven means to the process of education.

THE USER'S NEW COMPUTER

To get the most out of distributed processing the organization needs to get its users involved. The organization must make the commitment to return responsibility to the users and seek to generate enthusiasm to make the system responsive to their needs. This is no easy task. For the moment, we'll leave the communications features to the technicians and concentrate on the human aspects of change.

Getting the users involved, in our experience, was achieved when they were made aware of the new potential for them. One way to do this is to present the "corporate case" and explain how the new design affects the bottom line or, in a nonprofit organization, how the new design improves service. But most importantly, management must relate the computer to the worker and to his problems. Depending on the size of your staff and geographic considerations, a series of short seminars or briefings can be arranged to acquaint users with the new way of thinking. The presentation itself may be a formal slide show or a small, informal fireside chat.

The Computer and You

To set the stage, the discussion might begin with a description of the new concept of computing. Most users are not really familiar with computers. They think of computers in terms of a mysterious black box located somewhere in the organization—kind of an enigmatic monster with which they must somehow work. Many users have never even seen the mainframe computer, and those who have were simply awed. Others couldn't care less. Normally, users, particularly at the lower clerical levels, do not associate with computers, nor do they comprehend its usefulness to them in their jobs. Rather, they look upon their jobs as information fodder for the all-important machine. The irony is obvious.

The computer should be recognized as a tool for each department or function. How many companies have forgotten this in their zeal to put more and more applications on a machine that was idle for one shift! The computer was never meant to be a processor of data for processing's sake. In many instances, it turned out this way because of the extremely complex nature of the mainframe computers. As a result, today's computers are remote from most users, particularly for the lower-level working cadre.

Change and Transition

The new idea in computing encourages the user staff to consider what the computer means to them and how it can help them in their jobs. This positive approach uses "positive theory," which states that every question requires a positive response. There is no place for "I don't know" in positive theory. The user approach gets rid of the "I don't know" problem by stressing how the computer will help each employee to perform his job function.

In the new environment, the computer is very visible to the user—it is planted right on his desk in the form of a video display terminal. It represents a major change in his workday world, and the user must be made aware of the extent of the change: from centralized processing (the large-scale computer with sequential processing) to decentralized processing (the minicomputer with on-line processing). The user should be informed that the organization's new computer system means much more than the mere exchange of one black box for another. The new computer leads to a substantial change in organizational philosophy. It is an important move from a centralized scheme, running with a large-scale computer, to a decentralized scheme coordinated with on-line processing. It may also signal a transition to a powerful minicomputer.

The important words here are "large-scale," "sequential or batch processing," "minicomputer," and "on-line processing." You may say that a large-scale computer is all these things. It is large in size, expensive, requires a large number of electrical cables and switches, and is a large user of energy, including air conditioners and dehumidifiers. This is not to say that bigness is badness, as the mainframe has many powerful features.

But the mainframe is complex. It requires a staff of computer operators who must coordinate the running of systems in a "sequential" mode. Sequential processing, another name for batch processing, has been described earlier and will not be discussed here. It is important that the user understand, however, the very real differences between sequential and on-line processing and the advantages and potential pitfalls of each. For example, it is clear that the on-line system provides better response to user needs. It is just as apparent that when an on-line computer is not functioning, it has a very real negative impact on the user's ability to do his job. As we said earlier, it is far more disruptive than the less visible batch run with which he is familiar.

Traditional Processing

Sequential or batch processing can best be related to existing situations which are familiar to the user. For example, we have often referred to the traditional data processing organization and the diagram shown in Figure 23.

Traditionally, an organization that has employees to pay, meets the

Payroll	Pension	Labor Distribution
Social security number	Social security number	Social security number
Name	Years on job	Hours worked
Hours worked	Earnings	Job done
Pay rate		Rate

Figure 23. The three separate and redundant files of the traditional organization.

federal pension requirements, and controls personnel costs through a labor distribution system, sets up three completely autonomous systems. Maintaining year-to-date information on each, three different files carry the same information.

The problems of coordinating three files created by different people at different times is probably a common problem to us all. It should be described to users as a potential problem in coordination, as wasted effort, and as costly to maintain. Furthermore, the human error factor creeps in, since normally no one person or department is responsible for maintaining the integrity between the three systems. Sequential processing, simply stated, requires separate files.

Although the computer traditionally operated in sequential mode, the organization more naturally functions in terms of a continuous process. For example, in a manufacturing concern, the production line does not shut down waiting for the computer. In a service organization, such as a hospital, the patient intake does not stop at 5:00 to keep in phase with the computer. The user should learn that sequential processing is inadequate in meeting the demands of a dynamic service or manufacturing environment. The logical step is to recommend a change.

The on-line environment will place new responsibilities on the user, but it may well open up new opportunities as well. This can be achieved through a new concept in computing, the minicomputer.

In Name Only

The minicomputer is "mini" in name only, as we mentioned earlier. Its users should be apprised of the procedure undertaken to make the change to a new computer. Normally, the organization prepares a statement of its data processing requirements, which it then submits to the various computer manufacturers, or to the systems houses in the case of minicomputers. The potential computer suppliers, in turn, prepare their proposals in response to your request for proposal. A typical report is described in Table 10.

The suppliers' proposals recommended a number of computers that could handle the same workload and requirements specified in the request. Yet the large-scale computer averaged more than twice as much in monthly rental ($8,300 vs. $4,000), and did not even include on-line capability. But the story is not complete until the various features are compared.

We would recommend that you give an overview of the two types of computers in layman's terms. For example, you should discuss the following items with your staff.

Table 10. Actual responses to a request for data processing. Current rental = $13,100.

Manufacturer	Computer	Monthly Rental	Software Rental	Terminals	One-Time Consulting Fee
		MAINFRAMES			
IBM	IBM 370/115	$10,504	2,000	N/A	—
IBM	System 3/15	7,841	1,000	N/A	—
Honeywell	H 60/62	6,691	—	N/A	—
Sperry (UNIVAC)	90/30	6,919	—	N/A	—
NCR*	Century	7,031	—	N/A	—
Burroughs	B-1726	7,825	—	N/A	—
		MINICOMPUTERS			
Software house #1	Eclipse 300	$3,417	—	4	$86,000
Software house #2	DEC 11/70	3,903	—	4	80,000
Varian Data Machines	V/76	3,955	—	8	82,500
Hewlett-Packard	HP 3000	4,700	—	8	90,000

*After the decision was made, National Cash Register came in with an excellent proposal, but it was too late for serious consideration.

□ The space requirements to house the two types of computers.

□ The peripheral devices that can be used in each type of computer. Video display terminals, card readers, and line printers should be discussed. Disk space for storing information should be emphasized.

□ Processing speeds of the computers are in microseconds and nanoseconds.

□ Available memory for processing of user systems should be compared.

The minicomputer may be small in space requirements and price, but its performance is "maxi." It performs well because it can match or exceed the mainframe in peripheral devices, execution speeds, and in usable memory due to efficient software. But much more important, the minicomputer is a very people-"minded" machine.

SIX NEW WAYS OF THINKING

For the people who use it the minicomputer presents a very new way of doing one's job. We refer to it not as *a* new way of thinking, but literally six

DISTRIBUTED PROCESSING SYSTEMS

new ways of thinking, all of which are geared to improving job performance through increased interaction with the computer. These six new ways of thinking involve:

More time for analysis
More timely data for users
Improved accuracy
Instant access to information
Use of data from other systems
A means to converse

For the first time in the computer generation, the user has come into direct contact with the computer. The new thinking simply means that the users can be in charge. Let's examine its plusses.

More Time for Analysis

The first new concept that emerges from the new data distribution is the elimination of clerical time, which allows more time for analysis. There are several ways to accomplish this. The first is filing. The primary reason for massive paperwork files is convenience. Although the computer may store the very same information, clerical files are maintained so that the information is available when needed. The creation and maintenance of manual files is time-consuming. It is also costly. An on-line system eliminates the need for manual files in most cases. One exception, for example, would be for cases in which signatures and original documents are required by law.

The on-line system satisfies the requirement for convenience in that the data is always ready and available. The clerical processes of filing, indexing, and updating paperwork are replaced by entry of data through a keyboard. Experience and logic have shown that this process is tremendously more efficient than the traditional method of locating a file, pulling it, marking its vacant location, reviewing it, and refiling it. In an on-line system an employee can key in an identification and review the record, which comes up on the video screen. The savings in time is obvious and real.

A second obvious clerical savings to the organization is the preparation of coding sheets for input of data to a computer. Because data entry clerks in the traditional data processing organization are unfamiliar with the data that is submitted to the computer, source information is frequently transferred to data processing coding sheets and the remote (away from the user) data entry clerical function begins. We've discussed it before. It's nonproductive.

We will never forget our experience at one cabinet-level government agency. We had recommended source data entry to eliminate more than 30 nonproductive clerical positions. The savings in payroll costs would exceed

$400,000 and the savings in time would be substantial. This was more than seven years ago, and the bureaucracy is *still* studying the recommendation. The recommendation was logical and achievable, but because it ended one man's empire, it was politically not feasible. A sad commentary.

Source data entry means input of data by users at the origin of the information. In a December 1976 issue of a trade journal, a $100 million manufacturer of integrated circuits reported that source data entry has saved 40 percent in overall data entry costs. Source data entry also resulted in more efficient operations and a faster turnaround time, according to a company spokesman. The old method it replaced had consisted of keypunch machines with their excessive noise levels, reliability problems, format limitations, data redundancy, operational complexity, and soaring card costs.

This large manufactuer has proved what we have been saying all along about the advantages that can be realized. Source data input means:

- □ Reduction in the errors that result when an unknowledgeable remote data entry clerk makes inevitable decisions and interpretations as to the nature of the entry.
- □ Elimination of the lengthy error-correction process. Simply stated, department personnel correct errors at the time of entry.
- □ Total responsibility on the part of the end users for accuracy in their data. This has reduced the number of errors and created higher morale among personnel.
- □ Elimination of duplication of effort.

The end result of source data input is more time for meaningful tasks and less nonproductive clerical effort. As a side benefit, original source documents remain with the user department for reference.

Timeliness

The second new-think idea is timeliness of data. It is important for management to make this point to the staff, using illustrations that pertain to their specific jobs. The concept is not difficult to convey because the logic of updating files directly, as opposed to processing them with a series of clerical steps, should be evident. More important is the fact that each major file of information is on the computer at all times, which means that each file can be updated at all times, once the information becomes available. The computer and the data base wait for the information instead of having the information waiting for the computer to process it.

We referred earlier to the computer that was out of phase with the business or service organization. That is exactly the point here. Discuss the advantages of having timely data in phase with the inventory balance, which allows you to answer customer requests for shipment, the availability of funds for a new program, the status of "cash on hand," the accessibility of a skills inventory for each employee, the publisher's count of books sold and profitability per issue, whatever applies.

Improved Accuracy

In a recent experience we had with distributed systems, we discussed the improvement in accuracy that would result from this new way of thinking. We explained how the new-generation computers help users improve accuracy in their day-to-day operations, which would then give them a new sense of pride in their work. Enthusiasm for the concept was generated because the on-line concept "sold itself." Management may borrow from this experience. Basically, you can say that accuracy is affected directly by two unique features of on-line processing: the tutorial nature of the minicomputer and the new documentation capabilities. Let's discuss each in turn.

1. *Tutorial Function:* The very first minicomputer ever seen by one of the authors was on a Pueblo Indian Reservation near Albuquerque, New Mexico. On this reservation, and particularly in more remote areas, it is difficult to attract a sufficient number of teachers. In these cases, minicomputers can be programmed to become the teacher of math, English, and science, among other courses. The tutorial computer asks questions, elicits answers, and advises students of the accuracy of their answers. Here's how.

The student sits before a video display terminal and, using the terminal's typewriter-like keyboard, "types" in her name and lesson number, something like this:

HELLO, THIS IS MARIA
I AM ON LESSON 2

The computer responds:

HELLO MARIA
ARE YOU READY FOR YOUR MATH?

Maria replies:

YES

The first problem is transmitted to the screen and the student supplies the answer. If the answer is incorrect, the computer is programmed to back up and ask our student a simpler question. It then guides her through the lesson, step by step, explaining new concepts and showing her where her errors are being made and why. A record is maintained and a printout that contains the student's grade is generated for the principal or director.

The technique of the tutorial computer has ramifications for the business or service organization. After the user identifies himself and the system or information he is seeking, the computer should be programmed to ask questions and correct the answer for the user immediately. Figure 24 shows that after the user has identified the system as personnel, the computer asks for the employee number. After the computer receives the user's response, it responds. The user then *verifies* with a positive response before the computer proceeds to extract the information from the data base.

Verification is a valuable tool in improving accuracy. A visual check prevents making a change or alteration on the wrong personnel record, which could be disastrous. The same logic applies to a general ledger entry, which can be verified before changes are made. Other "edits" may be performed at the time of data entry, and the user is there to make sure that his new information is accurate. This hands-on concept with interactive conversation can improve accuracy dramatically.

2. *Documentation:* New documentation capabilities of the minicomputer also contribute to accurate processing of data. In the first place, forms can be drawn directly on the video screen. The form, pictured on the screen through a technique known as the "line-drawing set" in some terminals, allows users to "fill in the blanks." If, for example, your user (whose name is Dottie) has used one form for accounts payable for 20 years, that form can

Figure 24. An on-line system.

DISTRIBUTED PROCESSING SYSTEMS

be reproduced on the video screen and Dottie can talk directly to the computer using that good old form. Not only is the accuracy affected by direct input from Dottie, but training is virtually eliminated. The time and cost savings are obvious.

Another way the new minicomputer can be used for documentation lies in its ability to put instructions and reference or reminder notes into the computer for display on the video screen. One of the most clever uses of this concept that we have seen is called HELP. HELP is a series of instructions programmed into the computer that may be displayed on the terminal to assist the puzzled user.

How does it work? Let's say someone who is trying to use his particular system forgets how to perform a certain routine or function. That user simply types HELP into the terminal, and the terminal screen changes to a narrative description of the routine or function. It describes the purpose of the transaction and the individual steps necessary to complete the transaction or activity.

One general ledger system we observed had more than 35 HELP screens available in the computer for its users. HELP is a variation of the tutorial computer theme, and it can be very effective. The computer is also very patient. It waits for the user to comprehend the full meaning and procedure, by allowing the user to return to his activity when, and only when, he is ready to proceed.

HELP is only one of many ideas that can be employed effectively with the flexible minicomputer and its interactive communication. HELP can improve accuracy because it is really a sophisticated trainer. And the trainer is always available, as close as the keyboard and the four letters H-E-L-P.

Parenthetically, HELP is also effective in training new personnel and in providing documentation. When the general ledger system mentioned previously was adopted by a subsidiary organization, HELP virtually eliminated the need for additional documentation. HELP went along with the ledger system. Furthermore, this type of computerized documentation may be changed easily through editor software, which is standard with most minicomputers. Finally, HELP is easy to use.

Thus, with the new minicomputer the knowledgeable user can deal directly with the computer and his data base of information. This is most important, since the user is the person responsible for it. While each transaction is being requested or updated, it is edited by the computer and keeps the user informed and on top of the operation. For example, the employee number that was checked for accuracy had to be verified. In case the user gets a little forgetful, remember that HELP helps. Accuracy is the result.

To review, distributed processing with minicomputers represents new ways of thinking for your organization. To be effective, the users must be made aware of how this computer and new responsibility affect every one of them. Once the users are "in charge," they will derive benefit from having the interactive computer on their desks (in the form of terminals) because it frees them from many routine clerical functions, such as filing and filling out source code sheets. It can provide its users with more timely data and it can result in a definite improvement in accuracy.

Users of the new minicomputer will also become familiar with a fourth new way of thinking: they will have instant access to information. They should be made aware of the unavoidable time lags that result from batch processing one system at a time. Cite specific examples of large reports delivered at 8:00 A.M. that reflected obsolete data to make the staff aware of the problems that occur when the computer is out of phase with the organization.

They should then be introduced to the data base concept and what effects it will have on their work. Very simply, because each element of information in the computer system is always resident on the computer, the user can always get to it. We refer to this as *instant access,* and it has major implications for the user. Primarily, users don't have to wait until the next morning to know the status of an account or the cash balance in the bank. All they have to do is ask.

A good technique for conveying this concept is to diagram the data base somewhat like a typical manufacturing data base (look again at Figure 17 in Chapter 7). The users' attention may be drawn to their specific systems, such as the customer order/entry files, but the overall concept should also be stressed. The data base in Figure 17 includes five major systems and the information contained in each. This information is resident (or stored) on disks attached to the minicomputer. The arms of the disks rotate, continuously searching for the requested information. Users may access any information they are authorized to obtain at any time through their terminals. It will be retrieved from the disk and transmitted to the terminal as requested.

For the specific user, accessibility is invaluable. In customer order/entry, for example, the user can display (have appear on the video terminal) any customer from the customer file. He can obtain information on the customer address, shipping address, customer contact, and credit rating. From the pricing file, the user can find the price of each manufactured product. From the accounts receivable file, the user can find which customers are delinquent in their payments before any more products are shipped to them.

The sales file can provide the customer's historical purchasing practices or any other sales information that can prove valuable for keeping "in phase."

Instant access also reduces the need for maintaining manual records by customer and product and for receiving lengthy daily reports on customer orders and activities. The properly designed system can provide information to customers who call to inquire as to the status of their orders.

Instant access is a powerful tool for users and the organization as a whole. Its applicability to a business or service organization is limited only by one's imagination. Convey to your staff that they should let their imaginations soar.

Finally, instant access gives the organization visibility into all facets and activities. It permits the organization to look at future manufacturing requirements, future customer demands, and potential cash-flow problems. An incredible amount of information can be transferred between different but related systems and their data bases.

Use of Data from Other Systems

Computers that process one system at a time in the batch syndrome are limited in that interchange of information between related systems is complex and time-consuming. Not so with on-line minicomputers, which contain all information on-line at the same time. Let's examine Figure 17 once again.

The three circles in the figure represent three of many instances in which information can be shared between systems. Here are some examples.

Labor efficiency. The manufacturing manager needs to measure output in his plant. He wants to know where the inefficiencies are so that corrective action may be initiated. In order to obtain this information, he must know what was accomplished and what should have been accomplished. The labor reporting in the payroll system can tell us what was accomplished and in what period of time. The standards for performance, or what should be accomplished, are used for production scheduling in the manufacturing system. A daily labor efficiency report can be generated by comparing actual to standard production, the "what" against the "what should" idea.

Profit contribution. Should we increase our price on a particular product? This is partly determined by the profitability of each product. Beginning with the actual or standard cost to produce the product from the manufacturing system, the computer makes a quick comparison to sales price to determine the profit contribution per product. This can literally keep a profit-making organization from going bankrupt.

Cash flow. Mr. Dulany, the treasurer with a Harvard Business School degree, may want a sophisticated cash-flow report. Using outstanding purchase orders from manufacturing and other purchase orders from accounts payable (including payroll), a negative cash-flow report is generated. A more complete picture requires cash input from sales and the customer order/ entry system.

These are only three examples of sharing information in a way that will benefit the organization as a whole. The possibilities are limitless. This interchange of information can also be accomplished in batch systems, but it is cumbersome and requires making transfers of files on tape or cards. Human intervention is critical. In the on-line environment, transactions are passed from one system to the other with computer-programmed instructions. It is efficient, accurate, and very cost-effective and can make the whole new world of information processing a reality.

Users who previously had to exchange information between departments in a very inefficient manner find the change fantastic. It is simply one of the six new ways of thinking that must be conveyed to the users in a distributed environment of minicomputers.

A Means to Converse

The effect of this brand new way of communicating with the computer is the positive impact it has on job performance. It represents a "means to converse," since (1) the data files are on-line and available for accessing, and (2) the minicomputer is an interactive piece of equipment that allows the users to talk to it.

Every major minicomputer has an *information retrieval language* for nonprogrammers, that is, the users. If you come across one that does not, one of the authors (C.B.T.) can write you such a language in a short period of time. The information retrieval language, such as Hewlett-Packard's QUERY, allows the user to get into his own data base and extract data on the basis of any reasonable and understandable criteria he may require. The only requirement is that the system have a data base manager.

This has major implications for the user. How often does management come up with a new requirement that takes days or weeks to complete? Often the information is readily available but is either in the wrong format or is simply too voluminous for quick manual review and presentation. An information retrieval language strikes right at that problem and provides a solution.

An information retrieval language operates with understandable English commands. It allows a user to locate information, retrieve it, perform basic arithmetic computations, and either display on a terminal or print a report on the computer's printer. There are only two concepts for a user to understand: commands and connectors.

The intriguing thing about an information retrieval language is that it is designed to be easy to use by nonprogrammers. Most information retrieval languages also operate in the tutorial mode, prompting the user through the development of his request for information. A normal request may take about 20 minutes to prepare. If it may have to be repeated, the user can give the request a name (such as Retirement List) and call on it to be used later. The request will be stored in the computer and used again next week or next year.

The usefulness of the information retrieval language to the user should be obvious. If the information is available on the computer, it can be retrieved without weeks of labor. It can be retrieved without the assistance of programmers or the data processing staff. It saves the system's users the time of waiting in a queue for their reports. It also frees computer programmers from the pesty one-time requests so unproductive for them. With the information-retrieved language, everybody wins.

SUMMARY

The users should be taken through this type of logic on the way to advising them that the new computer philosophy is very new indeed. No more will they conjure an image of that strange black box located somewhere in the other part of the building. Now that computer will literally be sitting on their desks in the form of a video display terminal. Every job is affected. There will be more time for analysis and more timely, accessible data with a higher level of accuracy and flexibility. Finally, the user has a means to converse with this computer which simply means that he is in charge of his information, his system, and all its information processing implications.

But there are a few potential dangers and pitfalls that may await the user. These too must be explained to him, as they will surely surface sooner or later.

POTENTIAL PITFALLS

The primary pitfall in an on-line system is downtime. As we pointed out earlier, and as verified in a report for the *Harvard Business Review,* minicomputers are very reliable. They are generally more reliable than the large-scale mainframes because of their miniaturized circuitry. They have a greater mean time between failures (MTBF) than the mainframes do, but minicomputers do fail. And when they do, everyone in the organization is going to know it.

Let us recall a term that was discussed in Chapter 8. The term is visibility. The new minicomputer, which is distributed to the user, is constantly available to the user in the performance of his job. This is good, but you should know that whenever that little computer fails, the user knows it.

In the batch world, computer failures were visible only if they drastically delayed a needed report. If the computer failed, it was maintenanced and the system being run at the time was simply rerun. Few people, other than the data processing staff, ever knew of this hitch in the day's operation. But with on-line systems, when the computer fails, the terminal blinks and goes blank.

Unless it is a major hardware failure, the computer will be back in action in 5 to 10 minutes. This is, first of all, an annoyance and an inconvenience. The user is temporarily prevented from completing what he was in the process of doing. Unfortunately, he does not know how long he will have to wait. Meanwhile, in the computer room, the systems manager diagnoses the problem and documents it for future corrective action. He restarts the system with what he calls a "warm start," which is little more than resetting registers and pushing the start button.

The on-line system must have a failsafe, backup procedure to record every transaction and its effect on the data base. The systems manager makes sure the data base is intact (if not, he uses his backup system to bring it back to the condition it was in prior to the failure). He then advises users as to which transaction (normally only one) must be re-entered, and then the user is back in control. This is an inconvenience and an annoyance to be sure, and it will occur.

Ed McCrackin of Hewlett-Packard has been quoted as saying that the goal for manufacturers should be only one such failure per week, with just a quick warm start and only a short loss of time. This is reasonable and clearly workable in our experience. If there is much more downtime, however, user dissatisfaction will inevitably result. Visibility is the point here. If users are prepared for such failures, they will go on to other non-computer-related tasks when they occur. Now you can see why reliability is an important issue in selecting an on-line computer.

A related annoyance involves response time, that amount of time in seconds elapsing between the time a user enters the data and the time the data is either accepted or flashed on the video terminal. Response time should be less than three seconds. Six seconds is acceptable. Ten seconds is unacceptable. Why?

What is the importance of ten seconds when we used to wait 24 hours for the requested information? The response time is basically nonproductive time in which the user personnel must wait without anything to do. It is simply not realistic to ask someone to waste this time. It is unrealistic and demoralizing to put this type of barrier in front of someone who wants to get a specific job completed. If there is a slow response, which naturally prolongs tasks unnecessarily, it comes from poor systems design and can be corrected, or it may result from an overextended use of the computer coupled with a poor design. If poor response time is anticipated, the user must be made aware of the problem and asked to compensate either through shifting workloads or overtime. But this is only a temporary solution. Slow response time should not and cannot be tolerated. Corrective action must be taken.

There is one limitation to on-line processing that may be considered a pitfall, and therefore it must be faced. The video display terminal has physical size limitations and can only contain a finite amount of information. An average screen is 19 inches by 12 inches and contains 1,920 characters in 24 lines of 80 characters per line. If more information is needed, the user must display information on one screen, transmit this to the computer, call up a second screen, and continue. For example, a general ledger entry may be limited to ten debits or credits per screen. Once the data on the first screen is transmitted, it must be recalled for review.

Some users find this a limitation and we agree. Multiple screens for a single transaction should be kept to a minimum in the systems design. The primary point is to anticipate user dissatisfaction if response time is slow or if visual checks are lessened by use of multiple screens for a simple transaction. In other words, these pitfalls can be avoided with a proper systems design.

FINALLY, MANAGEMENT STEPS IN

Will management resist a change in favor of distributed processing? Although we cannot generalize, the new corporate entity, the "gamesman," will be an innovator. "Let's move ahead," he will say. Such rugged "decentralized management" advocates as Don Gaudian of Sybron Corp. will suggest decentralization from their division presidents, whereas some managers will hesitate. But managers must resolve two primary concerns: effect on profit (or outlay of dollars in the nonprofit organization) and effect of change on the organizational structure. These issues are explored in the next chapter.

10

Distributed Processing and Management

Historically, management resisted neither the unchecked growth nor the spiraling costs of computers. But the technological advances of the past few years have paved the way for management to make a break with the past and thus end the evolutionary growth cycle, once and for all.

The new generation will not be a case of stepping from one treadmill to another. For the elements that perpetuated the spiraling cost era will have been eliminated. The organizational dynasty that fostered and nurtured the escalation in equipment and costs will be replaced by dispersing the systems to their users through distributed processing. The nonsensical argument that a computer must be used to capacity will no longer be made, simply because there will be no centralized unit to make it.

What's more, management will have learned from the experience. The consequences of relinquishing control are what prompted us to write this book. We believe that the time to end the old era is now. Distributed processing is inevitable. Sophisticated communications are already being developed to handle future networks. Management must be in a position to evaluate these new developments.

COSTING THE MINICOMPUTER

Step 1: Establish the Need

The first step is to establish the requirements for a computer—no easy task, but it can, and should, be done. If your organization already has a computer, what kind of workload is it handling? To get an overview of the total system, management should obtain a profile of the systems currently being processed, and each should be documented in terms of the following information.

Flowcharts. Individual systems, such as payroll, manufacturing, and personnel, should be flowcharted to show the number of computer programs required to complete the process. Other information, such as program complexity, size, and language, is very helpful in evaluating the present workload.

Transactions. Each system is "driven" by transactions. It is important to document the various types of transactions required and then to document the quantity as well as the time of day they are processed.

Files. The major files should be documented by the data processing staff to explain how they are used and how often. Especially important is the size of the individual records and the number of records as well as the storage media: Are the files maintained as cards, on magnetic tape, or on disks?

Reports. The number and frequency of printed reports is important. You also need to know the volume (number of pages) and time required for printing.

This overview gives you an idea of your present data processing function. Included in this picture is the computer currently being used to process the various systems. Who manufactures the computer and what model is it? How much core memory does it have? What are the various peripheral devices, such as tape drives, disk drives, printers, and terminals? All this information, including the systems documentation, should be readily available in your data processing department. If it is not, then management has quite a different problem.

This information should be gathered and organized in a logical fashion with whatever other information may provide insight into the processing requirements of the organization. The next step is more difficult, as it requires taking a brief look into the future. It is management's job to identify future data processing requirements in terms of new files and reports. More importantly, management should attempt to spell out new systems requirements.

To clarify new requirements, it is helpful to have certain basic information. It is especially important to know the scope of the proposed system in terms of volumes of transactions, files of information, and potential reporting requirements. This information simply may not be available. It must be developed, however, if management is to have an impact on data processing decisions. It is important in evaluating the potential for distributed systems.

For the larger Fortune 500 company, the process of establishing requirements will take the form of analyzing individual systems for the potential use of minicomputers. For example, a major corporation may want to evaluate the potential benefits to be derived from stripping the customer order/entry system from the large mainframe and transferring it to a minicomputer. Citibank (formerly First National City Bank of New York) advocates this approach.

Citibank was one of the first to use minicomputers. Its new philosophy on data processing is that no job is too complex or too great that it cannot be broken into a smaller, more manageable task for a minicomputer. The bank is waging a war on paperwork with terminals and on-line distributed processing. And it appears from the outside that the bank is winning. Citibank recently reported in *The New York Times* that its clerical workforce of transaction processors had been reduced from 10,000 employees in 1970 to a present level of 6,000 employees. The result was a vast reduction in paperwork and estimated savings of $160 million.

Clearly, the large organization can also benefit from the analysis we propose. But in their world the approach may be a piecemeal evaluation of major systems, instead of an analysis of the entire computer configuration. Once the evaluation of present and future requirements has been documented—by either a large or small organization—the next step is to review these requirements with several computer manufacturers. This process may be referred to as competitive bidding or a request for proposal.

Step 2: Request for Proposal

Management should submit its requirements to various computer manufacturers and review the costs of recommended equipment. In the specific case study discussed in Chapter 11, a request for proposal was submitted to the major mainframe and minicomputer manufacturers. The responses were to identify specifications for current systems files, transactions, and future requirements. Specific applications, including payroll, accounts payable, and manufacturing, were also requested.

Each vendor gave his commitment to supply a computer that could handle the specified workload over a five-year period with only one shift of operation. Their assertions were tested and proved valid.

The mainframe manufacturers had to specify batch systems, which would only marginally meet the requirements. They did offer predesigned applications packages that would have to be modified to meet any specific organizational requirements. The mainframe manufacturers' projections were substantially higher in costs. The conclusions were obvious:

◻ The mainframe computers were quoted as high as $10,504 per month, not including the terminals.

Eight terminals would have added a minimum of $2,400 per month, but most of the recommended mainframe computers could not even support these terminals.

All proposed applications systems were batch-oriented, although the specifications called for an on-line manufacturing system at the very least.

□ The minicomputer manufacturers responded with quotes ranging from $3,417 to $4,700 per month.

These quotes represent enormous savings in hardware costs. If the minicomputer is indeed capable of replacing a large-scale computer ($10,000–$18,000 per month) the savings per month are $6,000–$13,000. Furthermore, the minicomputer requires less staffing. It is encumbent on management to evaluate this potential for putting an end to spiraling costs.

None of this is new. Kenneth H. Olsen, founder of Digital Equipment Corporation, made it clear in comparing his company's proposals to those of a major mainframe manufacturer:

There are major differences between the two companies, of course. We're cheaper, but they offer a lot more service.

Where do you think minicomputer got its name? It is "mini" in size and in costs; it is mini in no other way. The name says it, our experience and research confirm it, industry leaders openly acknowledge it: The minicomputer is a very cost-effective alternative for management because it can process the same data at substantially lower costs. Again, in analyzing one of the best minicomputers, *Datapro,* one of the recognized data processing research firms, said that it is true.

This much heralded (minicomputer) is a broad based minicomputer system that offers a variety of powerful features and high performance capability usually found only in much larger and more expensive traditional computer systems. . . . The most nearly cost effective systems available that can match the concurrent multilingual, multi-terminal capabilities . . . are the DEC System 10 from Digital Equipment, the Sigma 6 from Xerox, and IBM's System/370 Model 135. Against each of these systems [the minicomputer] is *considerably* more cost-effective, however.

What causes one of the leading research firms to make such an unequivocal assessment? The fact that it's true!

Yet some will question the validity of this assessment. In order to evaluate the potential cost savings effectively, certain questions that lead to this uneasiness must be answered.

First, some will attack the tangible issues of cost savings. The issues raised will be investment to date, the conversion costs, cost of outside assistance, and the other one-time costs. Second, management must be prepared to handle the issue of risks, such as loss of mainframe support and the security of staying with a large, established manufacturer. Each of these issues is discussed below because they will arise.

THE TANGIBLE ISSUES

Investment to Date

The first issue is whether investment to date is on too great a scale to be changed. We have seen systems "dollarized," whereby a dollar value is placed on the staff of programmers multiplied times the years of systems work. Management must ask itself in these instances whether current systems are satisfying current needs. How many systems emulate the problems inherent in the second-generation system? Do you still have the unit record mentality with its ubiquitous cards? This is the real question. The total spectrum of current systems must be analyzed objectively:

- □ Which systems are on the drawing board for redesign anyway?
- □ Which systems are ineffective and should be reevaluated because they do not provide meaningful data?
- □ Which systems duplicate data causing errors and problems of reconciliation in multiple entries of like data?

If none of these conditions exist, we would be very much surprised. Normally, these conditions exist in spades. How much effort, then, is required to work toward a meaningful data processor? Is this not the time to evaluate the total effort? The amount you have spent in the past hurts, but it is totally irrelevant when you are evaluating the need to improve your data processing ability. This is exactly the ploy your current vendor will use. Don't be swayed, for he will not make the same argument next door where he wants to replace a competitor's hardware. Ask your neighbor!

Some good systems will be found. But these may be converted within the total environment in which an organization functions. In fact, these systems must be reevaluated with respect to the new capability of the minicomputer (see Chapter 3). Systems are restricted today by the limitations of third-generation computers. Yesterday's good systems are not necessarily tomorrow's good systems.

A new approach may be needed, and the second-generation-to-date costs are way behind you. Forget them. They are a dead issue. Think of the savings that can be anticipated through an on-line network and what can be expected with timely and more accurate data.

The Cost to Convert

This is a variation on investment-to-date theme: Sure it's cheaper, but the cost to convert is so great, it just doesn't make sense. It is amazing how many managers never go beyond this premise, which they assume to be true. Management should start with the calculated savings ($6,000 to $13,000 per month) in hardware rental alone. Then offset these savings by the cost to convert.

To convert and redesign an ineffective system is a good idea at any cost. The cost to convert effective systems must be carefully weighed, but it is a mistake to calculate the cost of conversion using the existing staff. These are sunk costs, which the organization will pay regardless of whether it institutes a change to the new-generation computer. Unless an organization plans to terminate its systems staff, it should not refrain from change on the basis of the salaries of existing personnel.

This point cannot be overemphasized. Too often, those who are resistant to change calculate the cost of new innovations using an estimate of the time required multiplied by the salaries of the people involved. These costs are present and, unless someone can prove that these analysts will be used to obtain cost savings in some other specific task, management must consider them "sunk" costs, which have no place in your equation of "cost to convert." This is a potential pitfall that must be recognized. The economic theory of opportunity cost—the lost benefit from alternative use of resources—is pivotal to this argument. Without fear of contradiction, the cost to convert should not be used as a logical counterargument to change and improvement. But some will try, and some will acquiesce. If the potential benefits from alternative projects are so great, why aren't they being developed now?

The real issue here is not the cost to convert. The overriding consideration is the unlimited benefits to be derived from developing on-line systems. The improvement in processing data associated with timeliness could easily offset any cost to convert. These savings must be quantified. First, what are the savings to be realized from reducing multiple handling of data? Without a doubt, it is less expensive to enter data into the computer directly from source documents than to transcribe, keypunch, verify, and submit it to the computer. Second, fewer errors will result from direct input of data. And errors are costly. Finally, the timeliness of data can, in most cases, be quantified and translated into dollars. These are real savings which must be considered in the overall evaluation of current systems versus a move into an on-line environment with distributed systems.

The Cost of Outside Assistance

A minicomputer will have a dramatic effect on the data processing organization, as was pointed out in previous chapters. This raises fear and apprehension in the minds of the data processing manager and his staff, as we have said. It is true that staff reduction is possible with the elimination of specific functions. The two key functions (no pun intended) that are eliminated are:

All centralized key-entry functions, including keypunching and verification. User personnel, familiar with the data, enter it directly rather than transcribe to keypunch documents. Keypunching and verifying are eliminated.

Computer operators. The minicomputer does not require job scheduling and job control, as all applications should be on-line for operation. Batch jobs requiring no operator intervention are called in by the user.

We believe that much of the systems work can be effectively achieved with outside assistance from a reputable systems house. Their expertise in minicomputer technology is invaluable and can be passed on to the in-house technical staff. The extent to which a systems house is consulted depends on your organization:

Is the organization relatively stable in terms of new applications and systems? There are businesses in which systems are set and change is infrequent. These organizations may want to rely heavily on turnkey systems. More volatile businesses, which have frequent changes, may require in-house maintenance.

Is the major application stable? For example, a manufacturing system that has not undergone substantial change for five years may not require frequent modifications. In contrast, a management information system with its changing managers, new techniques, and shifting markets may require constant attention and in-house expertise.

We don't want to generalize. Each organization must review the extent of outside involvement in terms of its own unique requirements. But only in the most sophisticated environments would we consider no outside involvement at all. Use of a systems house means incurring a one-time cost, not an ongoing cost. And once concluded, there will be savings in personnel. To make the transition to on-line systems, such a cost should be incurred. (See Chapter 11 for the case study.)

One-time costs are one real part of the total conversion costs (tangible issue number two), but they must be considered separately. They are neither sunk costs nor continuing costs, but they should, and will, be incurred. Many data processing departments do not have experience in on-line systems. We recommend again that in the development cycle you employ a competent systems house to assist in the technical design. This will cost dollars in the short run, but it will save time and substantial dollars in the long run.

A simple cash-flow analysis should be prepared to reflect these one-time costs for systems development. The intent is to determine when the investment will be returned. How much of a return on investment will be realized differs from one organization to another, but certainly a one- to two-year period seems reasonable and desirable.

Cash-flow analysis serves another purpose. It forces management to define its processing costs and the potential for improvement in this costly area. It dramatizes the effect of potential savings in the user departments through on-line systems. And, in the end, it becomes a yardstick for measuring the original goals of the conversion to distributed systems.

One-time costs may be offset by profitmaking organizations with the investment tax credit (ITC). To spur development and investment, the federal government allows a 10 percent credit after taxes for new equipment purchases with an expected life of seven years. In addition, software may be bundled in with the hardware if a package is purchased from an original equipment manufacturer or a systems house to run on the hardware. For example, a manufacturing firm may purchase a minicomputer and the sophisticated Interactive Information System (IIS) manufacturing system, bundle the hardware and software, lease both over a seven-year period, and take a 10 percent aftertax credit.

Minicomputers run about $20,000 for a small system with two terminals, a disk, and a slow-speed printer up to $247,000 for a full-blown minicomputer with 100 million bytes of disk, eight terminals, tape drives, and a fast printer. (In Chapter 3 we said that the price of a minicomputer is less than $100,000. This is still true, but the peripherals make up the additional costs reflected here.) The investment tax credit, then, would range from $2,000 to $24,700 for the hardware alone. Less than a seven-year lease would reduce the credit proportionately, of course. The ITC is an aftertax credit, which has the bottom-line effect of doubling this amount. Therefore, $4,000 to $49,400 in actual savings is possible. This should most definitely offset a major portion of one-time systems help. And again, certain software packages may be bundled and included in the investment tax credit. This too should offset systems charges directly.

The full impact of a minicomputer, one-time costs, and the investment tax credit can be analyzed with a cash-flow analysis, as shown in Table 11. Certain conclusions may be drawn from this sample on the assumption that personnel savings will be realized once the minicomputer is implemented. Depending on your personnel policies, this may not be realistic, but it is important to reflect these as potential savings. From the table (pages 168–169) we see that:

□ The mainframe is maintained for five months along with the mini-computer. Increased costs are thus reflected incrementally because there are two computers.

□ One-time costs of $50,000 are clearly set out. This layout will be recovered within 11 months' time, as shown in the schedule of costs plotted against savings. By the 11th month, you will have realized a cumulative savings of $1,018.

□ An additional $50,000 has been amortized over the projected seven-year life of the system. These costs are incurred from the inception of the project.

□ An investment tax credit of $28,000, which includes hardware and software, is taken at year end. This partially offsets the one-time development costs.

□ Savings of more than $41,000 are projected in the first year (see sample). A more detailed cost analysis would include such one-time costs as shipment of the minicomputer, site preparation, and other incidental costs, which would not completely offset these savings after the first year.

The savings are supported in a comparative budget, set up in Table 11. Look at the savings in hardware, even if coupled with substantial software. Using our example, the substantial $100,000 software cost *could* be amortized over five years at $2,060 per month. Combining this with, say, a Data General Eclipse, would result in the following:

Item	Monthly Cost
Hardware (DG Eclipse)	$3,417
Software ($100,000, 5 years)	2,060
Total	$5,477

Is your organization paying more than $65,000 per year ($5,477 × 12 months) for hardware alone? If so, management should evaluate a distributed system using the minicost minicomputer. The Eclipse has been shown to be a superfast, superreliable minicomputer.

We feel it is definitely worth the one-time costs to obtain a new on-line system. The minicomputer manufacturer may well make his proposal to you through a systems house or an OEM (original equipment manufacturer). Either will quote you a price for hardware and software and will stake his reputation behind its success. Users will have the double-buffered safety factor, which we discussed previously. We have observed several extremely competent systems houses and OEMs and are convinced there are many more.

In recommending these one-time costs, we caution management to treat them properly from an accounting point of view:

☐ Don't be put off by the initial quotation. Analyze it in conjunction with the anticipated savings.
☐ Amortize these costs where possible.

Getting outside support may be seen as no different from relying on the manufacturer (which we have warned against). We urge management to maintain close control over costs and over the effort to implement it. In the past, the computer manufacturer has supplied the technical expertise. We're merely returning the base of technical expertise to the user with the help of a systems specialist. Management can get a better handle on the systems staff involvement, which is costly, than on the manufacturer's involvement, which is subtle and all-encompassing (see the discussion in Chapter 1). But the expertise has to be built. It could take forever to get the internal staff to educate itself. We found the transfer of knowledge from an experienced software house invaluable and time-effective. In the case study discussed in Chapter 11, the company used outside support to strengthen its own staff through new personnel and through training courses offered by the manufacturer.

To rely solely on software houses would be costly and shortsighted. But to do without them would be risky. What are the issues of risk?

THE INTANGIBLE ISSUES—RISK FACTORS

Support

Don't overlook the earlier remark of Digital Equipment's founder, Kenneth H. Olsen: "We're cheaper, but they offer a lot more service." This is true. One of the ways the minicomputer manufacturers keep their costs down is by avoiding a heavy commitment in technical support to users. Instead, they market their products through the OEM or systems house. So don't expect

Table 11. Sample cash-flow analysis.

Cost Category	Payback time in months											
	1	2	3	4	5	6	7	8	9	10	11	12
	MAINFRAME											
Hardware												
Mainframe	$13,000	$13,000	$13,000	$13,000	$13,000							
Maintenance	2,000	2,000	2,000	2,000	2,000							
Personnel												
Salaries	10,400	10,400	10,400	10,400	10,400							
Fringe benefits	1,248	1,248	1,248	1,248	1,248							
Overtime	500	500	500	500	500							
Education	300	300	300	300	300							
Outside assistance												
Keypunching	400	400	400	400	400							
Supplies	2,400	2,400	2,400	2,400	2,400							
Communications	100	100	100	100	100							
Total mainframe	$30,148	$30,148	$30,148	$30,148	$30,148							

MINICOMPUTER

Hardware												
Minicomputer		$ 4,700	$ 4,700	$ 4,700	$ 4,700	$ 4,700	$ 4,700	$ 4,700	$ 4,700	$ 4,700	$ 4,700	$ 4,700
Maintenance (90-day warranty)					1,500	1,500	1,500	1,500	1,500	1,500	1,500	1,500
Personnel												
Salaries						7,000	7,000	7,000	7,000	7,000	7,000	7,000
Fringe benefits						840	840	840	840	840	840	840
Overtime						500	500	500	500	500	500	500
Education						400	400	400	400	400	400	400
Outside assistance												
Amortized software ($50,000)		1,030	1,030	1,030	1,030	1,030	1,030	1,030	1,030	1,030	1,030	1,030
One-time ($50,000)		10,000	10,000	10,000	10,000							
Ongoing support						500	500	500	500	500	500	500
Supplies						1,000	1,000	1,000	1,000	1,000	1,000	1,000
Communications						100	100	100	100	100	100	100
Total minicomputer	$11,030	$15,730	$15,730	$15,730	$17,230	$17,570	$17,570	$17,570	$17,570	$17,570	$17,570	$17,570
Incremental (cost) savings:	($11,030)	($15,730)	($15,730)	($15,730)	($17,230)	$12,578	$12,578	$12,578	$12,578	$12,578	$12,578	$12,758
Investment tax credit:	—	—	—	—	—	—	—	—	—	—	—	$28,000
Cumulative (cost) savings:	($11,030)	($26,760)	($42,490)	($58,220)	($74,450)	($61,872)	($49,294)	($36,716)	($24,138)	($11,560)	$ 1,018	$41,596

much support from your manufacturer—he simply isn't the source, nor do you need him as such.

There are two considerations here. In the first place, management acquires a powerful, on-line computing system that is inexpensive and reliable. If it's a $200,000 investment, management can expect some technical assistance—just not as much as with the old mainframe. At a minimum, you should investigate the following:

Availability of manufacturer-sponsored staff training courses at their sites. They are available and are neither plush nor overly ostentatious. (What about the alternative for on-site training—at what cost?)

Maintenance support within a reasonable distance. The key is their local inventory of parts, which includes whole peripherals, such as printers and disks, and how long a downtime there will be before they will replace your whole unit. (But remember, reliability is far superior in minicomputers than in mainframes.)

The commitment of on-site technical support during the first month of installation. This is when the user will need help. So get all the full-time support you can during this 30-day period. Don't accept anything less than half-time.

Availability of a similar system for developmental work prior to the arrival of the minicomputer. With terminals and telecommunications capability, this should be no problem. In a recent experience, we observed one organization tying into a minicomputer for development over two months prior to installation. This greatly reduces the developmental cost.

The necessary support is available from the manufacturer with limitations and from his OEM or systems house at a cost. But eventually the user must assume the responsibility and become self-sufficient, which is good in the long run. The relationship between the data processing staff and the manufacturer has become much too cozy. That relationship must be broken now if evolutionary growth is to be contained.

Security

The needling question will be: "Do you really want to leave the security of dealing with a large mainframe manufacturer for an upstart?" Yes, we think you should evaluate it. Some minicomputer companies, such as NCR, Honeywell, and Digital Equipment, are large. Burroughs will soon announce a line of minicomputers. So this may not constitute an issue.

Considering the performance to date, even the smaller manufacturers do not offer very much risk. But, if the alarmist attacks, there are certain measures that can alleviate the fear:

☐ Keep the existing computer in-house until the conversion is complete, and then cancel. This approach means the organization will have to absorb some additional costs, but it is virtually risk-free.

☐ Discontinue the processor and establish a backup procedure on a service bureau or similar processor in case the schedules slip.

☐ Select a minicomputer that supports the organization's current language, such as COBOL and RPG. Varian Data Machines, Data General, Hewlett-Packard, and DEC currently support COBOL.

These are good compromises, but we would encourage new users of on-line systems to resist the temptation to merely convert batch systems to the minicomputer. On the other hand, certain batch routines that may be performing satisfactorily may be converted into COBOL, for example. Hewlett-Packard also has a translator for RPG, which makes conversion simple. Convert batch programs only if you are assured of their effectiveness, as batch programs will not make the best use of the minicomputer's extraordinary capabilities.

To analyze the risks is sensible. They can, and must, be overcome. It is imperative, however, that the minicomputer manufacturer support the implementation. This is only reasonable, considering the investment you are making. In addition to the specific technical support, the manufacturer's representative should personally assure management that the installation is feasible and workable, as well as successful. Management should place an order only after a commitment to the success of the specific installation has been made. That is true security.

THE COUP D'ETAT

Management should prepare one budget for conversion and a new operating budget after it has been accomplished. Nothing is more measurable than an annual budget by expense classifications. The ultimate coup d'état is a comparison of the proposed minicomputer operating budget with the current mainframe operating budget, as depicted in Table 12. It may not fit your organization but it is realistic, and we can prove it. It does tie in with the cash flow in Table 12. It indicates some of the benefits that can offset the risk of change. Here are some highlights of the analysis:

☐ The equipment rental is based on actual quotes. Most minicomputers are leased through a third-party lessor, including the largest banks in the country. The rate is one that was recently negotiated, for the sake of authenticity.

□ To be conservative, the budget includes a whopping $100,000 in development cost, with 50 percent amortized over five years. You may not need to do this.

□ When personnel costs are reduced, many related costs, such as training, fringe benefits, and overtime, are also reduced. Table 12 represents a conservative budget.

□ Supplies constitute a very dramatic cost reduction. The expensive Hollerith punched card is eliminated, and reports are greatly reduced due to inquiry capability of the minicomputer as described in an earlier chapter.

□ The training budget is increased to upgrade the professional capabilities and technical awareness of the user. This, a conscious decision, will pay off.

Table 12. Data processing budget comparison.

Centralized Mainframe	Expense Classification	Distributed Minicomputer
$123,800	Staff salaries	$ 81,000
5,000	Overtime	5,000
14,900	Fringe benefits (12%)	9,700
4,000	Contract keypunching [a]	—
—	Outside software house [b]	5,000
157,200	Equipment rental	56,400
22,000	Equipment maintenance	18,000
—	Amortized software [c]	24,700
29,000	Supplies	12,000
1,200	Communications	1,200
3,000	Education	4,800
$360,100		$217,800

Mainframe   = $360,100
Minicomputer = −217,800

Potential savings $142,300 × 5 years = $711,500

[a] Large peak loads at month's end were handled by contract labor.
[b] Contingency planning.
[c] Based on theoretical $100,000, as described earlier.

The important point is that the savings are attainable and quantifiable with a distributed minicomputer.

If management follows the steps we have suggested and prepares a document of current data processing needs, submits it to various mainframe manufacturers and minicomputer vendors, the cost variations will become clear. Some will challenge potential savings. The issues they will raise will, of course, be investment to date, conversion costs, personnel savings, and one-time costs. And the issues of risk will be support and security. The in-house staff will also question the savings. To avoid the potential pitfalls management has to have skill and guts.

There is no logic to an argument that does not acknowledge the substantial hardware savings of the minicomputer. Don't swallow the argument that a minicomputer requires the same staff as a mainframe. Consider the fact that the minicomputer can be plugged into a common wall socket and requires neither special floors nor expensive air conditioning. The "rugged-nova" concept is a reality in the minicomputer world. Prove the savings in supplies. Amortize one-time costs over the life of the system.

Management should accept our challenge and prepare a comparative five-year operating budget—the coup d'état—for a mainframe and a minicomputer followed by a realistic cash-flow analysis. Each has been illustrated in this chapter. If these two documents prove the obvious, management may be on the threshold of a break with the past, thus putting an end to the era of escalating costs and returning the systems to the users.

We have said it all along in many different ways: The problem in getting a minicomputer implemented really has nothing to do with the past history of your evolutionary growth to a mainframe, nor can we blame capability of the hardware, the availability of software, or any misconceptions about distributed processing. The real issues are a fundamental resistance of the human race to *any* change and, more specifically, management's own problems in grappling with the changeover in data processing techniques.

But grapple they must. The data processing manager, the systems analyst, and the ingrained mainframe manufacturer will resist. What about resistance on the part of management? The time has come for you to resist *them*—they are now on weak ground in resisting the inevitable.

> *He who fights the future has a dangerous enemy.*
> —Kierkegaard

11

A Case History

This is a true account of how one company successfully implemented a minicomputer and distributed data processing. We recognize that the concept of using minicomputers and decentralizing some important functions represents a new way of thinking.

This case study discusses the steps used to phase out the batch environment and move into a distributed environment. And it is written from the perspective of management, for it is management who should make this evaluation, aided by their technical staff.

STUDY OF REQUIREMENTS

The study of requirements in this case was initiated by management and headed by a member of upper management experienced in data processing. An outside consultant was retained to evaluate the need for a manufacturing system and the effectiveness of the present system.

This small study team worked closely with the data processing staff of 14 professionals. The goal was to document all the systems currently running on the company's centralized mainframe computer. Some documentation was available but as is true in most companies, most systems were not well documented. Some analysts are good at documentation, and some computer centers stress the need for it. Others do not. To fill the gaps, the small study team prepared gross flowcharts to get a better picture of the total existing requirements for data processing.

The study team also interviewed all major users over a period of three weeks to find out how responsive and effective they found the present systems in terms of their needs. Users were also asked what they saw as their future systems needs. Finally, top management in marketing, finance, and manufacturing was interviewed to round out the long-range company goals and ascertain where data processing might fit in.

The results of this study were neither unusual nor unexpected: Data processing in its present state was undoubtedly providing a valuable service to certain departments, but not from a company-wide perspective. Some systems were effective, but others had become obsolete because of changing technologies and requirements of the users. But the most interesting finding was that although this particular company was very progressive, growing rapidly, and a technical leader in all respects, its data processing simply was not keeping pace. Let's look at some of the reasons:

□ The company had many subsidiaries here and abroad, but no long-range plan was in effect for the data processing function.

□ There were no systems on the computer that had been designed to assist other subsidiaries or reduce overall systems development costs.

□ The manufacturing process was a continuous one, but the computer reports, produced in batch, caused an 18- to 42-hour delay.

In addition, the systems staff was putting most of its energy into maintaining existing but, in some cases, obsolete systems. Its only up-to-date system was a four-terminal order/entry application, which consisted of 75 to 80 percent of the daily processing that took place on the mainframe computer. Built into the order/entry system was billing, accounts receivable, sales (in a limited subset), and a finished goods analysis. The inventory control and bill of materials systems were run nightly, while the financial reports were shared between unit record equipment and the mainframe processor. The demands for a better manufacturing system and a responsive marketing system simply couldn't be met with the existing equipment and a staff that continued to hold onto outdated systems.

When visibility became possible and the maintenance effort relaxed, it was discovered that the existing batch computer could not process any new on-line applications without several thousand dollars per month of new equipment, which included memory and communications interfacing devices.

So the dilemma was real: a progressive company faced with a data processing function which, because of older systems and equipment limitations, could not provide the type of support it needed. At the same time, several progressive subsidiaries were getting into data processing on their own and were coming up against obvious problems. There would be no standardization, little exchange of ideas, and no organized means of control over total company expenditures for data processing.

An interesting sidelight was that the batch computer was really producing almost meaningless reports and volumes of source data for the manual preparation of meaningful reports. This was not reported to management as a criticism, but rather as a consequence of a very natural evolutionary process. Here, as in many data processing departments, the source of the problem was the unit record equipment. This is a limited device that can only store several totals and does not have the almost unlimited potential of the modern-day stored-program computer. But the systems mentality of the unit record days continues to pervade today's systems, which are designed to print totals without much thought to the user's needs.

The general ledger, for example, did list all accounts, but the profit-and-loss statements and balance sheets had to be produced manually and at considerable costs. This failure to meet the needs of users reflected the systems limitations that dated from the days of unit record.

The study generated a report to management that outlined a course of action for the company. As one part of that action plan, it was recommended that the current mainframe computer be evaluated against competitive equipment before more money was spent just to procure a bigger computer. It was recommended that the needs of the subsidiaries be included in considering a new computer. The action plan called for preparing a request for proposal to be submitted to all major computer manufacturers. The plan was approved by management.

REQUEST FOR PROPOSAL

The request for proposal, which was more than 30 pages long, detailed all the essential requirements for meeting the existing and projected systems load, along with an additional supplement, consisting of flow diagrams of two major systems. The information for the request came directly from the study team's efforts. There was no duplication of time or effort in this case. The intent was to set one standard document to which each manufacturer could respond and be evaluated. Their responses could then be measured and compared, and not be just a random, uncoordinated equipment listing of promises and credentials.

The request began with the selection criteria. The selection criteria provided the basis for choosing among the various manufacturers' submissions. The overall objective was the need for a computer that could meet the expanding requirements of a growing, progressive company. The guidelines were listed as follows:

◻ Implementation ease, including the number of new programs required, proposed time frame, and vendor support.

◻ New systems capability, with emphasis on materials planning and a responsive manufacturing system.

◻ Annual recurring cost savings in personnel requirements, hardware, and investment tax credits.

◻ Projected one-time implementation costs.

◻ Backup potential and vendor support during and after implementation.

◻ Ease of use, including the operating system and other systems software.

◻ Training capability of vendor.

◻ The hardware growth potential for new applications, increased volume, and communications capability.

These criteria were followed by a statement stressing the importance of having the recommended systems be transferable at minimal cost and difficulty to subsidiaries. Although it was not stipulated specifically at the time, the document called for some guidance for future installations in the total company.

In retrospect, the key criteria in the request were cost and a responsive manufacturing system, as was pointed out in the second criterion. The remainder of the first section of the request described the history and makeup of the company and its manufactured products. It also detailed the current data processing function to clarify the environment for the vendors.

The computer's projected workload was outlined. Each system and the time required on the computer for processing was listed. The time was separated into average minutes used for daily, weekly, bimonthly, monthly, and quarterly processing. Each system was then rated in terms of the percentage of total time required. This provided the vendors with the actual time required on the current computer to process the current workload. They were being asked to firm up the time that would be required on their proposed computer. This important request meant that the company wanted a written commitment of how many hours per day would be required by the computer to complete the workload.

Current systems were also described in the request for proposal. The configuration of the current computer was described with its core memory size, tape drives, printer, disk drives, and terminals. All software operating on the system was described including the operating system and the data base management system. The document reported that three languages were being used, but that COBOL was overwhelmingly predominant with more than 380 active programs written in this language. Each system was listed with the number of active programs cited.

The exhibit shown in Table 13 was provided to each vendor in the request for proposal. The Cards Read column listed the transaction volumes for the current computer. Print lines indicated the volumes of reports that must be produced by any proposed computer, and the central processing unit (CPU) time listed the current workload. Because most manufacturers have a range of computers from small to very large, these vital statistics were needed to select the model that best fit the potential buyer's needs. The potential buyer had already specified his processing requirements in order to hold the vendor to his representation in the event that the recommended computer did not perform.

The final analysis involved the use of files. Again, on a system-by-system basis, the study team prepared a disk- and tape-file analysis to alert ven-

Table 13. System inputs, print lines, and CPU times.

System	Processing Cycle	Cards Read	Print Lines	CPU Time (minutes)
Accounts payable	Weekly	114	†	6
	Monthly	1,030	1,470	8
BOMP	Daily	235	6,000	80
	Weekly	1,700	5,100	44
	Monthly	10,440	90,406	364
	Other	8	1,900	4
Order/Entry	Daily	500	16,700	106
	Weekly	126	15,300	32
Accts. payable	Monthly	70	3,500	5
General ledger	Monthly	2,560	44,000	68
Standby expense*	Monthly	1,300	22,000	34
Net earnings	Monthly	1,600	4,000	16
Payroll	Weekly	2,304	3,026	26
	Semimonthly	475	509	4
	Monthly	6,390	29,620	81
Sales				
Local	Weekly	800	2,800	4
	Monthly	3,225	38,100	50
Subsidiaries	Monthly	2,160	4,960	47

*Estimate without power. (Power accounting is a commercial software package, which is added to the computer's software to record the central processing unit minutes required to complete a specific application).
† Subsidiary processing.

dors as to the number and types of files that would be required in any new computer. For each computer file, the study team identified its purpose and developed the statistics on numbers of records and the size of each. This was all the various vendors needed to know. The stage was now set for an evaluation.

THE EVALUATION

The official request for proposal was submitted to the manufacturers as planned. The study team was expanded to include the data processing manager, the manufacturing manager, and the director of purchasing. These three people, along with the outside consultant and the representative of upper management, formed the evaluation committee.

The responses were timely in most instances because the specifications were clear. Each major vendor spent one to two days on site to review the requirements and better understand the company's needs. Each made a 4- to 6-hour presentation on his proposed configuration. Finally, each prepared written proposals for consideration by the evaluation committee. It was a time-consuming process, but the task was too important for half-measures.

The selection process had to be thorough, as the data processing manager did not really favor any change in the first place. The review was launched in earnest, though. Some of the major mainframe manufacturers withdrew from the competition because they could not meet the stated requirements. For example, one manufacturer submitted a conversion plan that would have taken more than two years for one system alone. This certainly did not fall within the concept of "ease of implementation." The problem was the major effort of converting to its hardware as it was designed. Another mainframe manufacturer recommended two computers: a large-scale and a dedicated small-business computer. This configuration cost more to operate than the existing system.

Because of local office personnel transfers, one mainframe manufacturer simply couldn't meet the schedule to submit a proposal. Another described a product that sounded great, but was not on the market yet. The evaluations of two configurations were compared with objectivity and at great length.

The minicomputer manufacturer offered an interesting contrast in its marketing approach. Digital Equipment Corporation does not pay its salesforce a commission, which reflects management's concern with overselling or pressuring potential users. Digital Equipment is very successful, with more than 72,000 computers now installed. One of their salesmen immediately recommended two systems houses that had the capability to install applications systems using Digital Equipment's minicomputers. Data General took the same tack. Hewlett-Packard and Varian salesmen recommended using their minicomputers for in-house systems development.

The evaluation committee found itself in the unique position of dealing with a number of very large and prominently established mainframe manufacturers, several large minicomputer manufacturers, several minicomputer original equipment manufacturers (OEMs), systems houses, and software firms. The OEMs recommended their own configuration of hardware and software with their own names affixed. For example, one might attach his name to a configuration that included a Data General computer, another manufacturer's disk, and their own unique operating system.

The systems houses, on the other hand, offered a standard marketed minicomputer, but with their own unique applications programs in a complete turnkey arrangement. The software firms basically offered programming support with, in some cases, some applications packages to draw on.

Each vendor was impressive in its own way. The manufacturers lent their support, offered reliable hardware, and approached problems with true professionalism. The smaller minicomputer manufacturers' representatives showed technical strength and enthusiasm for their products. And the OEMs, systems houses, and software firms came up with imaginative solutions to complex applications problems. One systems house vice-president detailed a bill of materials-processing technique that even smacked of genius. The evaluation team learned and profited greatly from the experience.

After nearly two months of deliberation, the decision was unanimous. They would switch from the mainframe to the new minicomputer and distributed systems technology, the primary considerations being cost and responsiveness. Having visited manufacturers in California and Massachusetts, the evaluation committee was confident of the technical abilities of the product, the commitment and integrity of the manufacturing companies, and their own need for on-line data processing.

The next questions were which minicomputer to select, and whether an OEM, systems house, or software firm would be needed. Since the company had no experience with minicomputers and very little with on-line systems, the selection committee made a critical decision. "It is imperative," they reported to the president, "that we develop our own technical strength, rather than rely on the minicomputer manufacturer or on a total turnkey application."

A technical consultant was retained to work with the company during the final selection and eventual implementation process. The projected cost savings and the real investment tax credit made it feasible to use the services of a consultant as well as a systems house for at least some of the development work. Not only would this help bridge the technological gap for the data processing staff, but the project could be kept moving while the staff was learning and a few new staff people were being hired.

Getting acquainted with this new world of minicomputers and distributed processing involves bringing the hardware and the systems capabilities together. For this company, the best solution seemed to be a very powerful minicomputer buttressed with solid systems expertise from the outside and strengthened in-house capabilities. With this in mind, the evaluation committee and the consultant got to work.

They would recommend a minicomputer to management after evaluating the capabilities of each computer in terms of meeting the specifications spelled out in the proposals. This decision to have in-house technical support contributed significantly in controlling costs, monitoring project schedules, training in-house staff, and integrating the final systems design. It represented a commitment to incurring the necessary one-time costs in taking a step toward distributed processing. The decision also gave management the decided advantage of being able to discriminate knowledgeably among the opinions and promises of the salespeople who were interested in the project. Not all salespeople are fully aware of the real capacities of and limitations to the equipment they sell.

The consultant's chief responsibility was to work with the selection committee to identify potential problem areas and pitfalls: Which minicomputer was the best suited from a technical standpoint? What was the best way to implement it?

Working with input from the data processing staff, the selection committee developed a more detailed statement and categorization of the technical requirements for the new computer. The three criteria they came up with for this particular company were hardware characteristics, software capabilities, and communications. The selection committee than reevaluated the responses and eliminated those companies that did not meet the technical requirements. These specific needs had to be excluded from the original request for proposal to avoid eliminating any really useful alternatives. These technical requirements constituted a second-stage filtering process in a careful comparative study.

They came up with three specific minicomputers that would meet the needs of the user and the technician in this particular company at this point in time. A report was generated by the consultant for the selection committee, which compared these three minicomputers from a technical standpoint. The report was labeled an *equipment analysis*. Appendix A is a sample technical evaluation.

The equipment analysis provided management with a document of what they needed to know about three equally qualified alternatives. Written in nontechnical language, it did not represent an ultimatum from the technical consultant or a data processing manager. Rather, it communicated technical information to management so they could make decisions regarding highly sophisticated equipment.

The equipment analysis defined such details as memory requirements and type of memory. Why was semiconductor memory preferable to core memory? The analysis listed six specific advantages. But it also stated why the company "could safely elect to use either form of memory."

The importance here was obvious. First, the absolute minimum core requirements were spelled out. All manufacturers had to meet this minimum requirement. Second, the type of memory was important only in that one—semiconductor—had six specific advantages over the other. Yet management was advised that either type could "safely" be used so that this did not have the fatal impact of memory limitations.

The evaluation committee had a long-term requirement for communicating with subsidiaries. The analysis therefore included a separate section on communications needs. This too was presented in a management perspective with the significance of each requirement explained. Again, the advantages of synchronous communications were explained. Furthermore, the limitations of asynchronous communications were defined in such a manner that this mode of transmission would not handle the projected workload. Therefore, management could either question the findings or conclude that asynchronous communications were inappropriate.

After this initial statement of specific hardware requirements was prepared, the evaluation committee reviewed them until a common level of understanding and agreement was reached. This required no more than one to two weeks (while committee members, of course, performed their other functions in manufacturing, purchasing, and running the data processing organization, respectively). Using the information gained from the proposals and the research capabilities of the leading computer evaluation firms, they compared the hardware.

Only three minicomputers are represented in Appendix A, but others were also evaluated with favorable results. Other considerations were incorporated into the final decision as well. Paramount was the support from the minicomputer manufacturers in terms of training and available documentation. But this equipment analysis provided the technical data needed for nontechnicians and technicians alike to make a reasoned selection together. Both technician and nontechnician talked extensively to the users themselves.

Recommendations

The committee's findings were then reported to the president with recommendations. The report referenced the initial study, which had launched this entire project only four months earlier. The report stated that "the earlier study indicated the need to review data processing costs and to evaluate the benefits and costs associated with implementation of more sophisticated information systems." The report outlined, once again, the reasons why the need existed to review costs and the responsiveness of certain systems. It stated that, as a result of the earlier study, a request for proposal had been issued and that the following report was prepared to provide the results of that effort and make recommendations for further action.

The evaluation committee's report recommended a change from the centralized data processing to a distributed user-oriented system. The emphasis from this time forward would be away from hardware and toward more responsive applications systems development. Systems, including output reports and the input of data, would become the responsibility of the end user. This would mean that video display terminals would be located in each user's department for data input and control over individual systems.

The committee recommended a detailed systems design phase for all major systems except the recently implemented customer order/entry system, which should be converted to the new computer with several innovations. The original language, COBOL, was to be used to make the conversion as easily and quickly as possible. This requirement for COBOL had a major bearing on which minicomputer was recommended.

The detailed systems study allowed the company to define its own unique requirements rather than trying to adopt packaged software. To reduce the immensity of the redevelopment effort, the committee recommended that an established systems house be retained to implement their tried and true manufacturing system and customize it to the company's specific requirements. After a satisfactory on-site demonstration of the system, the evaluation committee made arrangements to visit three live sites to observe the system in actual operation. The projected benefits were included in the original report to the president and are included in Appendix B of this book.

It was further recommended that all systems be designed to function interactively with integrated data bases. By interactive, the report stated, "We mean that the computer guides and checks the user through each step of data entry to increase accuracy and timeliness of data." By integrated data bases,

"We mean related files are updated only once by the user to prevent duplication of data and reduce processing time and costs." It was further recommended that the company use its computing power in a multitasking mode which would permit different systems and applications, such as order/entry, manufacturing, and accounting, to be processed concurrently. Thus, the report concluded, the application of cash, the processing of purchase orders, and the entry of inventory activities could be overlapped with any other necessary transaction.

The Report

A minicomputer. To accomplish this in the earliest time frame at a reasonable cost to the company, the evaluation committee recommended the newly announced Hewlett-Packard HP 3000 minicomputer. The configuration included 256 million bytes of memory, 94 million bytes of disk capacity, one tape drive for backup processing, a 600-line/minute printer, and eight video display terminals. This computer, ranked in power and capability with the IBM 370 Model 135, would be leased for a rate of only $4,700 a month. The Hewlett-Packard was only one of several minicomputers evaluated that would handle the unique requirements of the company. It was concluded that the other three could also produce the desired cost-effective results. At the time, however, several factors weighed heavily in the selection of Hewlett-Packard's HP 3000:

□ It could be expanded to double the recommended configuration.
□ It was the only minicomputer at that time with a vendor-supported data base manager (IMAGE).
□ It was the only minicomputer that offered a full COBOL compiler.
□ The HP 3000 operating system, MPE, had been field-tested for more than three years.

The proposed configuration was compared with the existing configuration to let management know that this was, in fact, no ordinary minicomputer in performance capability. The comparison is shown in Table 14. One top manager responded, "What took you so long?"

Financing. The report continued with proposed financing and a projected budget. It was recommended that the manufacturing system be bundled into one package along with the hardware and that the combined total be leased through a third party. As an aside, the software recommendation was not followed, and the cost of the software package was expensed as incurred. The hardware was to be leased over a five-year period. One-time costs for the manufacturing system were outlined, and the use of one pro-

Table 14. Comparison of hardware.

Characteristics	Present Computer	HP 3000
Memory (bytes)	192,000	256,000
Disk capacity	125,000	94,000
Tapes	3	1
Printer speed (lines/min)	600	600
Cycle time (speed)	1,500 ns	350 ns
Virtual memory	No	Yes
Terminals	4	8
Terminal capacity	4	16
Data base manager	Yes (Total)	Yes (Image)
Inquiry language	No	Yes
Languages	All standard	All standard
Manufacturer's lease cost	$18,000/month	$4,700/month

grammer to assist in the conversion of the order/entry system was included. With the projected savings in hardware alone, the one-time costs were recoverable within approximately 9 months.

When the conversion effort was completed, the committee concluded, the revised budget would represent a conservative savings of $150,000 per year for five years, or $750,000. It should be obvious that the equipment savings alone represented nearly $100,000. Other projected savings were maintenance costs of $5,000, personnel savings of $35,000, and paper and supply savings of $10,000. The reduction in paper was estimated from the fact that a daily list of inventory status was no longer required and the tremendous expense of punched cards would be eliminated.

Subsidiaries. The evaluation committee proposed a recommendation that each subsidiary that needed computer capability be analyzed with the same thoroughness that had just been completed for the head office. The systems being developed locally would encompass, wherever practical, those requirements of the various homogeneous subsidiaries. It was suggested that each subsidiary would have two alternatives after implementation of the proposed systems, referred to as the *core* system. A core system was defined as a generalized system that would fit multiple subsidiaries with minor modifications or "customizations." The two alternatives open to each subsidiary were:

□ *Terminals* that would be connected to the localized computer via common voice telephone lines. This alternative meant that the subsidiary would share the same computer programs as the local company but would maintain its own data base of information.

□ *A stand-alone minicomputer* that could use the same core systems already designed with specific modifications. This alternative, for the larger subsidiaries, would represent a substantial reduction in software costs.

Either way, the company would have a truly distributed data processing network with all its advantages. The choice of alternatives would be predicated strictly on the economics of the issue.

Benefits. The president's report included a section on expected benefits. To summarize, the report listed the following tangible benefits:

Cost savings.
New emphasis on systems instead of hardware.
On-line data entry with localized editing.
Immediate file update.
Six major systems operating concurrently.
A real-time manufacturing system.
An on-line data base for personnel.
An updated general ledger system.
A real alternative for subsidiaries without duplicated development costs.

Risks. It came as no surprise to anyone that the proposed change to a minicomputer meant a complete break with the past. Although the possibility that the systems house would not perform was one of the risks in making a change, this is a common concern when any outside consultant is called in. The evaluation committee believed it could establish sufficient controls and milestones to monitor performance adequately.

The area of most concern was the ability of the minicomputer to handle the company's workload. To reduce this risk, it was recommended that the selected manufacturer commit in writing that the proposed computer would meet the processing requirements stipulated in the request for proposal, and that it should also commit its resources to the success of the venture.

Second, it was recommended that the present computer be retained until all systems were operational. Having both computers on site would mean some overlapping, but as the two major systems became operative, the present mainframe could be stripped down, and unused memory, terminals, terminal multiplexer, and supporting system software removed, thereby reducing the cost. When only a few minor systems remained, the company had the option of using a service bureau if it was found necessary. Thus, there would be at least two sources of backup for each system, that is, either the present mainframe or a service bureau.

The worst possible eventuality would be that the minicomputer would not be able to handle all applications. Yet the company would still benefit from a dedicated manufacturing system with its on-line capability. Coupled with the related customer order/entry, this would have a favorable impact on the operations. What would the lost, however, would be the projected savings. The committee concluded that this was a reasonable risk to take if the manufacturer were to stand behind its computer. The manufacturer did just that.

The president's report concluded with a plan for implementation. It was tentatively approved and sent to the board of directors for final approval.

Implementation of the Minicomputer

The implementation was neither easy nor without problems. Some precautions had been taken, however. To lessen the risks, an initial training and familiarization program was set up at the manufacturer's regional computer center at no charge to the company. Terminals were placed on-site and operated on a timesharing basis with the regional personnel. The terminals were loaned from the local sales office so that the only cost to the company was the telephone line charges. Through this arrangement, the data processing staff was able to get valuable hands-on experience and training on the minicomputer prior to its delivery and the actual systems development.

At this stage, there were three major technical tasks to be performed before any serious developmental efforts could begin. The first task was to acclimate the users to the new system. At the onset of this project, the data processing staff was trained and experienced primarily in mainframe processing. All the existing applications were programmed in one language, COBOL. Most programs were large because the batch philosophy encourages the creation of large multifunctional programs. This required large amounts of memory and the inevitable escalation of costs. It was common practice in this batch environment for programmers to be less concerned with systems efficiency and more concerned with creating very large self-contained programs with even larger systems developed around them.

The minicomputer environment eliminated this problem. It was recognized that these same large programs had to be made efficient so that many programs and users could share the resources of the computer. It would no longer be a case of running a big inefficient system at night. Rather, the new environment would permit many users to talk simultaneously to the computer. Conservation of computer resources was a fundamental lesson that had to be learned. Previous requests for more memory by data processing personnel had been a function of the extravagant way in which applications had been designed and implemented.

It became everyone's responsibility to become aware of the differences in philosophy of systems design and programming and to learn to think in terms of this new environment. Some analysts simply would not make this adjustment. Although experience differed with the individual personalities, it was found that young, unbiased college graduates were very easily trained in the new way of thinking. Acclimation to on-line processing was one of the early, major technical tasks that were undertaken.

A second technical task, which fell mainly to the technical consultant, was to put the minicomputer to best use with its existing capabilities. As a timesharing system, the new minicomputer lent itself well to handling the communications with multiple terminals, but it lacked a sophisticated screen-handling capability. Therefore, the development of screens (video displays) for input or retrieval of information was not directly available in the system.

Moreover, the computer's architecture was designed to be most efficient in an environment in which one program (or small group of frequently used programs) was being executed by many users. Therefore, it was important to structure the applications systems so that it could operate as a set of routines (or subsystems) under one control program. In the heavy processing environment of this company, failure to implement this concept could amount to a loss of hours of potentially available time each day. It was therefore important to optimize the use of a single program to call in all other programs as subsets or subroutines.

Realizing that it may take as long as two minutes to call in a new program and that screen handling was inefficient, they had a second technical task—to develop a single central control program, called the *monitor,* which would handle screens easily and maintain fast user response time. All applications programs would be called in and controlled by the monitor.

The use of a central control program also afforded the company the unique opportunity to develop one set of programming standards and one total systems design criterion. This would ensure that all systems conform to common editing rules, satisfy internal security requirements, and maintain the integrity of each data base by system. Therefore, the monitor program was written to:

Monitor and control all system inputs.
Edit all incoming transactions.

Secure the system from unauthorized users.

Maintain and control all video screens within the system.

Log all incoming transactions.

Initiate the processing of all application functions.

The result was immediate. All design criteria were established. The conventional approach of designing individual systems without consideration of the overall effect on the organization and effectiveness of the computer was dropped. The potential for interfacing related systems and sharing information had proved feasible.

These communications and interrelationships were critical to the new on-line environment. Response time (the time required for the computer to respond to a user's request) was at stake. Data base integrity, information accessability, and overall systems performance became critical issues. A built-in control program not only represented an attractive opportunity to integrate systems, it was a necessity. In addition, the requirement that each applications program conform to the monitor's specifications would help police and administer strict programming and systems standards, a long-sought-after goal of the truly professional data processing manager.

In the conventional systems environment, it was the programmer's responsibility to (1) maintain screen formats, (2) receive transactions and data, (3) edit the data, and (4) process the data through a unique applications program. This created the need for very large programs. In contrast, the new on-line environment with its central control program extracted the first three of these four functions and placed them in the monitor area, retaining the last function for the applications programs. The net effect was smaller applications programs.

Underlying this approach was the fact that the major portion of operating time would be spent performing the first three functions, while only a small portion of time would be required to accomplish the last function. Therefore, a general-purpose program to issue screen patterns, receive inputted transactions, edit the transaction upon entry, and, only after satisfactory completion, turn control over to an applications program would greatly enhance the overall capability and throughput of the system and would eliminate the necessity to prepare additional applications programs to satisfy these functions.

Furthermore, it had become extremely important to limit the amount of time required for a particular applications program to tie up the data base, since other applications might be waiting to use it. The minicomputer system was a multitasking system, driven by the response rate of the operating system and data base. No applications function should tie up the data base waiting for a terminal operation's response. For this reason, the central control program–applications program was separated into two areas:

Central Control: To handle terminal interaction.
Applications: To handle data base interaction.

Although seemingly simplistic, this technique defined the domain of each of these areas. Screens, transactions, and edits required terminal interaction, which fell into the central control area, while file processing (information retrieval, updating, and posting) was a function of the data base and unique to a specific applications function. Thus the central control (monitor) program was designed and programmed.

The third technical task to be resolved before serious development could begin was to establish a common language in which to program all systems. This issue was an emotional one. Most of the existing data processing staff preferred COBOL, whereas the systems houses and consultants favored the more efficient FORTRAN or interactive BASIC for the on-line applications. The manufacturer's representatives took the position that it was the company's choice, on the basis of the skills of its present staff and the nature of the individual systems involved.

A very detailed comparison of mainframe and minicomputer COBOL characteristics was undertaken. The result was that the COBOL on the HP 3000 was similar to the COBOL presently used by the data processing staff and that it complied with established standards (ANSI COBOL). Since the choice was not clear, a compromise was reached. All new development was to be written in FORTRAN, but the large order/entry system currently in COBOL was to be converted into COBOL for the HP 3000 minicomputer.

This decision made a dramatic impact on implementation. Later, after the decision, a benchmark program was developed at Hewlett-Packard's Eastern regional facility in Rockville, Maryland. The test was performed on an applications program, which tested the computational efficiency of the various languages. The program merely added the value of 1 to a counter for each execution of the program. The results were measured for four different programming languages, including FORTRAN and COBOL. The evaluation criterion was the number of times the computer could execute the programs in each of the four languages with all four programs running simultaneously. The end result proved that the decision to undertake all new development in FORTRAN was sound, as shown in Table 15.

To convert a staff of COBOL programmers to FORTRAN presented another quite different problem. It became a question of professional confidence and security. The answer was clearly education and training. In addition, sound

Table 15. Benchmark test executions.

Language	Program Executions
Scientific Programming Language (SPL)	150,000
FORTRAN	125,000
COBOL	75,000
BASIC	45,000

programming standards were developed to ensure that all FORTRAN programs were well organized and structured. The set of standards resembled the COBOL standards of program identification, data definition, and procedural comments, all very familiar concepts to a COBOL programmer. Structured and generic (use of common subroutines) programming standards were described and documented by the technical consultant.

With the three major technical issues resolved, several months of work had passed. But using terminals linked to the regional computer, the staff was now prepared to undertake a very exciting, if demanding, project.

Development began in earnest. It was controlled over a 14-month period according to a detailed implementation plan.

Project Control

The new system was put into effect under the direct control of a project leader who represented upper management. Three development teams were formed each under the direct supervision of a team leader who acted as line manager for that team's required tasks. The technical consultant held the additional role of final arbitrator in all technical decisions that had to be made. The three teams were:

□ *The manufacturing team,* which was responsible for implementation of the manufacturing system procured from the systems house selected.

□ *The order/entry conversion team,* which was given responsibility to convert the customer order/entry system in COBOL to operate on the minicomputer. This team also became responsible for the sales and forecasting systems.

□ *The financial team,* which was given responsibility for implementing payroll, general ledger, and accounts payable systems. This group was given additional funds to use consultants or to purchase software packages if any could be found. But at this early stage in the study, no good packages had been identified.

The implementation plan was monitored through the use of a time-phased chart known as a Gantt chart, named for its originator. Tasks were identified, responsibilities set, and beginning and target dates established. Overlapping tasks were identified and conflicts resolved. A manning chart was also developed. The manning chart was a statement of each analyst's tasks and responsibilities so that one analyst was not expected to do more than he could achieve.

The project leader originally developed the administrative section of the implementation plan and monitored progress of each task and each system. This document was then entered and maintained on the computer, a sample page of which is illustrated in Figure 25. By putting the schedule on the computer, it was easily updated and rerun just prior to any critical status meetings. It was also reorganized automatically according to responsibility, to provide the important manning chart.

The legend at the top defined the status of each task. That is, the task might be complete, past due, open, canceled, or extended, or it might be a new task. The plan included a description of the task to be performed, the initials of the individual or team leader assigned to the task, the estimated work days required, and the chart, indicating starting and projected target dates. Finally, the current status was summarized on the right side of the plan based on the reported status from the team leader.

This plan was essential for controlling the multitude of tasks that had to be accomplished. Each team leader submitted a detailed plan of tasks for each system under his responsibility. The total plan was more than 25 pages long. In the manufacturing system, a more detailed implementation plan filled one ring-binder notebook. But this project schedule was developed at the level of detail needed for the project leader to monitor the progress of the various tasks, to determine which were coming due, which were behind schedule, and which were ahead. Allocations or reallocations of resources were decisions made from the implementation plan.

Weekly status meetings were held at which time progress was measured against the schedule and potential problems discussed with each team leader. It was the responsibility of the technical consultant to resolve all technical problems that arose during the entire development phase. It was the responsibility of each team leader to keep his tasks on schedule.

The establishment of these disciplines made monitoring the project straightforward. The project leader had complete visibility into the overall status of the project, but he had to rely on the team leaders for detailed prog-

```
   10      STATUS:4/9/76
   20      C-COMPLETE
   30      P-PAST DUE          ———— ———— HP3000 PROJECT SCHEDULE          ——   —— 
   40      O-OPEN        ·                                            DATE:3/5/76
   41      X-CANCELED
   42      E-DATE DUE EXTENDED
   43      A-ADDED AFTER 4/9/76
   44
   60                 ASSIGNED  MARCH     APRIL     ·MAY      JUNE      JULY      S
   70      DESCRIPTION RE MAN   1 1 2:    1 2 3:  ·1 2 2:   1 1 2:    1 2 3     T
   80       OF TASK    SP DAY   5 2 9 6:2 9 6 3 0:7 4 1 8:4 1 8 5:2 9 6 3 0     S
   90      -----------------   -- ---   - - - -:- - - - -:- - - -:- - - -:- - - - -
 1100      COMPUTER HARDWR  JB  -      . . . : . . . . . ·: . . . : . . . : . . . .C
 1110      SELECTION        JB  -      . . . : . . . . . : . . . : . . . : . . . .C
 1120      APPROVAL BOARD   JB  -      . . . : . . . . . : . . . : . . . : . . . .C
 1130      ORDER            JB  -      . . . : . . . . . : . . . : . . . : . . . .C
 1140      SITE PREPARATION LF  5      . . .*. : . . . . : . . . : . . . : . . . .P
 1150      INSTALLATION     LF  5      . . . : . .*. . . : . . . : . . . : . . . .C
 1151      ADDITIONAL EQUIP LF  -      . . . : . . . .*: . . . : . . . : . . . .A
 1160
 1200      UNIT RECORD SHOP LF  -      . .   . : . . . . . : . . . : . . . : . . ·. .O
 1210      DOCUMENT USE     LF  5      . . .`. : *. . . . : . . . : . . . : . . . .C
 1220      PLAN TO SELL     LF 10      . . . : . . . .*: . . . : . . . : . . . .O
 1230      SELL             LF  5      . . . : . . . . . : . . . : . . . :*. . . .O
 1240
 1300      STAFF REQUIREMTS JB  -      . . . : . . . . . : . . . : . . . : . . . .C
 1310      PREPARE REQUESTS JB  -      . . . : . . . . . : . . . : . . .(. . . .C
 1320      HIRE ANALYST ONE JB  -      . . . : . . . . . : . . . : . . .(. . . .C
 1330      HIRE ANALYST TWO JB 10      . . . :*. . . . : . . . : . . . : . . . .X
 1340
 1400      USE OF CONSULTTS     -      . . . : . . . . . : . . . : . . . : . . . .C
 1410      ROLE - FINANCIAL JAB 2      . . .*: *. . . : . . . : . . . : . . . .C
 1420      ROLE - I         NS  -      . . . : . . . . . : . . . : . . . : . . . .C
 1430      ROLE - II        JB  -      . . . : . . . . . : . . . : . . . : . . . .C
 1440
 1500      STAFF TRAINING   BT 10      . . . : . . . . . : . . . : . . . : . . . .C
 1510      JERRY B.         BT  8      . .*****: . . . . : . . . : . . . : . . . .C
 1520      BRIAN W.         BT  8      . .*****: . . . . : . . . : . . . : . . . .C
 1530      NINA S.          BT  8      . .*****: . . . . : . . . : . . . : . . . .C
 1540      GERRY F.         BT  8      . .*****: . . . . : . . . : . . . : . . . .C
 1550      FRANK M.         BT  4      . . . .*: . . . . : . . . : . . . : . . . .C
 1560      LEW E.           BT  2      . . . .*: . . . . : . . . : . . . : . . . .O
 1570
 1580                 ASSIGNED  MARCH     APRIL     MAY       JUNE      JULY      S
 1591      DESCRIPTION RE MAN   1 1 2:    1 2 3:  1 2 2:    1 1 2:    1 2 3     T
 1592       OF TASK    SP DAY   5 2 9 6:2 9 6 3 0:7 4 1 8:4 1 8 5:2 9 6 3 0     S
 1593      -----------------   -- ---  - -- - -:- - - - -:- - - -:- - - -:- - - - -
 1800      SYSTEMS OVERVIEW BT  -      . . . : . . . . . : . . . : . . . : . . . .C
 1810      DATA BASE DESIGN BW 20      . . . :*. . . . : . . . : SYSTEM SET UP    .O
 1820      TRANSACTIONS     BW  5      . . . : . .*. . . : . . . : INFO CATALOGED  O
 1830      INTEGRATION      BW 10      . . . : . . . .*. : . . . : . . . : . . . .O
 1840      EDIT RULES       BW 10      . . . : . . . . . :*. . : . . . : . . . .O
 1850      SECURITY         BW  5      . . . : . .*. . . : . . . : . . . : . . . .O
 1860      QUERY TO USERS   BW 10      . . . : . . . . . : . . . :*. . : . . . .O
 1870      TERMINALS & USE  BW 20      . . . : . . . . . : . . . :*: . . . : . . . .O
```

Figure 25. The manning chart.

ress. A weekly review of the updated project schedule was unable to decide
whether to hire new analysts, to reassign staff from some areas to those that
were falling behind, and to assign new task priorities.

OUTSIDE PROGRAMMING SUPPORT

The company had board approval to retain a systems house, which would install the manufacturing system. One month prior to delivery date of the new

computer, a senior programmer from the systems house arrived in order to familiarize himself with the company and its new computer. This programmer became a member in the manufacturing group. He participated in training courses and contributed significantly from his knowledge of on-line systems and minicomputers. In conjunction with his efforts, a second programmer remained at his home site and assisted in the development over phone lines through a remote terminal. He wrote programs and "debugged" programs without ever appearing on-site.

The resident programmer remained on-site for more than four months. His firm was paid both an hourly billing rate and his living expenses. Instead of staying in a motel, the programmer chose to lease an apartment and brought his family with him. The company paid living and travel expenses. This project lasted exactly four months, and he returned to his home base on schedule. These two programmers were not retained to design a new system, but to convert their field-proven manufacturing system from BASIC, in which it was originally programmed, to FORTRAN, which had been selected as the company standard. (BASIC was also supported and would therefore run on the HP 3000.) However, because of the desire to standardize on one language for new development plus the fact that the Hewlett-Packard data base manager did not operate with BASIC, the company decided to use FORTRAN.

The detail systems design for the manufacturing system had been approved previously by the manufacturing department, and customizations were considered to be minimal. The work began.

The financial team studied innumerable software packages, but none seemed to satisfy the company's needs adequately. The heart of the financial reporting was the general ledger, which included the asset accounting system, the departmental budget and expense control system, and the source of the profit-and-loss statements and the balance sheets. Its importance convinced the financial team that this system should be designed and implemented in-house. The simplicity of the accounts payable system plus the need to incorporate it into the general ledger made it a candidate for in-house implementation.

The payroll system required a combination of in-house expertise and outside support. The financial team leader selected a contract programmer to assist in the initial design of a payroll system, who thereafter took full responsibility for programming in FORTRAN. The payroll design called for a salaried payroll, an hourly payroll with a labor distribution subsystem, and automatic entries into the general ledger. Finally, the system was to take advantage of the data base management system and provide the capability to make on-line inquiries into the personnel information file.

Staffing and Training

The new concept of on-line systems required some additional expertise beyond the existing data processing department. The new analysts were hired. One, who was found early, was a young systems analyst with on-line experience at a very large mainframe installation. Her transition to the minicomputer was smooth.

There was a longer search for a second analyst, as real and relevant experience was not readily available. Many systems analysts simply did not want to work with minicomputers and FORTRAN. It was decided that the existing staff could handle the workload until time was available to recruit and train new analysts who did not have built-in prejudices for mainframes and batch-type processing.

Early in the development phase, all the analysts were scheduled for the manufacturer's commercial business users' course at its regional office. Courses had to be staggered, which made it impossible to get all analysts trained prior to the beginning of the development phase. Furthermore, some staff had to remain on site to keep the existing large systems on the mainframe computer running. The staggered courses usually lasted five days. The operations manager was promoted to the position of systems manager and was sent to the systems management course. One programmer/analyst was sent to the comprehensive data base management course. Approximately $1,000 per person was invested in training.

There was even more extensive in-house training during the early stages of implementation. The technical consultant held a three-day seminar on the technical aspects of the new system. Then the staff attended the commercial business users' course discussed earlier, having a better understanding of the basic concepts. In addition, the manufacturer presented a comprehensive five-day on-site training program for the entire staff the first week the minicomputer was delivered. This brought the staff into closer involvement with the new minicomputer system, since unlike the formal courses offered, a more relaxed and informal atmosphere could be maintained.

Site Preparation

The computer was delivered in April to the shipping dock. It consisted of only the basic mainframe, four terminals, a printer, and one disk. The full complement of memory, an additional disk drive, and more terminals were scheduled for a later delivery. Development could now begin with an on-site computer.

A small room had been prepared in advance according to predetermined manufacturer's specifications. An electrically "clean" line to the source of power was required, with a dedicated transformer. One air conditioner was installed with a temperature requirement of 20°–30°C (68°–86°F). One dehumidifier was installed with a target of −1°C (30°F). There were no other special electrical requirements nor was there a raised floor.

The computer was moved into the room on small dollies and installed within 2 hours. The manufacturer tested the computer for 1½ days before giving it the go-ahead. The printer was placed in the data processing department and was connected through a partitioned wall to the minicomputer. This provided security to the system, yet allowed programmers to retrieve printed reports without the need to enter the computer room. An alarm system was installed to sound an alarm if the room ever reached a temperature of 29°C (85°F). The door was locked, and only the systems manager was authorized to enter the room. The minicomputer was turned on, after which it ran night and day.

Going Live

The next 14 months were spent in intensive developmental effort. At the same time, the original mainframe was retained, resulting in some long hours and hard work for the department. The first system to go live was the manufacturing system, developed by the outside systems house. The reprogramming was handled very professionally and accomplished very smoothly. The data base management software proved instrumental in the conversion effort. The manufacturing system ran in full parallel at a remote location for a period of only one month prior to being cut over to the minicomputer. At the local site, the system was phased in by the manufacturing department over a 14-month period of time. Enhancements to this system were to be continuous, as is frequently the case in a dynamic environment.

The payroll system was the next to be implemented. Its stand-alone nature precluded any interference by other systems or considerations. When the system first went live, response time suffered. It became obvious that programming efficiency was a key element in on-line processing. A one-month audit of the system improved response dramatically, but a lesson had been learned. Large processing-bound programs should not be put into a position of contending for the resources of the system with the more critical on-line update and status functions. It is more critical that a manufacturing supervisor know the status of his order than that a calculation be made that generates a check for a payroll not due for three days.

The biggest single problem encountered was the conversion of the order/entry system, the only system to remain in COBOL. The batch programs, such as printing of shipping labels and closed order reports, were converted successfully. An entire new design philosophy was needed. Large, inefficient programs had to be redesigned and segmented into smaller efficient programs. The monitor's power and effectiveness in program execution were necessary.

The mainframe conventions were not necessary and a new way of thinking was needed. After four months, the conversion task was dropped, and the system was reprogrammed in FORTRAN with exception of the batch programs, converted by an in-house programmer. The reprogramming took the original design into account. A new team was assembled with the new team leader who was the technical consultant. The new team was made up of three energetic recent college graduates who had an academic background in FORTRAN programming. The programming was begun and completed in five months for 60 programs. The many users ran in parallel on this system for a full four months before going live in March, 11 months after the computer had arrived.

Objectives Confirmed

The objectives of the on-line systems were realized. Those benefits that had been presented to the president by the selection committee had become a reality:

□ Cost savings were reflected in the new data processing budget because the hardware alone represented a $100,000 cost reduction with the minicomputer.

□ The manufacturing system clearly demonstrated a new emphasis on systems to support a progressive and expanding company and contribute to a competitive edge.

□ There was local editing for general ledger, payroll, accounts payable, order/entry, and manufacturing. Each operated on-line and became the responsibility of the end user.

□ All files for each system above were maintained on-line for immediate file update. Voluminous reports in inventory control were discontinued. The 18-hour information lag disappeared.

□ All systems were operational during the day, simultaneously, with as many as 14 active terminals at one time.

□ A real-time manufacturing system, an on-line personnel data base, and a very sophisticated general ledger became realities.

Improvements were in the order/entry system that had not been anticipated. Even though the system had been termed an on-line system on the mainframe, there were several batch-type inefficiencies in the original design. For example, the mainframe required that a partition of 54,000 bytes of core be set aside for on-line processing. Twice a day the system would be shut off so the core could be used for generating shipping papers and invoices. If shipping papers were needed at other times, they were prepared manually, thereby circumventing the system.

With the truly on-line system, invoices and shipping papers could be printed on request. Thus, if a truck arrived unexpectedly at the dock, shipping papers and packing labels were printed on a small printer in the production department. Not only did this eliminate the manual processing, but it meant that the on-line system could operate continuously, rather than be shut down twice a day for batch processing.

Another enhancement of the new system was the ability to receive transmissions from customers directly from the computer, rather than through mail and data entry. Clerical effort and the time of processing customer orders were reduced by at least four working days. This feature greatly enhanced production planning and order scheduling in a very competitive environment.

The on-line nature of all systems improved responsiveness to user requests. A substantial reduction was shown in lead time from receipt of customer orders to execution of a manufactured order. All major systems required considerably less time for processing than had been possible in the batch environment. Payroll processing alone was reduced by 40 hours of clerical effort. Manufacturing began to realize the benefits described in Appendix B.

The new systems were transferred to one remote subsidiary with plans to expand this elsewhere in the company. Remote terminals, operating over common telephone lines, have adopted those systems, which had to be designed and programmed only once. This was the objective—confirmed and realized.

EPILOG

In retrospect we have learned much from our experiences in implementing distributed systems, and these experiences have been favorable ones. Yet there are mountains to be climbed and obstacles to be faced if the benefits of distributed systems are to be realized. We have taken this trip and believe it to be timely and rewarding. A Chinese proverb says it all:

> *I hear and I forget.*
> *I see and I remember.*
> *I do and I understand.*

We have done, and we understand.

We understand, first of all, that it took a very special person in top management to encourage the initial pioneering efforts described in this study. But now that the facts are before us, others in management positions in business, service organizations, and government can take the initiative to evaluate the potential in their own environments. We can now assure them that the theoretical benefits of returning the control of information to the users are real.

We also understand the user's natural reluctance to accept the new responsibilities of which we have written. But we have also been struck by the new enthusiasm generated by the awareness of the computer's power and its direct accessibility. And we have witnessed the nontechnicians applying their educational experience to solving their own problems and enhancing their own job performances with the new computer.

But a word to the wise: Technical expertise is essential in the development and implementation phases. In the preface we described this as a "why to" book in a world of "how to" sources. Perhaps the time has come for the "how to" minicomputer book.

APPENDIX

Data Processing
Equipment Analysis

1.1 Scope

This report concentrates on two basic areas of computer selection criteria—hardware capabilities and software capabilities. The strengths and limitations of several computer systems are discussed in terms of these two areas, in a totally nontechnical, business-oriented presentation. No recommendations are made—it simply sets forth the data processing needs and compares the performance of three minicomputers. The report does not go into other major issues, such as support, training, and financial statistics.

1.2 Objective

The purpose of this report is to evaluate systems and ensure that the selection is the best for the company. As a format, the report first defines local and network requirements and then describes the minicomputer's capabilities in meeting those requirements.

1.3 Systems Evaluation

Evaluation data has been compiled on three computers: Hewlett-Packard, HP 3000; Digital Equipment Corporation, DECSYSTEM 20; and Varian Data Machines, V76. Each of these systems has been given an excellent review by Datapro Research Corp., the foremost data processing research consultants in the country. Each system is considered to be in the same basic performance class, although each has concentrated on a different market. The HP 3000, in existence for three years, has heavily penetrated the educational market, where it has replaced many large mainframe systems in the university timesharing/student record-keeping environment. The DEC 20 (a small edition of the DEC 10), which was introduced in January 1976, is addressing the hospital and banking markets as well as the manufacturing market. The Varian V70 series came out in 1973 and is equipped to handle an on-line network of distributive systems. Its emphasis has been on servicing industry with data collection front-end processors, distributive processors, and process control systems.

The HP 3000 and the DECSYSTEM 20 are classified as timesharing systems, while the V70 would be considered a real-time system. Both systems offer on-line capability. The timesharing systems focus on developmental environments (where the programming development is considered more important than the supporting applications, as in schools and universities), in contrast to the real-time systems, which direct their resources to the production environments (where the processor is dedicated to the applications, with a secondary emphasis on program development). Timesharing and real time can service a company's needs and are considered among the finest computers available today. For online applications, they are by far the most cost-effective computers in existence.

2.1 Hardware Capabilities
In order to make the best decision as to which of these systems would be best suited to Company X, evaluation criteria have been established that represent the organization's basic requirements and serve to clarify these most important features.

2.1.1 Hardware Criteria of Evaluation
The following paragraphs itemize the basic hardware requirements of the system in serving the local requirements and the future network of subsidiaries and divisions.

2.1.1.1 Memory Requirements
Systems must support memory of at least 64,000 (64K) words, with expandability to 256K words by means of hardware memory mapping or direct addressability. To support the ongoing system requires 128K bytes of memory. However, additional memory could improve the throughput if it becomes a problem.

2.1.1.2 Type of Memory Available
The manufacturing of computer memory is bidirectional. Conventional memory is manufactured in metal oxide and is known as *core memory*. Core memory resembles a lattice structure (horizontal and vertical rows of electrical core), is produced in 4K, 8K, and 16K word units, and can achieve cycle speeds of up to 600 nanoseconds. *Semiconductor memory* is the new form of memory. It is playing a more prominent role in today's computer manufacturing and reflects the present state of the art. The advantages of semiconductor memory over core memory are:

Less power required to maintain it
Less space required to house it
Direct isolation of defective memory components
Greater long-run reliability
Extremely fast execution (200–600 ns)
Low cost

Within the next five years memory will be found only in the semiconductor form. All vendors offer semiconductor memory within their product lines in one form or another. Today, it is being offered principally to be interchangeable with, or in a combination of, core and semiconductor memory. Tomorrow core memory will be obsolete. In terms of Company X's needs, however, the organization could safely elect to use either form of memory.

2.1.1.3 Processing Time
The processing unit must have high-speed memory in order to ensure adequate response time to the user. This requires a processor with memory cycle time no greater than 1,000 nanoseconds (1 microsecond). For processes that operate serially in executing instructions, a 600-ns rate would be very desirable. It is difficult to evaluate processing throughput on the basis of statistics alone, but the statistics do provide guidelines. To exemplify the problem of using raw statistics, if we were to evaluate the HP 3000 on the basis of memory cycle time alone, this machine would be classified the slowest on the market, with its 1,000-ns rate, whereas the DEC, Data General, and Varian processors have considerably faster core memory at 660 ns. However, the HP 3000 achieves, in effect, a faster rate by doubling up or paralleling the instructions for execution, and the difference is washed out in the total picture.

2.1.1.4 Separate Input/Output Processor
To relieve the input/output (I/O) burden of having to service multiple low-speed devices by the central processor, the system selected should have an internal I/O processor. This unit usually shares the central processing unit. The result of this configuration is a substantial improvement in throughput.

2.1.1.5 Firmware Capability
In order to address the commercial market, minicomputer manufacturers expanded their instruction capabilities to handle the kind of processing indicative of commercial applications satisfactorily—high-precision decimal arithmetic, rapid flow of data, multiple comparison operations, and extensive table manipulation. This was achieved by adding "firmware" or microprogrammable high-speed memory (normally 20-ns cycle time) where the new instructions were kept in a hard-wired form. If the firmware area is accessible by the user, frequently used subroutines can then be placed there, which reduces memory requirements and increases throughput. The organization requires firmware capability to improve the overall throughput of the system.

2.1.1.6 Hardware Registers
The system that is selected must contain a sufficient number of hardware registers to minimize the overhead factor or bottlenecking of data manipulation. In general-purpose systems, 8 to 16 general registers and two to three index registers are sufficient. For stack machines, fewer general-purpose registers and more index registers are needed. There should also be a number of hardware stack registers for better calling of subroutines and overall efficiency of memory usage.

2.1.1.7 Arithmetic Capability
Company X is not interested in the strong scientific capabilities of these machines, such as floating point and complex arithmetic or trigonometric functions, but we are concerned with the machine's ability to do high-precision integer arithmetic and decimal arithmetic calculations. High-precision integer arithmetic is dependent on the machine's resources to

perform 32-bit binary addition, subtraction, multiplication, and division on hardware registers, instead of through slow software manipulation. Comparing binary to packed decimal arithmetic, binary operations normally take one-tenth the time of comparable packed decimal operations. However, a good portion of one system is now in packed decimal form and is about to be converted into binary for improved performance.

2.1.1.8 Supporting Peripherals
The system should support a wide variety of peripheral equipment in order to satisfy the needs of:
> Mass storage disks
> Nine-track tapes (industry standard)
> Video terminals
> Teletype printers
> High-speed line printer
> Card reader

2.1.1.8.1 Mass Storage Disks
The system must be able to transfer high-speed data in order to support the large-scale units. Overlap/seek capability would be desirable and would definitely increase the throughput and optimize the response time (overlap/seek allows two users to retrieve information simultaneously from multiple disks). These large-scale disk units are manufactured by such companies as Control Data Corporation, Information Storage Systems, and Calcomp. Normally, the vendor develops an interface compatible to these disk units and capable of supporting up to eight individual disk drives off one interface unit. This interface is placed inside the computer manufacturer's central processor and is directly linked either to the central processing unit (CPU) or to the I/O processor. Different manufacturer's disk units have different storage capabilities:
> CDC   90 megabytes of storage
> ISS   47 megabytes of storage
> Calcomp   90 megabytes of storage
> Memorex   20 megabytes of storage

2.1.1.8.2 Nine-Track Tape
Nine-track tape is an industry standard, in the field of commercial data processing. This standard has been set by IBM's 2400 series and has become a standard method of off-line communication between the large mainframes, like the 360/370, and the newer processors, such as DEC, DG, and HP.

2.1.1.8.3 Video Terminals
Two types of video terminal are currently available—asynchronous (teletype compatible) and page-buffered (IBM 3270 compatible). Either one may be used for processing by the organization. The teletype compatible units are an industry standard and almost every minicomputer manufacturer makes its own model. They are linked directly into the processor through a multiplexor and require continuous on-line servicing. Each character

is transmitted at the time of entry to the central processor. The IBM 3270 type is a more sophisticated unit, which contains internal error-checking features and feeds the processor in a burst, rather than a character at a time. As a result, the processor is not tied up until a message requesting servicing by the central processor is transmitted.

2.1.1.8.4 Teletype Printers
These devices operate like a video terminal but can perform the function of issuing hard-copy output. It is envisioned that a terminal of this type will be located in the warehouse for preparation of bills of lading, packing slips, stencils, and so forth.

2.1.1.8.5 High-Speed Line Printer
Off of the central unit the organization must have a high-speed line printer to capture required batch reports. This printer must be capable of speeds no less than 600 lines per minute—otherwise the system will be backlogged in processing reports.

2.1.1.8.6 Card Reader
Initially, development must take place through the video terminals and program card units. For this reason, a medium-speed card reader is required as a stopgap measure. After the on-line systems development effort levels off, this device will no longer be necessary. All entries will then be made through the terminals.

2.1.1.9 Communications
The organization will be interested only in the area of terminal communications (discussed in Section 2.1.1.8.3). Communications with other divisions is discussed in the paragraphs relating to the Company X network.

2.1.1.10 Analog-to-Digital Communications
If the organization chooses to place counters on the machines, which can then transmit information as to start-time and end-time along with customer orders back to the main processor, this would be a function of A/D communications processing. If we use the HP 3000, we would then have to purchase a separate processor, the HP 2100, to satisfy the A/D communications, whereby transmissions would be sent by means of a data link from the HP 2100 to the HP 3000. However, this function is now being supported in the Varian V76 system without any additional equipment (other than the counters themselves).

2.1.2 Hardware Criteria for the Company X Network
In addition to the corporate worldwide communications effort, the network must service the divisions and subsidiaries. Bearing in mind that we are concerned only with the system at home, any network requirements must be considered separately.

2.1.2.1 Memory Requirements
To satisfy a worldwide network, additional memory modules would be required. The memory would be dedicated to the expansion of I/O buffers and the capability to execute

a greater number of routines simultaneously. The present configuration accommodates the execution of eight concurrent tasks. With the additional request made by the network, a configuration of ten tasks should be adequate. The initial bulk of memory recommended by Varian and DEC for their systems might not necessitate the expansion in their configurations, but the HP configuration would most probably have to expand.

2.1.2.2 Separate I/O Processor
Considering the network, the burden of communications on the central processor would absolutely necessitate a separate I/O processor. Without this feature, the system would degenerate by 40 to 60 percent.

2.1.2.3 Wide Range of Processors
It would be extremely desirable, but not mandatory, that a manufacturer be selected that has a series of processors that support a wide range of small to large applications models using one set of systems software (that is, one operating system, one data base manager, one terminal processor, and the same set of higher-level language compilers). This could reduce the cost of the programming development by establishing one set of programs that would act as the system's standard. Confining the applications programs to small program units ensures that these programs can be used in both the host and its satellite systems. This can be accomplished adequately only if the system software is the same for both processors. The only manufacturer that has a product line that spans such a range is Varian with its V70 series, which begins with a very inexpensive 32K processor and extends to a medium-price 512K processor.

2.1.2.4 Supporting Peripherals
Added to the complement of supporting peripherals must be the single-cartridge disks, which would be used in the smaller satellite systems at other facilities. These devices have a capacity of 10 megabytes/unit.

2.1.2.5 Medium-Speed Printer
The satellite systems do not require the speed of the high-speed line printer (600 lpm printer), and could be satisfied through an inexpensive 200 lpm printer on the medium-speed 300 lpm printer.

2.1.2.6 Communications
To serve the network communications requirements adequately the computer system must be capable of handling the following types of communications—asynchronous and synchronous or bisynchronous. *Asynchronous* communications refers to the conventional teletype form of transmitting data to and from the terminals. However, a more efficient manner of transmitting data is in high-speed batches, rather than character-by-character transmissions. This is accomplished in a *synchronous* method with restricted protocol at a rate of 20K bits of information per second. The protocol is a technique of identifying the beginning and end of the transmitted data, along with the number of characters transmitted. This system is used to ensure that information has not been lost or modified in transit.

The remaining technique is called *bisynchronous* and has become an industry standard for high-speed data communications. This method operates at 40K bits of information per second over special lines, utilizing a very sophisticated hardware-secured protocol to ensure data reliability. To ensure the integrity of data transmitted from the subsidiaries, bisynchronous is highly recommended. All processor-to-processor communications are handled in a bisynchronous manner, and would be handled as such in any Company X network. To make the best use of terminal communications, the IBM 3270 bisynchronous-type terminals would minimize the amount of time required to tie up the long-distance communication lines. This technique can reduce actual on-line time to seconds, whereas minutes or even hours might be required to accomplish the same communications linkage in the asynchronous system (see Tables A1 and A2).

2.2 Software Capabilities
The method used in evaluating the hardware will be the same for software capabilities. Establishing suitable criteria is essential to determine which system is most suitable.

2.2.1 Software Criteria for Evaluation
In order for a system to qualify, it must possess these minimum software characteristics:
Operating system software
    Terminal independence
    Multitasking
    Reentrant applications
    Overlay management
    Dynamic program loading
    Common subroutine linkage
    Data stacking
    Logical I/O handling
Data base management
QUERY (or report generator)
Low-level and high-level language support
Password protection and user control
System utilities and recovery routines
Each of these specifications is elaborated on in subsequent sections.

2.2.1.1 Operating Systems Software
The operating systems on the advanced minicomputers are highly sophisticated compared to those of the mainframe systems, which now monopolize the market. To perform the on-line functions the mini was designed to handle requires the addition of several very sophisticated, independently written system software packages:
    POWER   To accommodate the multitasking operations (multiple programs executing concurrently in the processor).
    CICS   To accommodate the video terminal communications between the various users and the system.
    TOTAL   To accommodate the data base access techniques.

Table A1. Hardware comparison.

Hardware Capability	HP 3000	V76	DEC 20
Memory			
Quoted	64K	128K	128K
Expandable to	64K*	1,000,000	512K
Word size	16 bits	16 bits	37 bits
Memory map	Yes	Yes	Yes
Direct addressability	No	No	Yes
Type	Core	SC	Core/SC
Speed	1,000 ns†	660 ns	1,280 ns
Processor			
CPU	Yes	Yes	Yes
I/O Processor	Yes	Yes	Yes
Error-checking processor	No	No	Yes
Firmware			
Expanded instruction set	Yes	Yes	Yes
Programmable	No	Yes	Yes
User programmable	No	Yes	No
Hardware registers			
General purpose	—	8	16
Index	10	3	16
Stack	4	2	2
Firmware	0	8	8
Arithmetic capability			
High-precision binary	Yes	Yes	Yes
Packed decimal	Yes	Yes	Yes
Supporting peripherals (quoted)			
Mass storage disks			
20 MB	No	Yes	Yes
47 MB	Yes	Yes	Yes
90 MB	No	Yes	Yes
9-Track tape units			
800 BPI	Yes	Yes	Yes
1,600 BPI	Yes	Yes	Yes
800/1,000 BPI	Yes	Yes	Yes

Hardware Capability	HP 3000	V76	DEC 20
Video terminals (teletype comp)			
HP 2644	Yes	Yes	Yes
Hazeltine	Yes	Yes	Yes
Teleray	Yes	Yes	Yes
Data General	Yes	Yes	Yes
Super Bee	Yes	Yes	Yes
Video terminals (IBM 3270 comp)			
3270	No	Yes	No
Sanders	No	Yes	No
Teletype printers			
Teletype	Yes	Yes	Yes
DECwriter	Yes	Yes	Yes
GE-Terminet	Yes	Yes	No
High-speed printers			
300 LPM	Yes	Yes	Yes
600 LPM	Yes	Yes	No
1,000 LPM	Yes	Yes	Yes
Card reader	Yes	Yes	Yes
Asynchronous communications	Yes	Yes	Yes
A/D Communications			
Direct	No	Yes	No
Other processor	Yes	Yes	Yes

*Hewlett-Packard is now modifying its equipment to provide a method of expanding memory to 256 words.
†ns = nanoseconds.

Each of these packages is sold separately to the user at a substantial cost and uses a substantial amount of memory. By simultaneously using DOS, POWER, CICS, and TOTAL, which represent two-thirds of the mainframe's memory, a 192,000-byte processor is consumed. Comparing memory requirements for identical functions on a typical minicomputer system would fall within the range of 32K bytes, leaving a substantial percentage of memory available for user programs. However, each manufacturer's operating system is quite different from the next, and it is our responsibility to determine which is best suited on the basis of the following requirements.

Table A2. Hardware comparison for network.

Hardware Capability	HP 3000	V76	DEC 20
Memory			
Host processor	128K	128K	128K
Satellite processors	N/A	40–64K	N/A
Satellite supporting peripherals			
Single cartridge disk	Yes	Yes	No
Medium-speed printers	Yes	Yes	No
Communications			
Asynchronous	Yes	Yes	Yes
Synchronous	No	Yes	Yes
Bisynchronous	Emulated	Yes	No

2.2.1.1.1 Terminal Independence

An on-line system monitors and maintains communications among many independent users and the central processor without requiring scheduled intervention. This is the exact opposite of batch processing. Instead of *one* scheduled request coming into the processor for servicing, calling a lengthy operation to execute to completion before turning control over to the next scheduled request, dozens of requests are being fed into the processor simultaneously, and each is being serviced independently of the other. This is normally accomplished through the use of video display terminals; however, other devices, such as teletypes and low-speed keyboard printers, are also frequently used (as shown in Figure A1).

2.2.1.1.2 Multitasking

In mainframe systems, multitasking is supported only in the large units, such as the IBM 360/50 and 370/155. In the minicomputer field, however, even the smallest systems offer multitasking. Multitasking is the ability of the processor to perform many operations (tasks) at the same time. This is done by partitioning memory into user applications segments, loading the various applications into the computer, and running them simultaneously. In an on-line environment, this allows the system to service many user requests at the same time, optimally reserving a task for every user terminal in the system.

2.2.1.1.3 Reentrant Applications

In order to make the best use of memory, routines on applications that are frequently used could be coded in such a way that many users could access them concurrently without holding separate copies in memory, that is, only one copy of the routine(s) need to be in

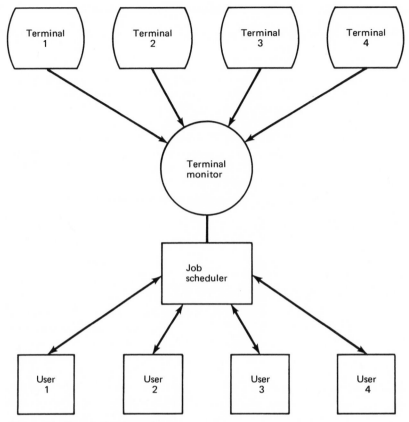

Figure A1. Terminal independence.

memory at the time of execution. The concept of reentrant applications is meaningful only in a multitasking environment, where many tasks need servicing by the same routine. If the system does not have this feature, then additional copies of the routine must be available as memory.

2.2.1.1.4 Overlay Management

Segmentation of programs into autonomously executable units is normally accomplished through a root-overlay structure. The root segment of the program remains resident in memory over the entire period of execution and controls the requests of other nonresident segments which can be called for execution separately and, therefore, use a common memory area. The technique is called overlaying because each segment is requested and loaded into the same area of memory in which the last segment resided. This sharing of common memory minimizes the amount of memory required to perform a particular function. The largest of the programs can be divided into efficient overlay segments to be executed in the smallest processors.

2.2.1.1.5 Dynamic Program Loading

Up to 1976, only timesharing systems were capable of dynamic program loading. But since the fever of on-line systems has spread, the real-time systems manufacturers have modified their operating systems to support this feature. The idea is to utilize available memory upon demand, not to set fixed partitions in the memory, but to restrict the area where an application can be loaded. This is a function of memory management, and the more advanced processor allocates and maintains its available memory through hardware functions, alleviating the operating system of additional overhead.

2.2.1.1.6 Common Subroutine (Run-time) Library

The more efficient systems have used the technique of creating one common library of subroutines for all reentrant-codeable applications, loaded into memory in one central area to be used by multiple user programs. The user applications, most frequently the result of a compiled program, access the routines in the run-time library through branch and return functions, passing parameters to and from the two functions. This technique definitely conserves memory while it improves throughput (see Figure A2).

2.2.1.1.7 Data Stacking

Like overlay management, the concept of a data stack is to provide a common area of memory that can be used as a scratch pad by multitasking user functions. The area is dynamically assigned to the user upon request at execution time—and freed upon completion. New data stacks overlay old, used data stacks, which place the new interim task data values onto a reusable stack area, to conserve memory requirements and allow reentrancy of code. As memory becomes more critical, so does the data stacking. As a note of interest, the large-scale system never offered this feature.

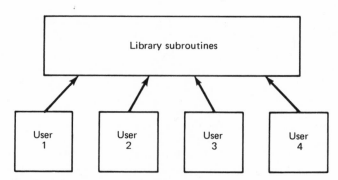

Figure A2. The subroutine (run-time) library.

APPENDIX A

2.2.1.1.8 Logical I/O Handling

The purpose behind logical I/O was to remove the application from the restrictions of having to identify the physical I/O devices prior to use. Using logical methods, the applications program communicates the use of a run-time device by providing a symbolic identifier, which is later equated to a physical device. This provides the system with greater flexibility at run-time, and simplifies the task of reassigning devices.

Furthermore, this feature was not offered by IBM under its DOS operating system, but required the customer to upgrade to a system 360/50 configuration, which supported an operating system that did provide the OS feature.

2.2.1.2 Data Base Manager

The key ingredients of a true on-line real-time system are multiterminal access, multitasking, and integrated data base. The integrated data base requirement ultimately leads to data base management. This feature alone is often considered the foundation of on-line systems, since without it the system could not survive. The concept of a data base is to create a structure that centralizes information in a related fashion, eliminates the redundancy of data found in conventional file systems, and maximizes the space required to house the information. The purpose of the data base manager is to provide a traffic controller that supervises the accessing and updating of information already within the data base. The following sections discuss what is required to support the Company X data base.

2.2.1.2.1 Data Base Access

There are currently two types of data base access methods: a multikey ISAM method and a master variable file method. The latter technique is the most widely accepted today. It consists of a master record hookup through the algorithmic listing of a key, followed by the reading of related chained records called "variable" records. This technique makes on-line inquiry possible, and eliminates many of the requirements of large batch passes of the files and presorts for reporting. The three systems discussed have both functions of data access incorporated into their software.

2.2.1.2.2 Multithreading of the Data Base

Owing to the extensive amount of data base accessing required to service an on-line system, it is extremely desirable to allow many users access into the data base concurrently, as long as the integrity of the data is preserved. This feature is called multithreading. Many systems, such as the Hewlett-Packard, simplify data base processing by single threading, allowing only one user at a time into the data base. This works quite satisfactorily under normal conditions, but multithreading eliminates the possibility of bottlenecks.

2.2.1.2.3 Multiple Chains

Any sophisticated application would require the ability of the data base manager to perform multiple chain processing. This means that variable detail vends should be accessible via different masters; for example, we might want to keep routings by part and also keep routings by work center. In Hewlett-Packard's IMAGE DBM, there are 16 separate linkages into a variable detail file, whereas in Varian's TOTAL, there are up to 256 linkages. The DEC 20 system allows the user to go one step further, and set up a data set binary, such that parts used could point to an operation record, and this vend in turn could point to a note vend. IMAGE and TOTAL will not permit this by definition. However, it is a desirable feature to have within the system.

2.2.1.2.4 Network Data Management

There are currently two accepted forms of data management—hierarchical and network. The first permits the user to access data down a chain of related files, such as customer to order to item to special instructions, whereas the network approach allows the user to access information by crossing over the range of data. Figure A3 represents a hierarchical structure, whereas Figure A4 represents a network structure.

The flexibility of a network structure is an extremely valuable tool in the formation of a manufacturing data base. The best example of this is the bill of materials processor. Its data base structure is a network, as shown in Figure A5. Therefore, a network data base manager is a definite requirement.

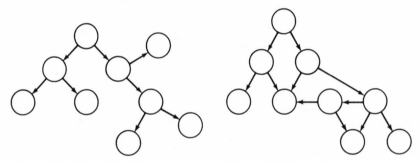

Figure A3. Hierarchical structure.   Figure A4. Network structure.

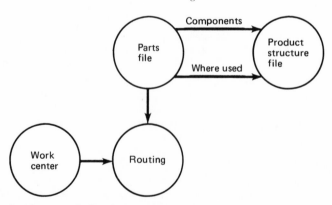

Figure A5. The network data base manager.

2.2.1.2.5 Data Base Security and Recovery

The centralization and accessibility of corporate information make it necessary to provide the system with extensive security. This is to prevent unauthorized use of the data base. Advanced data base managers are able to restrict access on the basis of the item, rather than the application on the entire vend. Take the example of two clerks wishing general access into the personnel/payroll files, The one might have authority to access salary data, whereas the other would be allowed to access only name and address data. In this circumstance the data base manager would void the employee's record, filter out the data by replacing unauthorized data with blanks, and pass the information to the respective users. Therefore, control of the system is a direct function of how rigorously the security is maintained.

Recovery is another feature of extreme importance. Each of the systems under evaluation has excellent provisions for data base recovery, minimizing the amount of time required.

2.2.1.3 QUERY Language

The availability of a QUERY language is directly dependent on the establishment of a data base management system. This function of a QUERY language is to allow non-technical (nonprogrammer) users to independently select information from their data bases and report it in a manner they specify. This is done directly at the user's terminal, and requires only a few hours of training to be proficient.

What this does for Company X is to reduce the turnaround time and communications problems between the data processing department and the various users. One-time application should most definitely be done through QUERY, while the data processing department remains responsible for permanent requests.

2.2.1.4 Virtual Memory Management

In order to conceive memory requirements, more advanced systems have a function called memory management, which is a separate operation performed on the final program prior to its being placed in the production library. The program is examined by this operation, and optimally split into various executable segments. The two techniques used to date are segmentation and paging.

Paging separates the program into fixed-length components that can be called into memory in an overlay fashion, as discussed in Section 2.2.1.1.4. *Segmentation* requires a considerably more sophisticated manner of managing logical memory partitions. The programs are segmented as efficiently as possible and depend totally on the logical structure of each program; therefore, the sizes of the segments are all different. This imposes an additional burden onto the memory management system to maintain the availability of memory space and the location of presently running applications.

Both features are totally acceptable for the local need. The Hewlett-Packard system uses the segmentation method, whereas Varian and DECSYSTEMS use dynamic paging.

2.2.1.5 Low-Level Language Support

The trend in today's technology is the development, on one hand, of increasingly higher-level languages moving toward the QUERY approach, and, on the other hand, more and more efficient lower-level language support. In years to come, the necessity of intermediate languages will be less significant. Lower-level languages are defined as the assembler languages, a macroassembler language, and a microprogramming language.

The assembler language is a one-to-one correspondence with the hardware to execute various machine functions, such as loading registers, adding registers, moving data from one location in memory to another location. No higher-level language will achieve the efficiency of a good assembler program; however, the selection of what programs shall be written in assembler language is critical. *No* user application programs should ever be coded in assembler language. Yet, the subroutines used in the higher-level languages should most probably be assembler routines, such as date conversions, I/O processing, and intricate bit manipulation.

One level away from the assembler language is the macroassembler language, to ease the effort of writing assembler code. These macroassemblers can be very sophisticated, such as Hewlett-Packard's SPL, which to the average programmer resembles the BASIC language. Using a macroassembler language improves productivity.

The latest processors are offering the most efficient tool development in recent years—read only memory (ROM). This is a highly efficient semiconductor memory that operates in speed well in excess of any existing conventional memory (normally 20 to 50 times the speed of standard memory). However, to use this feature requires that the programmer write in a language known as microcode. Only highly trained technicians can adequately write microcode programs, due to the degree of technical knowledge required. Recently, there have been breakthroughs in this area to assist the furtherance of the practice—microassembler languages. In years to come, this area of technology will become a common practice among minicomputer programmers. *It is this area of development that makes the minicomputer as powerful as the large mainframes.*

2.2.1.6 Higher-Level Language Support

The system must be able to support COBOL and FORTRAN. It would be desirable, but not necessary, for the system to have such languages as BASIC, RPG IV, and RPG II.

COBOL is required owing to the extensive programming development to date invested in the present order/entry system. This system must be converted with as little effort as possible. COBOL is a new development in the minicomputer area, and requires the support of firmware in the central processor. All systems under evaluation satisfy these requirements; however, each has its idiosyncrasies.

FORTRAN is the most efficient higher-level language for these systems and has become an industry standard as COBOL has been an industry standard for the mainframe systems. New developments should be done utilizing this language in its commercial version.

The other compilers available to the systems are merely frills to satisfy external applications. The major on-line system will be supported under COBOL and FORTRAN.

2.3 Communications Software
In the timesharing systems the communications software is part of the operating system and is handled on a character-by-character (asynchronous) basis. Interprocessor or network processing is not inherent in these systems, and must be satisfied by user application code. In the real-time systems the communications software is serviced by a separate systems software package supported by the manufacturer, and usually becomes the basis to a fully operational terminal and network communications monitor. Programming development to support interprocessor communications between the HP 3000 and the HP 2100 will be substantial, whereas Varian and DECSYSTEMS have turnkey software already available.

2.4 A/D Software
To control the input and processing of counters requires special hardware and software features not found in the HP 3000 and DEC 20 systems. These features are currently available in the V76 unit. Here again, we must weigh this against the programming cost of developing suitable software to handle this function in the HP and DEC systems. The HP 3000 cannot directly handle the load of the A/D processing and would have to be supported through a communications link by an HP 2100 processor whose function would be specifically to handle the A/D processing, passing its results intermittently over the HP 3000. However, if we are not seriously considering counters, then this will have no effect on the evaluation (see Table A3).

Table A3. Vendor software comparison.

Software Capability	HP 3000	V76	DEC 20
Operating system capability			
Terminal independence	Yes	Yes	Yes
Stack capable	Yes	Yes	Yes
User reentrant codable	Yes	Yes	No
Supports multitasking	Yes	Yes	Yes
Supports overlays	Yes	Yes	Yes
Dynamic program loading	Yes	Yes	Yes
Common subroutine linkage	Yes	Yes	Yes
Logical I/O handling	Yes	Yes	Yes
Data imbedding codable	No	Yes	Yes
I/O independence from code	No	Yes	No
CRT paged buffer processing	No*	Yes	No
Disk-release capability	No	Yes	Yes
Data base management support			
Type	IMAGE	TOTAL	IDMS
Multithreaded	No	Yes	Yes
Multilevel access	No	No	Yes
Network access	Yes	Yes	Yes
Number of unique items	256	32,000	32,000
Number of detail files supported	16	256	256
Password security	Yes	Yes	Yes
Recovery provisions	Yes	Yes	Yes
QUERY languages feature	Yes	Yes	No
Virtual memory management			
Segmentation	Yes	No	No
Paging	No*	Yes	Yes
Overlaying	Yes	Yes	Yes
Lower-level language support			
Assembler codable	Yes	Yes	Yes
Macroassembler codable	Yes	Yes	Yes
Microassembler codable	No	Yes	No
Higher-level languages			
COBOL	Yes	Yes	Yes

Table A3. Continued.

Software Capability	HP 3000	V76	DEC 20
Higher-level languages (*cont.*)			
FORTRAN	Yes	Yes	Yes
Optimized FORTRAN	No	Yes	Yes
BASIC	Yes	Yes	Yes
RPG II	Yes	Yes	Yes
RPG IV	Yes	Yes	Yes
Communications software	No	Yes	No
A/D Software	No	Yes	No

*Under development in Rochester by Hewlett-Packard.

B

Economic Results
Attainment Report

A new manufacturing system may have substantial impact on a business. George Plossl, the premier manufacturing expert, calls the control of inventory and production the last frontier for profit. This appendix contains analyses of three companies, Company X, Plant X, and Company Y, that installed an on-line manufacturing system.

Company X is a $75 million manufacturer of sophisticated, computer-based process control systems that are sold and serviced worldwide. Manufacturing shipment volume has been running between $40 and $45 million annually during the past two years. Their mini/maxi manufacturing planning and control system has been fully operational since April 1974. Results to date include the following:

1. Manufacturing, engineering, marketing, and finance are now working as a unit with the same plan and set of supporting data.
2. Prior to the implementation of the minicomputer modules, all manufacturing systems were operating in a batch mode on an IBM 370. The manufacturing organization was being charged an average of $15,000 per month for data center resource usage. Since the implementation of the minimodules, the manufacturing organization has been charged an average of $4,000 per month for IBM 370 data center resource usage, which comes down to an average monthly charge reduction of $11,000 for the manufacturing organization.
3. Inventory record accuracy has improved by approximately 30 percent during the past 18 months as a result of on-line data-entry validation as well as cycle-counting features of the system.
4. Manufacturing cycle time has been reduced from an average 6 months to an average 60 to 90 days over the past 18 months. This has provided a tremendous competitive impact.
5. Work in process inventory has been reduced substantially since the beginning of 1974 from $2,600,000 to its current level of $1 million.
6. Manufacturing stock or component inventory has been reduced also from its 1974 beginning level of $13 million—a $4.5 million reduction.

7. The inventory service level has improved from 65 percent to more than 96 percent during the past two years. The inventory service level for each month in 1975 has been above 95 percent.
8. Back-ordered line items have been reduced by more than 80 percent over the last 18 months. There are currently less than 1,500 line items in a back-ordered position. This represents less than 150 purchased components and less than 500 inventory items overall.
9. The inventory turnover rate has increased by more than 30 percent during the past 18 months.
10. Engineering change control and overall configuration control have been significantly improved over the past two years.

Plant X is a $20 million manufacturer of an industrial chain utilized primarily in conveying equipment and drive applications. Under their mini/maxi system, the bill of materials, inventory management, and materials requirements planning modules have been fully operational on all products since January 1975. The shop floor control module was installed in October 1975 and is currently working on a pilot basis. Results to date include the following:

1. Customer delivery performance during the past 11 months has improved from 33 percent on time in January 1975 to an average of more than 60 percent on time during the past 3 months in terms of the customer promise date.
2. Average manufacturing cycle time has been reduced from 16 weeks to 8 weeks during the year.
3. In 11 months, the value of back-ordered items has been reduced from $2,300,000 to its current level of $890,000.
4. Productivity defined as the dollar value of work produced per standard hour of production has improved by 15 percent over the previous year.
5. The inventory investment has been reduced by more than 10 percent during the past three months on an increased shipping volume level. The rate of inventory turnover has improved significantly; this trend is expected to continue.
6. Accuracy of inventory record keeping has improved by more than 15 percent, with a built-in tolerable error factor of 3 percent.

Company Y is a $30 million manufacturer of valves, steam traps, and metering pumps for the utility and process industries. Under their mini/maxi system, the bills of material and inventory management modules have been operational since April 1975 for all products. The materials requirements planning module was installed back in July 1975 and is currently in effect for products representing 50 percent of shipment volume. Results to date include the following:

1. On-time deliveries to customers based on the promised delivery date have steadily improved monthly from 33 percent in May to 63 percent in November.
2. During the same May–November period, the inventory turnover rate has remained constant.

3. Relative to on-time delivery performance, shipments were more than 10 days late 46 percent of the time back in May. Steady monthly improvement has occurred since then with November 10-day-late shipments occurring only 25 percent of the time.
4. A substantial inventory investment reduction is anticipated in the first and second quarters of 1976. The results of recent materials requirements planning processing for those products currently operational on MRP have been carefully validated, and $1,900,000 worth of outstanding purchase orders have been either canceled or rescheduled.
5. The materials staging area in which materials were pulled in advance of order release (to check for shortages) has been eliminated.
6. Better controls now exist on both record accuracy and engineering change control (the process of recording and controlling changes made on engineering drafts), although it is difficult to quantify improvements at this stage because of poor or nonexistent monitoring and control mechanisms that existed before the new system was installed.

INDEX

vacuum tubes, 35
Varian Data Machines, 44–45, 57, 180
  applications of minicomputers of, 64, 75
  minicomputers of, 60, 130, 171
verification
  on CRT terminals, 150
  of keypunching, 105, 140–141, 164
Viatron, 80, 100
video terminals, *see* cathode ray tube terminals
virtual memory, 30, 78

visibility, 136, 156
von Neumann, John, 27

Weiner, Norbert, 26–27
Whirlwind computer, 27, 42
White, Robert B., 132–133
word processing, 72–73
workloads, 139–141

Xerox, 161

zero-base computing, 17–20